Wisdom
Now and Always

BY

Miguel Mendonça

First published 2020 by Miguel Mendonça

Copyright © 2020 Miguel Mendonça

All moral rights reserved

This book or any portion thereof may not be reproduced or used in any manner whatsoever without the express written permission of the authors except for the use of brief quotations in a book review

Cover design by Miguel Mendonça
Front cover photograph by Miguel Mendonça
Back cover photograph and image by Louise Applegate

ISBN 13: 9798674347774
ISBN 10: 8674347774

www.miguelmendonca.com

About the Author

Miguel Mendonça is an Anglo-Azorean writer based in Bristol, England. His education has incorporated forestry and horticulture, journalism, a BA in Geography and History, and postgrad studies in social science and environmental ethics. He worked as an author and campaigner on sustainability while serving as Research Manager at the World Future Council and Communications Manager at The Converging World. At that time he authored or co-authored three books: *Feed-in Tariffs*, *Powering the Green Economy* and *A Renewable World*.

Following that work, Miguel published a short fiction collection, titled *Quick! Act Normal*. He then studied metaphysical topics, and published a trilogy: *Meet the Hybrids*, *We are The Disclosure* and *Being with the Beings*.

In addition to exploring fresh subject areas in nonfiction, he dabbles in music, poetry, photography and stained glass.

To my mother and father,
Thank you.

Knowledge speaks, but wisdom listens
— *Jimi Hendrix*

Acknowledgements

First of all, my deepest thanks to the contributors. Each of you has taught me so much of value, and I enjoyed our discussions enormously. It is my great pleasure to share your experiences and perspectives with the readers.

I wish to thank all those who helped connect me to some of the contributors. Johannes Mosskin at the Right Livelihood Foundation was a fantastic source. Also, Herbie, Fay Vale, Danielle Silver, Philippe Ullens, Elisabet and Isabelle. I am also grateful to Jakob Von Uexkull, who founded the Right Livelihood Awards and co-founded the World Future Council. Both have made important contributions in bringing together people that embody and exhibit great wisdom in their lives and work.

I would also like to thank those whose contributions did not fit the final version. They were thought-provoking and much appreciated.

Kurt Vile, Hans Zimmer, Julia Gjertsen and Jóhann Jóhannsson for providing some wonderful editing music. And there were many other Scandinavian composers who contributed. Somehow their music conveys the richness, depth, beauty, complexity and occasional sorrow of these discussions.

Also Darlene, for her support early in the project. And the proofreaders. It's generally wise to have a second pair of eyes on our work.

I am ever grateful to my family and friends, and their willingness to listen to me chatter away excitedly about the project of the moment. Matt Thomas and Dave Bennett especially.

And Lou, my moon and stars. One of the wisest people I know, and an eternal inspiration.

And Dexter, as always.

Contents

Introduction 11
Failautusi Avegalio, Jr. 16
Isabelle Axelsson 33
David Bailey 50
Lyn Buchanan 63
Rachel Corby 74
Jane Davidson 88
David Eby 107
Michel Ferrari 117
Herbert Girardet 135
Randy Hayes 153
David Krieger 173
Satish Kumar 182
Kim Langbecker 196
Reuben Langdon 211
Frances Moore Lappé 223
Francesc Miralles 234
Juan Pablo Orrego 247
Tiffany Patterson 272
Elisabet Sahtouris 289
Mollie Semple 310
Vandana Shiva 320
Sulak Sivaraksa 340
Wendy Stephenson 349
Julie Taylor 363
Mike Wallis 379
Conclusion 393

Introduction

The value of wisdom came to me early in life. It was 1981 and I was about seven years old, sitting in class in Highfield Junior School in Eastbourne, England. Our teacher told us the story of the wisdom of King Solomon. Two women came to Solomon's court to seek justice, both claiming to be the mother of a baby. He considered the situation and declared, "There is a simple solution. I shall take a sword to the child and you shall have half each." At this, one of the women fell to her knees and begged the king to give the child to the other woman. And Solomon knew he had found the true mother.

I experienced literal illumination, an explosion of light around my head, and I understood clearly: the purpose of life is to acquire and use wisdom in order to solve problems and make our lives better. That moment is perfectly fresh, though it was almost 40 years ago.

However, as my father was addicted to watching the news, that floodgate was open at every opportunity, filling our home with images of war, terrorism, famine and economic hardship. Not at any point was this comprehensible to me. As schoolchildren we had been told, explicitly, that wisdom is a feature of the human experience, and a valuable resource. So where was it? In the ensuing four decades I have been looking for it, consciously or otherwise. I have found it in many people occasionally, and a few people often. And I now realize that I have gravitated to those who seem to have more of it, more often. So it makes sense that I would end up working with such people on environmental and social justice issues. The fact that these efforts go almost entirely against the grain of the prevailing political and economic order is still bewildering to me. Perhaps it would not be, had I never heard the story of the wisdom of Solomon.

But it was not until recently that the subject of wisdom came up for me in a pointed way. A year ago I found myself pursuing several threads, during research for a screenplay. I read many books on cults and their leaders, which led me to read up on narcissism and sociopathy, which in turn led me to read about resistance, rebellion and revolution. And there was a moment when a voice said: read a book on wisdom. The idea brought with it an excitement, an echo of that first childhood encounter. I scoured numerous sources, both in person and online. I wanted a book that took a deep and wide look at wisdom, in terms of what it is and how it can be developed and applied. I sought something which would give me a global perspective, from people who have lived wise lives. I thought I would quickly find several titles that would meet my needs. But if the books are out there, we did not find one another.

Fast forward to 2020, and we are living with a global pandemic, racial violence, climate chaos, Brexit, rising geopolitical tensions, a global economy sliding towards the abyss, and much of it is being overseen by the inept and the sociopathic. We are, more than ever, desperately in need of a flourishing of wisdom. I therefore decided to create the book I wanted to read, and which I feel could benefit every reader in this moment or any other. Wisdom is a perennial resource, something which will always have a vital role in human affairs.

The outline and questions were developed with this broad scope and ongoing utility in mind. The interviewees were selected on the basis of their ability to speak to both contemporary themes and the eternal nature of wisdom.

Identifying the interviewees was a mix of easy and challenging. I knew many from my sustainability work, and from my circle of friends. I listed a number that I felt would offer powerful and insightful stories. That category included Herbie Girardet, my former boss at the World Future Council, and some of the council members and people we worked with, including Frances Moore Lappé, Randy Hayes, Vandana Shiva, Sulak Sivaraksa and David Krieger. Through the Schumacher Society annual lectures in Bristol I had met Satish

Introduction

Kumar and Elisabet Sahtouris. Elisabet introduced me to Professor Failautusi Avegalio, Jr., an academic colleague of hers at Chaminade University, and a man of Samoan warrior king lineage. While working for the Converging World, another NGO, I had worked with Wendy Stephenson, the CEO.

From my friends I wanted to interview Mike Wallis, someone who has had a powerfully positive influence on the development of my character, and the course of my life. This book simply would not exist had I not met him. David Bailey is an incredibly insightful craftsman in Bristol who I have had the pleasure to know for some years.

During my research on the extraterrestrial topic I met the multitalented Reuben Langdon, and had interviewed the remote viewer Lyn Buchanan. As I like to spend time at Stanton Drew, a 5,000-year-old stone circle near my home, I thought it would be interesting to get a Druid's perspective on wisdom, and found my way to Mollie Semple. For another screenplay project I had interviewed Julie Taylor, a nationally recognized school guidance counselor, and she made a huge impact on me. I asked my friend Philippe Ullens for some recommendations and he suggested Rachel Corby and Francesc Miralles. Herbie had suggested Jane Davidson, given her work on the wellbeing of future generations while serving as a government minister. David Eby is a musician I discovered while looking at information on the spiritual community that a friend had joined in Oregon. I found Michel Ferrari's work on wisdom, having wondered if and how academics might study the subject. My search for someone who could discuss issues around race and civil rights was rewarded when I interviewed Tiffany Patterson, Associate Professor of African American and Diaspora Studies at Vanderbilt University. It was a very powerful way to conclude the interview stage of the book.

I found many more people who would have been excellent candidates, but not all worked out, for a variety of reasons. Some sent material that I could not quite find a fit for, but all of it added to my perspective, and is appreciated. Others were more interested in payment than in wisdom. The management team of one of my favorite rappers said, and I'm paraphrasing, 'Sure, he can give you an hour. That will be $12,000 please.' I will leave it to the reader, by the end of the book, to determine how that relates to their personal definition of wisdom.

I reached out to numerous indigenous wisdom keepers, but that was also a challenging process. Some were perfectly willing, but given the complexity of working through translators, and time constraints, those did not work out. So I am glad to have interviewed Professor Avegalio, whose chapter is the perfect opening to this book. His story about moving from his Polynesian culture to that of America is fascinating. And his tale of experiencing wisdom through an excruciating personal ordeal is unforgettable. We also benefit from the observations of those who have spent many years living and working with indigenous peoples around the world. Their stories are particularly arresting.

From the beginning I was looking for someone to interview about wisdom as it relates to race relations and civil rights. And a few weeks into the interviewing, George Floyd was murdered, on camera, by a white cop. I have never seen the video, though I have heard it described by many who have. The discussion with Professor Patterson was an experience that will stay with me. It took me back through my whole relationship with racial issues. I was three years old when my family moved from Rhodesia to England. Given my 'foreign' name and olive skin courtesy of my Portuguese ancestry, I was subjected to a range of racial slurs which typically pegged me as being black African or Pakistani. This was my introduction to racism, and its generally impoverished knowledge base. All my life I have witnessed in my fellow humans the almost feverish taste for racial hatred. And it has never ceased to baffle me. As individuals we love novelty. In fact much of our global economy is based on feeding populations in the Global North a ceaseless flow of stuff that is slightly different to the stuff we already have. And we love to travel and display photographic and material evidence of the difference that we encounter abroad. So we tend to like difference. But politicians are adept at the divide and rule strategy. On the domestic level, the things that make us slightly different are cast as suspect, threatening or downright dangerous. Religion and 'values' are used to open up a chasm between us, and set up culture clashes, and in some cases, war. It is the oldest trick in the book, yet we still fall for it. All the time we fight among ourselves we fail to unite to create a fair, balanced, safe and sustainable world.

My response to all this is my own act of rebellion: the production of a book about wisdom. Given my methodology, which mainly involves listening and transcribing, my role is to organize and MC 'paper conferences'. I set the subject, invite and introduce presenters, then offer some closing remarks. I have found this to be a highly effective way of gathering and sharing a large amount of information quickly.

My advice is to read this book closely, and slowly. And read it at least twice, as some things take longer to be absorbed. You may benefit from keeping notes, and certainly from discussing what comes up for you. You may be reassured by both the wisdom and the humility of the contributors, and what that implies regarding your own reservoir of wisdom.

The people you are about to meet have more than 1,500 years of collective life experience, across three generations. They represent a wide range of professional backgrounds, including education, governance, the military, science, industry, the arts, journalism, activism and nonprofit, religion and spirituality. Between them they have traveled to most of the countries of the world. They come from 11 nations, on five continents, and speak at least 10 languages. They have produced around 200 books, which have sold millions of copies. Their careers have benefited countless people. I feel incredibly grateful to have brought them together for this project, and it has been a hugely life-affirming experience. I believe we have collectively moved toward a solid sense of wisdom, and its shared benefit, now and always. My greatest wish is that this book will help you recognize, cultivate and share your own wisdom.

Failautusi Avegalio, Jr.

Papali'i 'Tusi' Avegalio was raised on a coastal village in American Samoa and entered college in the US as a scholarship recipient in 1968. Returning to Samoa as a graduate, his teaching and cross-cultural-based leadership style was rewarded by unprecedented job promotions from the classroom to the Central Office in one year. He pursued advanced degrees in Education and became president of the local community college in American Samoa. After serving as an East West Center Research Scholar at the University of Hawai'i, he was recruited as a professor in its College of Business, where he is Director of the multi-national award-winning University of Hawai'i Pacific Business Center Program. He was conferred the Papalii title in 1980 as a senior heir of the Malietoa Talavou (warrior king) line of Samoa. He is an advocate for the weave of indigenous wisdom, values of aloha and spirituality with modern science, knowledge and technology.

What comes to mind first when you think about wisdom?

The Moana. The Pacific Ocean. The land is the heart, but Moana is the lungs. As a little boy growing up on an island, you run from the heart to the lungs, learning how to breathe with the ocean. This is a practice which grandmother encourages, to teach us through play about balance, about floating and breathing with life. We are a seafaring, voyaging people, so much of our wisdom centers around the Moana. The wisdom passed down by our ancestors tells us that all humans have two mothers and two fathers. The two mothers are our biological birth mother and Papa, our Earth Mother. In Polynesia a newborn's umbilical cord is wrapped in Ti leaves and ritually buried in the sacred ground. The physical act of burial, ritually conducted by elders, symbolically connects the newborn to Papa, our Earth Mother.

Today the modern meaning of fanua in Samoa is land. Its original and ancient meaning is placenta or afterbirth. Eleele today means dirt, and palapala is mud. The original and ancient meaning of both words is blood. Ma'a today means stone but its original meaning comes from the word fatu ma'a, which means heart. The very language of ancient Polynesia discerns our Earth as alive, and as our mother who birthed all life and matter from the progenitor of the heavens, Tagaloa Lagi.

Do you recall the first time you witnessed wisdom in action?

When we were eight years old my grandmother gave us a taro plant to care for. We call them 'uli'. You plant them as many baby taros, and when they grow you separate them and then they become large taros on which you feed the family. So she gave one to each of us, my brothers and me, to grow and care for. So we put them in little coconut shells with soil and water. But at that age, caring for anything is not something that comes naturally. You enjoy, you play. It's a given that the children have no sense of responsibility. So I didn't care for my taro. The soil dried out, the uli got no water and the leaves dried. About a week later she called me to bring my taro. And then I remembered, and thought, 'Oh my God, my taro.' It was dried out and looked dead. She acted like I had allowed something precious to die. I was so sad, so remorseful. It had that much of an impact that even today, when I think about it, it makes me reflect in a good way. I thought it was dead, not knowing any better. But the taro is a very resilient plan. All you have to do is water it again and it will come back. So she said, "How do you feel?" I was so apologetic. I said, "What can I do?" And she said, "Well, if you can care for it and love it, it might come back." So, I became very dedicated. Every day I watered it and checked on it. I made sure that it got just enough sun, then I put it in the shade. About a week later, the first green started to show, and in two weeks the leaves were there and it came back to life. That was the greatest lesson I had ever learned about respecting life. Life is not something that you should take for granted or abandon. So that kind of wisdom at that age was fundamental to building my character, and actually the character of most children in our village.

I grew up in a coastal village in American Samoa, in the South Pacific. Those are the kinds of experiences that I tried to simulate in some way with my grandchildren. They can learn the importance of caring for something that to us is our kin. Be responsible, love, respect and care for it, so you learn about caring and respect for life through that activity. At the same time, you also learn humility. All of this came to me wrapped up around a little dry, shriveled and seemingly dead little taro shoot. Grandmother guided my first steps on this journey that will continue to affect my entire life with such love and kindness. Such lessons were planted in my soul and grew with me as I matured. That deep feeling, the euphoria, that gratitude and love as a result of the lesson of the baby taro, has guided my life ever since.

Who have been your wisdom teachers?

Our elders. They have been fundamental, because our method of teaching is by first weaving a relationship with a story, within which the lesson is planted and grown. The story creates context that requires doing, showing and connecting action to emotion that underpins values. We don't have conversations before the lesson has been shown; for example, by bringing the taro back to life. The experience was the planted seed that the elders know would mature in time and be the reference point, where meaning begins to flower and conversation like the nourishment of rain and warmth of the sunlight touches on the emergence of wisdom. So now you have a basis for a conversation. Too much conversation with little basis in experience or in reality is an abstract conceptualization, more essence than form.

There was no formal discussion, because through your lifetime the elders are watchful and the memories remain intact so that at the right moment, when it's appropriate, a particular wisdom will hit you. For example, we were out fishing with my uncle in our canoe and the wind picked up. It was very rough and he told me to hold on to the ama, the outrigger. I reached over and we both held on to the ama. The outrigger stabilizes the canoe in rough waters so it won't tip over. So, when the squall passed us the water settled and we continued fishing. So, the ama was the example of the importance of balance. Then, in life, when there are rough seas we will need an ama. As an adolescent our ama were our parents, who were all the elders of the village. Then as young men entering puberty, it was the older and mature middle-aged who led the 'aumaga', or men's (youth and mature) organization. This provided general service to the village as a whole, and was the primary force for its protection.

As adults our ama becomes the knowledge and wisdoms of life learned for self-nourishment. As a mature adult/elder who has aligned with the tofa (wisdoms of life) of our cultural values, one understands the ama is more than the veil of what one can see, feel and touch; it is the awareness and ability to attune to the omnipresence of the universe manifested in what Polynesians call 'mana'. Mana is the spiritual energy of the universe manifested through life. You reach for it so that you can survive that particular squall. So, that's the teaching moment, versus sitting under the coconut tree and all of a sudden my uncle talks about reaching for the ama while we're on land. It wouldn't make sense. They taught us the way they were taught. It's not a scheduled conversation for a moment of teaching. Life is the curriculum and will set what needs to be emphasized at any particular moment in any setting.

We're not a literate people. We record history through oratory and through chants. Using this method, our navigators can name every constellation in the sky. Most people just know the four winds; north, south, east and west. But for a voyaging people, there are over 100 winds. It's the same thing, as I understand it, for the people in the Arctic. They have many words for the various types of snow, because they live in that. So, although we don't write what we know, we have detailed knowledge of the natural world. Our ancestors could find a tiny bit of an atoll 2,500 miles away by navigating by the stars. Even modern technology has a bit of difficulty doing that. So even with this precision and quantifiability that scientific knowledge emphasizes, this is only one way of getting where you need to go, but it is not the only way. One relies on a manufactured navigational instrument; the other is that the navigational instrument is the voyager himself.

Our current generation is not learning the same way. With the cascade of technology and media, the distractions of imported processed foods, and the hip social norms, these are greatly distracting, so ideally our best and brightest will be grounded on the island before they go out into the larger world. That way, they can learn the best that they can overseas and then bring it back to the island. Of course, the higher purpose is having the internal strength to hold on to the tofa (wisdoms) while learning a different but dominant western worldview far from home. The challenge at first was not to be overwhelmed and swept away by the compelling weight of Western technology, astonishing science and formidable power. I was raised in a fundamentally stone age culture. Polynesian cultures had no metals and utilized sharpened basalt stones and shells as the primary material technology, and wood from tropical trees as the primary resource. So the exposure to Western technology can extinguish and supplant the wisdoms of millennia where it would do the most harm. Most of the scholarship recipients of my class were primarily the heirs of traditional leaders. Hence, in my case, a descendent of a warrior heritage, I possessed the temerity and confidence to stand my ground, politely but firmly, during discussions at university settings, while voraciously reading and experiencing the machine paradigm by reading and learning theory, literature, arts, science, technology and religion to understand its underpinnings. In time, I was able to weave the traditional wisdom and knowledge of my living/organic world view with the prevailing Western mechanistic paradigm of modern science and technology.

Technology is just a medium, a means to do something. It cannot feel or love, so it is just a medium. The important thing is the person who uses it and the essence behind the purpose in using it. If they intend to teach and convey wisdom, they'll use the appropriate tool. The outrigger is a tool. The wisdom is in utilizing the tool to most effectively convey the wisdom that the tool can teach.

I have had many other wisdom teachers. In the university, during my graduate and postgrad studies, the greatest influence for me academically was Dr. Elisabet Sahtouris. When I first entered university, I was a child from essentially an organic living world. My worldview was a living universe in which I am part of everything in nature, and they are part of me; they're my kin. Over time, I studied the 16th and 17th century paradigms, the enlightenment, and the idea that the universe operates like a giant machine that functions with machine-like regularity. This was new to me. I was beginning to learn the mechanistic paradigm, the mechanistic view of our Earth by Western science. As I progressed further into my graduate studies, I was close to letting go the hand of my organic mother, and replacing it with the hand of my new mechanical father. It was at that moment that I read *EarthDance* by Elisabet Sahtouris, and realized that not all eminent Western scientists and academics think this way. Some actually believed that my world is real too. It was a pivotal moment in my life. Over time, I went on to read other works with great delight such as: *The Web of Life* by Fritjof Capra, *The Whispering Pond* by Ervin Laszlo, *Wholeness and the Implicate Order* by David Bohm, and more recent publications of the same genre. I started to realize that I don't have to give up the hand of my organic mother, my natural mother. But I can also hold the hand of my mechanical father. It's like the bird has a left wing and a right wing, but one body. The learning from these wisdom teachers shaped and guided my life. I shudder to think of my hand slipping away from the living and guiding hand of Papa, my Earth Mother. In fact to this day, I cannot help lowering my head with my eyes watering at the thought. I would have been transformed into an extension of a mechanistic paradigm that continues to cause her unprecedented pain and suffering, rather than one of her many children dedicated to mitigating and stopping it.

Looking back on your life, what is the wisest thing you ever did?

When I decided to get my tatau. This is the traditional tattoo of my people. It's become westernized, which is where you get the word 'tattoo'. In our culture, the tatau covers your skin from the knees to the middle of your chest and often takes up to nine days. It's done with a mallet and a comb that's carved out of human bone. It can get so painful at times that you lose consciousness. I gained greater wisdom through that ritual than anything I had ever experienced. There's a certain point in the tattooing process where they deliberately build the crescendo of pain. The tattooist knows exactly what he's doing. Particularly as the razor-sharp comb of bone needles is tapped into the flesh within a 16th of an inch around your anus, and in between your anus and your testicles to connect the thighs. You can choose to stop at any time, and the ritual ceases. However, you will be incomplete and subject to the timeless disgrace associated with quitting one of the loftiest rituals of all Polynesia. I felt such severe agony; pain appeared white and my thinking was delirious. I knew I could quit so that my suffering would stop; or, I could endure it because I did not want to shame my family and all those that I love. Because this is a very sacred ritual, to not complete it will scar you and your family for generations. It's that severe. When it got to the point where it bifurcated—it's you, or it's who and what you love—I had to make that choice. Any thoughts of self were buried under the image of my mother—who passed while I was away in college in the US—my elders and ancestors who shaped me, my extended family, my village, and of all things, the picture of a little dried and shriveled baby taro in a half coconut shell—everything other than me. All of a sudden, my attitude shifted radically from a near-ignominious slobbering of woe is me, to staring death in the face and yelling defiantly in my mind, 'Screw you; kill me. I won't quit.' It was a feeling I thought I'd never experience. I was really ready to die. The wisdom I gained from that was the realization that there are more important things in life than yourself. I learned that I am willing to endure great hardship and pain for my mother nature, my family, my people, my culture, everything that I hold sacred. I've been tested and know I will step forward as needed to protect it, to defend it, and to assure that it endures, so that my children and their children can also carry it forward. That was an amazing lesson for me and a great wisdom.

I submitted to the tatau ritual in 1980. The military and the missionaries had banned it in American Samoa. However, it was still being done surreptitiously in independent Samoa so you had to go away into the bush and do it. In spite of that, several of us said, "This is our birthright. This is our heritage." And we were willing to go to jail. When we did it, our peers were highly critical of us, because our generation for the most part had been socialized in an imported modern system to see it as a heathen ritual. My boss wouldn't give me leave from work, so I hobbled back and forth to work in my lavalava, with blood oozing through the material. I recall getting onto a bus, and an old man was sitting there staring at me. I went and sat down next to him, and he grabbed my lavalava and nearly yanked it off so I was bare-naked. And when he saw the raw tatau he just called out, "Auwe, auwe!" It's an expression of great joy or sorrow in Polynesia. He said he thought he would die without ever seeing this again and was so grateful and happy that our ancient ritual still lives.

The generational difference in reactions was amazing. The elders were so moved. However, my generation, because we were educated in a different way and had been trained to move away from these heathen practices, reacted as if we had regressed and turned native, so to speak.

We were among the first group to be tattooed on the island since 1930. There were two other groups that were being tattooed at that time. Today there are over 400 Samoan men and women who are tattooed in the traditional manner. With its revival in the Samoas, it has grown in Samoan population centers in New Zealand, Australia and the US. Even greater numbers are having discussions with their extended families for permission to undergo the sacred ritual as more are sensing the suffering of Earth Mother and being guided by her mana to act, speak and heal on her behalf. The revival of the tatau has been extraordinary in its renaissance, and compelling in terms of the young responding to the call of the ancient ritual. Many of our young, highly educated Samoans are tattooed, and others, inspired by their example, are seeking theirs. Equally compelling are the numbers of Samoan women seeking the malu, or special tattoo for Samoan women of nobility. The tatau and malu have undergone a cultural renaissance and its growth continues, no longer impeded by the religious and foreign policies that sought its eradication in the 1930s.

What is the hardest-won wisdom that you have?

I would say the tatau. Your lessons are etched on your skin, and the blood, your life essence, is an important part of it. I think that act embraced my soul in a way nothing else would have. I don't know if I could have attained that level of wisdom without having gone through that experience.

In coming from my culture to the US, I don't know if it was difficult as much as it was new. It was more about curiosity and adaptation. As they say, "You can't direct the wind, but you can adjust your sails." Adjusting and adapting is part of a voyager's life. I think Polynesians in general tend to get along well under almost any circumstances. So I was more curious and fascinated than feeling intimidated or discriminated against. Even if there was discrimination, I wasn't aware of it to the point where it bothered me.

As a young person, you're always taking the risk of losing your soul. You're in a new norm, a new culture. The local young men have different values so I found myself becoming like them without realizing it, because part of being adaptive is that you're not aware that you're also being absorbed. I was being absorbed into new values and behaviors that I almost took for granted until tensions started to build up and I began to feel uncomfortable. At times, but not always, the dissonance was great enough that I actually stepped back and took a look at it, then readjusted my sail to align with my comfort level as to who I was. I find that common with many people. When you enter a new culture, you want to adjust and adapt. Sometimes you're aware that you're becoming absorbed, but at times I saw friends and relatives absorbed to the point that I didn't recognize them. For example, when you sit down as a Samoan, you naturally share your food. However, I met with someone after a few years of our adapting and they would eat in front of me without offering to share some of their food with me. Something as simple as that is a clear sign that they've adapted and adopted a norm. You get your own food and you take care of yourself. It's not that it's bad, but that's the norm. Many of them stayed and married locals in the United States and often they become Americans of Samoan ancestry. There is nothing wrong with that. It's neither good nor bad, I'm not making a judgment. For me, I realized that I nearly crossed the line on that one.

In the world today, where do you see wisdom, and its lack, being demonstrated?

In leadership. Again, it goes back to the mechanistic world. Western culture says that if something's wrong, you need to 'fix it'. You go see a doctor and they say, "Let's work out what's wrong and see if we can fix it." These terms are used by a mechanic. So, when it comes to complex human intentions, it may not be appropriate to say, "Let's fix it." How do you fix hate? You don't—you heal it.

Then, there is a confusion between healing and curing. Curing is removing all evidence of the disease, but it doesn't necessarily mean you're healed. So, you could cure without healing. Healing means to make it whole. The focus of most leaders, from my perspective, is on curing and fixing.

Tensions are usually caused by pain to the body, the soul or the spirit. If you can heal those, that can move you closer to the desired state of harmony and balance that we all see as peace in the world. The same language was used by Nelson Mandela. He used the word 'healing'. That was the first time I'd ever seen a leader use that kind of language. He had suffered horrific violence, but he saw that only healing was going to build his nation, not fixing.

That emphasis came from a lesson from my grandmother. When I was in independent Samoa, my grandfather, who was a ranking traditional leader, was having a meeting with other chiefs. He saw me running over there and knew I wanted to go sit next to him and disturb their discussions, so he called over to my grandmother, and said, "Please take him over there and tell him stories." I was very eager, because I loved her stories. She took me to her little hut in the back. I wanted her to regale me with the great feats of our warrior ancestors. You know, the big pile of heads and bodies. I asked her who was our greatest warrior, and sat there with great anticipation. She replied, "Our greatest warrior did not wield a battle club." I thought she meant he must have had powerful hands. She said, "Our greatest warrior never killed anyone in battle." I thought, 'Oh, maybe grandma's getting older and senile.' Then Grandma said, "Our greatest warrior was not a man. She was a woman. She was the one and only queen in our history. When she reigned, there was no war for her entire lifetime." It was during her time that the medicinal plants, the voyaging and the great architectural buildings flourished. It's similar to the Pax Romana. It was the Pax Samoa. The blossoming of our voyaging civilization occurred about that time and she was known for her healing. That's where I learned an expression that has stayed with me. She said, "Good leaders lead, but great leaders heal." This has been fundamental to my interpretation of leadership.

We are among the most warlike people, under cultural circumstances. We're a very ferocious people, yet it was the principle of healing that this woman brought into our history; and that healing brought peace and harmony.

The machine paradigm has been pervasive so much in modern life that when there is a problem, particularly when it involves a human being or life form, the tendency is to view the solution as a matter of 'fixing' the problem. As I had learned from the wisdom of my grandmother, healing is different and a deep dimension of alofa (love). Similarly, I had always been moved by Mandela's compelling advocacy of reconciliation and healing. Our wise elders and ancestors guide us to seek remedies to the negative legacies of the past, and through that process we heal as a people, move forward as a nation, and embrace as humanity.

How do you apply wisdom to the care of your mind, body and soul?

Most cultures have rituals or ceremonies that address that, because all indigenous societies promulgate or teach through their rituals and ceremonies. Our culture has such ceremonies. One of them is the tatau. How do you teach it? You need to experience it. You cannot develop an ability to do something unless you have a level of experience. You need to learn healing, serving, sacrificing, suffering, loving, spirituality and meditation. All of these kinds of things contribute to a foundation on which you can grow wisdom. Wisdom is not an installation. You don't need a mechanic; you need a gardener.

So, you cultivate these learnings. Every society, I'm assuming, would usually have such rituals and protocols to help their youth, so that they can sustain their level of wisdoms for the next and future generations. We are now seeing societies that are trying to recreate them, or fashion new ones, or import others. As far as I'm concerned, if the end result is a wiser human being, it's good for humanity.

Is wisdom a uniquely human concept?

That would almost imply that animals do not understand wisdom, or are incapable of some level of intellectual learning. I think of Starlings in murmuration, the complex flight of hundreds of them. I knew that with fish before I saw it in birds. You see schools of fish being approached by a shark, and then they break into many shapes and contours, and the shark will get confused and frustrated because it can't catch the fish. That has to come from somewhere. It's simplistic to say it's a survival thing. I think there's something a little bit more there, so I'm not sure wisdom is limited to humans. Where there is life, there has to be some level of wisdom. Otherwise, how does life endure over the millennia? It's through its ability to adapt and adjust. I'd like to think there's an element of wisdom in all living things.

Do you have a favorite parable or anecdote on wisdom?

Good leaders lead, and great leaders heal.

How do you ultimately define wisdom?

I guess it's the ability to gain insights into life, by experiencing healing, serving, sacrificing, suffering, loving and spiritual meditation. All of those I experienced with the tatau; so it's more than just concepts and words. I actually went through a process where I felt as if I met each dimension personally.

How can each of us develop wisdom?

I would suppose it depends on your purpose. We were taught what we call in Samoan, the 'tofa'. There are four major tofa. Tofa means wisdoms, plural.

When you say 'fa'amaulalo', it means humility. So the four tofa: Tofa fa'amagalo (wisdoms of humility), Tofa fa'a aloalo (wisdoms of respect), Tofa alofa (wisdoms of love) and Tofa fa'amagalo (wisdoms of forgiveness) are the foundational pillars of my values that are gifted from our elders to guide the lives of each new generation.

The basic teaching order of the wisdoms follows this sequence: Always engage with wisdoms of humility to all people, large or small, important or unimportant; and to all life with balance and harmony. This is followed by embracing the wisdoms of respect and sustaining with the wisdoms of love. When the three wisdoms are out of alignment, usually it is due to discord, so the fourth, the wisdoms of forgiveness, is conjured. The wisdoms of forgiveness can be construed in another way or expanded into another dimension, the dimension of healing. The tofa fa'amagalo can realign the other three in a way in which realignment can regenerate the healing energies of their collective wisdoms to heal the discord. The wisdoms of forgiveness tend to focus on those who hurt you, but there's a deeper forgiveness there, which is to forgive yourself within your own mind and heart. Until you can forgive yourself, you cannot heal.

These are the wisdoms that help guide you to the greater meaning of life and purpose, which is the foundation of how we interact with all life on this Earth; the all embracive higher tofa (wisdom, singular) of alofa (love).

As I said before, these were not taught formally. Each time, at the right moment, the appropriate one was brought to my attention. It was just like the ama when we were out fishing. My uncle was the one who taught me that teaching and learning are in the moment. It would not be unusual that several elders will approach you about the same incident and remind you of that particular wisdom, to reinforce it.

Is there anything else you wish to add?

In our culture—and I believe it—the foundation of wisdom is alofa, meaning love. When you have love as your foundation, everything else falls into place. I never saw it as something external. It was very much part of growing up, so I didn't really distinguish it as something different. It was something normal. I wasn't as aware of all its manifestations until I got much older. Now I truly understand how central it is to our existence and everything that we do.

How did it feel to discuss wisdom today?

I'm delighted. I'm very happy because this kind of conversation doesn't happen often enough, unless I'm with my family or with others who share the same spirit and values. It's not a common conversation, which is unfortunate and sad, but I try to make it as common as possible in my home, for the benefit of my children and my grandchildren.

I also bring it into my teaching. When I work with the Executive Leadership Seminar Series, my approach is very different than the conventional leadership principles that are taught. For example, specificity, clarity and directness, "When in charge, take charge," connotes the warrior ethos expected of a CEO or corporate executive. I always found disconcerting the absence of alofa, spirituality and an appreciation of the intimate connectivity of all things in the business and leadership literature. Intimacy with one's environment and the universe is the basis of understanding balance, harmony and the life cycle of regeneration where one gives back what energies and materials are taken from the earth to restore, renew and revitalize them. In other words, give back in full measure what is taken.

That's a little different than using metaphors. In our language we convey meaning through metaphor, allegory and analogy. It's irritating when I run into colleagues who insist that it doesn't exist if it can't be measured. They say, "Why are you talking about this metaphorical nonsense?" And I say, "What do you mean nonsense? My understanding is pretty central to your culture and your literature. Haven't you read John Keats, Lord Byron, Shelley or Tennyson? They can teach you a lot about metaphors, analogies and allegories."

Essentially, we're trying to teach life and the principles of life to these young executives, and I think the more holistically we offer the topic to them, the more effective they will be as leaders. Otherwise, you're teaching mechanics. This generation has a very enthusiastic response to this approach. When I first started in the 90s, the industrial paradigm was still very strong. But it's a different generation now. This generation is really concerned about burgeoning disease often associated with human activity, health, chemical dependence for food production and processing, pollution, clean air and water and the general health of the planet. They want to do something about it. I love it because it's easier to guide them towards the essence of wisdom, and into love, because if they really examine what they're doing, that's where it's coming from. It's not coming from the mind alone. A lot of what touches the heart and moves the spirit is in the wisdoms. Many find it difficult to express this love, because it's not taught in a meaningful way. We could encourage every kid to seek and be guided by the wisdom of their elders. To familiarize and learn from the world's life forms by discerning the rhythms, patterns and currents of (mana) life energies, expressed by cultural and world literature, poetry, art, music and philosophies, and discern the kinship ties of all things globally. I'm sensing a movement in this direction and I'm really excited about this generation.

In Hawai'i, 'aloha' is an attunement of life's energies that restore, renew and revitalize the energies of life. In our context aloha is very profound. This is the foundation of life. Otherwise you're just an organism that's alive, but you have no soul. Only acts of aloha strengthen aloha. The only ones that I am aware of that radiate aloha are our elders. They've accumulated this through their lifetime. It just runs within them. Just by them touching you, it's a channeling of energy that we can sense. We get it from people who can manifest this ability because of how they live their lives. Our elders are our greatest gifts as they are the repositories of wisdom who pass it on to each new generation. We must do all we can to assure their health, welfare and happiness as the treasures they are. We must be worthy of our elders as the sacred gifts they have always been in our histories.

I'm not Hawai'ian, but I've sat in on Hawai'ian ho'oponopono. My best description of it is the pure healing power of aloha. However, you need individuals who can channel that to the group. And it's the foundation of healing also, in many different ways. I've seen other people try to practice it, who don't have the cultural roots. It's not something you pull off a shelf. It's something that is planted, and then it's cultivated, grown and fruits within you.

What we practice in Samoa is called the 'ifoga', which is the ritual of forgiveness. Regardless of how horrific the crime, it can be forgiven through the ritual of ifoga. Murder can be forgiven. Wars have stopped or been prevented through ifoga. It's a ritual of humility and forgiveness. The individual who may have been responsible for the problem, let's say a murder, will have his entire village assemble and come before the village of the injured. The most respected and esteemed elder of his family (an elderly mother or father) will be presented with a mat draped over their head. Essentially, it's an ancient form of blood sacrifice to atone for a grievous action. It would be the traditional right of the aggrieved to approach the individual with a war club and bash their head in, killing them instantly. The offending party then wraps the body in the mat they were draped with and withdraws with profound grief. Then it's over. That's one option. The other is a test of the nobility of the aggrieved. They may choose to remove the mat from the head of the elder and invite them into the chief's dwelling to share food and hospitality. With the removal of the mat, and assisting the elder into the dwelling of the offended, then treating them with love, respect and hospitality, the 'crime' is forgiven and the two villages celebrate with subdued joy. So you have these two options. One is healing. The other would be perpetuating conflict because it would be blood for blood for blood, and so on. It's very rare that one would choose to kill the elder, because it calls to the highest nobility of spirit and reminds everyone of this. If the aggrieved decided to actually bash in the head and take the life of the one representing atonement, he and the village will be cursed with misfortune as punishment by the gods. Or, his nobility of action will be exalted for generations, reinforcing the power of forgiveness and healing. It always gets back to reconciliation, forgiveness and healing, because fundamentally Samoans believe that all humans are caring and loving people. In my experience, I have yet to witness or experience anything better.

Isabelle Axelsson

Isabelle Axelsson is a Swedish climate activist from Stockholm. She has been an activist and an organiser of Fridays for Future Sweden since December 2018. In January 2020, she attended the World Economic Forum in Davos along with other climate activists including Greta Thunberg, Vanessa Nakate, Loukina Tille and Luisa Neubauer.

She is currently studying for a bachelor's in Human Geography at Stockholm University, focusing her studies on the social aspect of the climate crisis. She plans to use this knowledge as much as possible in her climate justice activism. During her time as an activist she has amongst other things authored an opinion piece in *TIME* magazine about hope, and given speeches at several events, notably the big climate strike in Stockholm in September 2019, and the Nordic Council's televised award ceremony in 2019, rejecting an environmental prize awarded to Greta Thunberg. fridaysforfuture.se

What comes to mind first when you think about wisdom?

I think of knowledge, and the ability to use knowledge. Also, time comes to mind; the accumulation of knowledge over a long period of time. But I also think that wisdom is something that is difficult to put your finger on and really define.

Do you recall the first time you witnessed wisdom in action?

It's difficult to go back in time and pick out one moment because I think even in very small everyday things there can be a lot of wisdom.

For example, I was talking with my mum the other day and she was saying that when we were children she could tell by the sound of our cries if we were hungry or if we were upset. She could differentiate. So there is a lot of wisdom in knowing and having to understand another person. So I guess when I was a baby I would have experienced wisdom for the first time.

Who have been your wisdom teachers?

Pointing out the wisest person is really difficult because I think most people have wise moments and wise aspects to themselves, which they express in the way they go through life. But they are not necessarily always wise. People develop wisdom within their subjects. An accumulation throughout the life of other people's wise aspects is what contributes to your own wisdom.

I think my parents are pretty wise. And some of my school teachers too. For example, I really liked my history teacher. And my social studies teacher, who taught us to discuss, to listen to each other, and to learn through talking rather than just reading. A lot of that comes from people that I meet in my everyday life, and conversations I have with lots of different people. And of course, there will have been wisdom in books I read growing up, but I can't point out any specific ones right now.

I listen to a lot of music, a lot of punk and DIY music, and there's a lot of social justice elements in this. So from the perspective of wisdom for society, I think there's a lot of wisdom in thinking about other people and seeing injustices in the world, and doing what you can to prevent them, and avoid perpetuating them.

A lot of my understanding has come from finding interests that I like, and then applying that to real life. An example comes from *Star Trek*, the original series, which I used to watch a lot. In some ways it's very outdated, but they raised a lot of important societal issues, and some of them are still relevant today. And that is also something that makes you think.

Through popular media, music and the internet, I have learned a lot about what the world looks like. But you also pick this up in school, and through discussing what I've learned with other people, and being open to many different perspectives. But the most defining thing for me was when I really learned about how connected everything is to each other, through getting involved in the climate movement about a year and a half ago.

I've always been very interested in nature, the climate and the environment. My twin sister wanted to be a marine biologist from a very young age, so growing up we watched a lot of nature documentaries, instead of just watching what was on TV. So we have quite a deep connection with nature in my family. And then when we started learning about how humans are destroying the planet, it was something that really connected with us. And it's horrible. This led to making personal changes in our lives and then getting involved in activism. So a lot of it has to do with how we were raised, to always be listening and to be aware of our surroundings.

Looking back on your life, what is the wisest thing you ever did?

I don't necessarily think that I have had time to make a lot of deliberately wise choices. I still have a lot to learn about the world and how life and everything works first. Though something that I did that I realized would be good for the future, was when I decided to listen to my parents and seek help to get my Asperger's diagnosis. I was struggling in school, and though I thought I had it under control, I obviously didn't. So that has helped me understand myself a lot more. So I guess that was pretty wise.

In trying to help the world and make a positive impact, joining the Fridays for Future movement was important. It allowed me to take my worry and anger about the state of the world to the next level and actively try to shape the world. Though I do have a tendency to overwork and constantly push myself to the brink of burnout, which isn't very wise. So I guess there are wise and unwise aspects to actions.

And I think it's difficult to put your finger on what is wise if it's not wise for both yourself and society.

I got involved through my best friend Ell. She found out about the strikes a couple of months after they had started in Stockholm. She basically said, "Hey, Isabelle, we're both really interested in the climate. We want to do something about it, and are both angry about the situation. We should go to this." So we went, and then we never stopped going. We went every Friday that we could, and started organizing and helping out, doing everything that we could manage. Of course we can't really strike at the moment because of Covid-19, but we're still active and trying to do projects and continue to learn and influence.

Organizing is very organic. Fridays for Future is a grassroots movement, so there's no central organization. I know some countries like perhaps Germany have some form of organization, but in general, it's incredibly loose. At this time we have no legal foundation or institution in any way.

In the beginning, it was simply about striking. It has since become more of a movement where we're pushing and doing more projects, but everything we do began with people coming together, talking and getting to know each other. We started meeting more often to plan things. And I think that happened all over the world as well, that people would meet up in their towns and cities and start planning. We also reach out internationally on social media. So now we have organized group chats. We don't have any real centre or hierarchal system. We have no positions, everything just very loose. That can have its drawbacks, but it has worked for us so far. And I think that's also part of the power of the movement. We aren't stuck in power politics in the same way as other people. It does happen on occasion, since we are products of the society we're raised in, and in my experience, it can be difficult to change behavioral patterns.

The first strike I went to, in December 2018, I actually had an exam that day. My plan was to go in the morning and then leave to do my exam. But once I got there, the strike felt so much more important.

And I thought that I could probably redo the exam at a different date, and my teacher will understand. So I decided to stay the full day. On the one hand, by getting a good enough grade I would get into university and get my career on track. But on the other hand, by standing up to for my opinions and for facts, I could possibly influence our politicians to make decisions that will influence the entire world, and therefore the futures of many millions of people.

At that first strike it was a freezing cold winter day. It started at 8 am and finished at 3 pm. There were maybe 20 of us there all day, and around 100 that came at different times. There were also quite a few adults there, keen to show their support. The mood was quite cheerful if I remember correctly. I think people felt like there was strength in what we were doing. And at the same time, people were trying not to freeze. There was also a sense of anxiety and anger as the problems we are protesting are real. Our governments are ruining our environment, our climate, our planet, and it's affecting so many people and they just carry on as usual.

The strikes started at the end of August, so they had been going on for three months when we first joined. I didn't really know who Greta Thunberg was when I went to the strike for the first time. I knew she was the one that started the strike but it wasn't until after I started going that she became well known. To us in Stockholm she's a co-activist, like the rest of us. She would strike every Friday, the seven full hours like everyone else, unless she was traveling. When she became known worldwide it did end up changing the strikes a bit because, in the beginning, it wasn't taken very seriously at all. But then suddenly there was a lot more interest from the media and there were constantly individuals coming by and saying things like, "You're doing such a good job." People did that before, but not to the same extent. And there were always journalists at the strikes, people taking photographs. And it increased as the year progressed. By spring or summer 2019 there were journalists everywhere, and sometimes it felt like we were standing in a fishbowl.

In terms of the politicians, it has always been a very 'them and us' thing. And even now, because we won't engage with our politicians in the way that people expect us to. Some want us to debate and negotiate with them for climate laws. But at least in the movement in Sweden, our view is that we're only here to be a megaphone for the science. We want our politicians to listen to the science and to do it with climate justice in mind.

Climate justice is the principle that our transition to a so-called green society should not harm people. It shouldn't leave poor people behind, and it should be done with justice towards Global South countries. So for example, countries like Sweden, England and the United States have historic emissions that we need to make up for. And so-called 'developing' countries don't have the same kind of infrastructure we have had time to build. Therefore, countries in the Global North need to transition a lot faster than what they expect Global South countries to. So climate justice is the concept that we have to transition, but we can't leave anyone behind. And some people shouldn't have to bear the brunt of it just because they aren't as rich or because they don't have what they need. We have to take responsibility for history as well as the present.

What is the hardest-won wisdom that you have?

That it takes a long time. Time is the most difficult thing for us climate activists because we know we don't have a lot of it. For at least 30 years we have known that climate change exists and that it will be horrible. And we learn more facts almost daily that prove this point. And yet it's still seen as something you can debate, that you don't have to prioritize. Our politicians don't seem to be taking it very seriously, and prioritizing the change that is needed. Yet we can see how it is affecting the planet. We know that we will soon pass a tipping point at which it is completely irreversible. So we want to reduce the amount of suffering that climate change will cause. Time is frustrating because we don't see our politicians acting and yet we see climate change happening.

In the world today, where do you see wisdom, and its lack, being demonstrated?

I definitely see a lack of wisdom in our politicians. Because they aren't seeing the world from the perspective that is needed. I don't think they have a very holistic view of what affects the planet and how climate change affects other social justice elements, such as sexism, racism and poverty. In pursing those agendas we will also partly be helped by working on the climate crisis and stopping that. Which is a difficult concept of course. But they should still be listening to the science.

I see wisdom in a lot of the youth, who are taking the lead and identifying what needs to happen. We are learning and taking responsibility for something that we shouldn't have to take responsibility for.

I also see wisdom in indigenous peoples. They are some of the wisest of us because they see nature for what it is, and live with nature rather than living off of it, most of the time. I think that is something that we need to learn from a lot more. We would benefit greatly from respecting that, and their undying devotion to nature, and how far they will go to protect it. Seeing the news from the Amazon in Brazil, with all the land defenders being killed, is so heartbreaking.

The question of good examples of climate leadership is difficult. I certainly haven't seen any city do enough yet. Sweden and the other Nordic countries are seen as leading on climate issues. But for those that live here and do read the science, we see that we're doing nowhere near enough. An interesting article was published recently by Uppsala University and Manchester University, authored by Andersson, Stoddard and Broderick. It is a study of the extent to which the UK and Sweden are following the Paris agreement, and how our climate goals line up with that. And they say that Sweden is fulfilling about 50% of what we need to be doing, yet Sweden is seen as one of the leaders on climate change. It is horrifying that the country or the areas that people look up to are doing the bare minimum.

I did a speech in Stockholm after our demonstration last September. We had about 50,000 people there. I was terrified. But when you're on the stage it's fine. Actually, I find it less scary to talk to that many people than to talk to 10, because then you can see every reaction. That was probably one of the craziest things we organized because we weren't expecting that many people to come. It was so cool afterwards watching the news, because there were so many interviews with people that went to the strike. It was one of the biggest demonstrations that Stockholm has seen in a very long time. There were people there that have never demonstrated or even considered being activists before. Many had left work or taken the day off work to come to our demonstration. And many of them were older adults or even retired. It was crazy that we had managed to motivate people who had never thought about getting together to fight for the climate.

In terms of the way our government has handled Covid, it's been very easy for me at least to continue my life pretty much as normal, besides not being able to go and strike. I know for many people, the way that we've handled it has been absolutely terrifying, because when you go outside it appears very normal. I work in an ice-cream shop so I do go out and work. There are signs everywhere about social distancing, and people keep their distance on the tube and on public transport. But when you walk down the street, it looks almost like normal. Although, while you're outside, you only see the people that aren't taking it seriously, and not the ones who are isolating and taking care of themselves and social distancing.

The government has a lot of trust in its people. And the people do have a lot of trust in the government, whether we like to admit it or not. So I think we would have followed their guidelines if they'd been more strict. And while we do have a lot of deaths, we also count more of them than other countries do, so not only the hospital Covid deaths, but also deaths in retirement homes. Our way of handling it has been easier on the people. Though it's still really difficult. For example restaurants aren't making enough money. But people can still go outside. People aren't cooped up at home, being frustrated. People can go to work and haven't been thrown into poverty in the same way that other countries are. So while I think we haven't limited the spread as much as we could have, it also hasn't affected people's lives or mental health as negatively as others. I can't really speak to the effectiveness of this way of dealing with it compared to other countries, because I don't know the facts and I'm not a scientist or epidemiologist.

The hope subject is something that a lot of people ask us about. People say, "You are giving everyone hope." They expect us to have lots of hope for the future. However, through a lot of discussions with other people in the movement it's clear that a lot of us don't have much hope for the future, but we're doing this anyway, because we have to. There's no option to not do everything that we can. And I don't think this hopelessness is a bad thing necessarily. It means that we are very realistic. We know the science, so we know the facts and we know what will happen if we don't change. And at the same time, we don't see the action needed from our politicians.

So we are realistic about the fact that climate change is happening and there's nothing we can do about it besides telling our politicians to act. And they're not doing that. The system in place isn't working. So unless they do something there isn't a lot of hope. Humanity is not going to end, there's not going to be an apocalypse, but there's going to be a lot of suffering. That's something that we have to accept and understand, but we still need to do everything we can to stop or mitigate it. We have to try to influence our politicians to change, even if they aren't showing any willingness or action.

And I think having a lot of hope in seeing that we can solve this within this amount of time, sure it can be very motivational, but I also think that it can bring about the opposite. When it comes to climate change the highest chance is that we will fail in our mission as activists in trying to basically save the world, and that will bring even more hopelessness. And I think a lot of people will give up. That's something we have seen within the movement already. People say,

"We've been doing this for a year and nothing's happening." But I think we need to see that things are changing, slowly. They're changing too slowly, but we also have to understand that we can't change them as fast as we want to and need to. The politicians and the system doesn't allow things to change faster, which is stupid. I could rant about this for a long time. But I think hope is something that people want to have, yet I don't think it's something that we need to have. I think realism is a lot stronger, and being realistic and understanding the situation and still doing everything you can, is amazing. So many of the youths understand that this is basically inevitable, but are still going to do everything they can to stop the suffering and the inequalities that this will cause. Even if I'm putting lots of time and effort into this and it hardly pays off in helping others, I will still do it because someone needs to. I think that is such a strong approach: doing something even if it seems impossible.

How do you apply wisdom to the care of your mind, body and soul?

In terms of taking care of ourselves, there is very little of that in the movement. There is a lot of burnout, a lot of people working so hard and not making sure that they themselves are doing okay. I know a lot of people have so much anxiety and anger about the climate crisis, and the failure of our politicians, but that is their way of trying to be heard, even if it's not as successful as we would want it to be. So I guess I have a similar issue, in that I do work a lot. I'm so busy. I hardly ever have free time anymore. But one thing I do that helps is to get good sleep. At least seven to 10 hours a night. Sometimes I get less, but sleep is so important to me in my processing and being able to manage. There's a lot of all-nighters pulled by people in the movement, but I try to never do that.

I like going on walks in the forest or by water, which is really nice. Either I'm with someone else and discussing things, or I'm listening to a podcast, usually about the climate. But I find it relaxing, walking in nature. I do feel connected to nature, because I know that life is sustained by the water, by the air, by the vegetation. We couldn't exist without it. That is something that we don't really appreciate when we're out walking and looking at nature. We just see something beautiful rather than something that sustains us. And if we ruin it, how do we sustain ourselves? We won't. At least not in the way we are doing today. There is a big disconnect between humans and nature. And I'm not as connected as I would like to be. We don't realize how much we are depending on nature, because we live in big concrete buildings.

I don't have a spiritual practice. I'm an atheist, but I do respect people's religions and their way of seeing the world. One of my best friends is a Christian, and another is Muslim. I think it's fascinating and I really respect their faiths, even if I don't understand it myself.

I'm not sure that there are some unique, pre-existing cultural conditions that led to the school strike movement. It could have happened anywhere really. I think it takes the right person at the right time with the right things happening just to set it off. And I think that's what it was: a catalyst. We do have lots of nature in Sweden. We are mostly forest. If you exclude Russia and Ukraine, we are the third biggest country in Europe by area, just under 174,000 square miles. But we are the 16th largest by population, with 10.1 million people. So there's a lot of nature here and a lot of Swedish people really like nature. It's common to go out camping, skiing or hiking.

But one significant influence on the strikes was the summer of 2018 when we had the big forest fires here. From early May to late July we only had half an inch of rain. May and July were the hottest ever recorded here. In mid-July, temperatures were 10 degrees C higher than normal. We had around fifty fires, covering an area of 100 square miles, or 250 square kilometers. There were also forest fires in Norway, Denmark and Finland. And I think that's when a lot of people realized, 'Oh crap, this is actually happening.' For a lot of the time we feel like climate change doesn't really affect us in Sweden. We get warmer winters, which means we don't have to freeze as much. Summers are generally quite warm as well. We can go swimming in the lakes which is also quite nice. But we don't always realize how bad something is until it directly affects us. Like the forest fires did. That could have been a catalyst in Sweden, or at least the youth learning more about the climate crisis through direct experience. I also think that it is something that a lot of kids think about, because we do learn about it in school, and then can learn about it ourselves. But I think this could have happened anywhere really. it could have happened in the United States, France or the Philippines. But it happened here because the right person had the right idea at the right time, right before our elections. And then it caught on.

When the media covers the strikes, it's often focused on Greta. I think people like finding a figurehead to relate to, or someone to focus on. I understand it, even if it's perhaps not optimal for the movement or for her, or for the climate. But the way the media reports on climate has changed since we started striking. They do write more about the climate crisis, rather than just climate change. And they write about what it is, and about the responsibility of politicians. However, it's still very focused on us, and what we're doing, and not enough on the actual science and what needs to be done. So I don't think the science is being communicated properly. It's a lot more about personality and fun, rather than on science and what needs to be done based on that. So it's easier for politicians to dismiss us as just teenagers skipping school, rather than addressing the science, and what is happening. And it also opens up to be more of a debate, I've noticed. But it's harder for the politicians to debate the facts themselves.

Everything is at a bit of a standstill at the moment. I was supposed to be traveling this summer. To be honest, Covid-19 has had a bit of a silver lining for me because I have finally been able to slow down a bit. This year has been absolutely crazy, because I started it by going to the World Economic Forum and spending a week in Davos, talking, networking, watching panels and speaking on panels with lots of world leaders and so-called stakeholders. It was kind of crazy. And then two weeks later I went to Berlin for a meeting and then two weeks later I went to Brussels for a demonstration. And then just after Brussels I came home and went into isolation for Covid-19—all of this while studying full-time at university.

I was planning on going to Vienna, and to France for a summit, and to Italy for a meeting. And plenty more places. It was all cancelled, and it's kind of a blessing that there's less organizing to do so many of us can rest up. However, it is slowing down climate action from politicians as the focus is elsewhere. So when Covid is over we'll be able to go full-on again and demand change.

So my plans are just to work during the summer and chill at home, and do some backlog stuff like emails. I've already finished university for the term, and it doesn't start until the end of August. So I'm basically free. I'm doing a bachelor's in human geography, society, the environment and global processes. So it's a lot about how humans use the land and our relationship to it. It's really interesting, and next term I'm doing a couple of modules focusing on the climate and how it affects society and vice-versa.

Is wisdom a uniquely human concept?

No, I don't think so. We have observed many animals learning and using knowledge. And they pass it down to their children. Like orcas. They learn hunting techniques, and different forms of them have different ways of hunting, and different prey. Some are more specialized in hunting seals and others in hunting whales, or fish. They teach it to the children, and they have some really cool techniques. I think that is very wise, that they learn how to adapt themselves to the climate and location, and they a find a way to teach it to their children. So there's definitely wisdom in other animals, and in nature and how it adapts to a changing environment. Though the climate is changing so fast that a lot of species are struggling to adapt fast enough.

Do you have a favorite parable or anecdote on wisdom?

None that I can think of specifically. I think it's been running through my life. My mom has passed on a lot of things that I use daily.

A lot of useful knowledge or maybe even wisdom. She's an educator, a preschool teacher. She focuses a lot on listening and philosophy with children. So we've had a lot of discussions about what listening means and what listening is, and how to be open to other people.

I was raised without my parents giving me and my siblings any political ideologies or anything. So we didn't talk about those things until I learned about them in school.

Instead, we would watch nature programs, which are very factually-based. We would talk about listening to and understanding other people's perspectives, and respecting other people. That has given me a lot of opportunities to choose how I see life, and how I view the world and politics. It has given me a lot of advantages in the climate movement. For example, if there are arguments in any of our chats, I can see what's going on and say, "Both of you have points in this argument. This is how I see what has happened objectively. You're not listening to each other, so we're not going to get anywhere." That is so important when you discuss things. You have to genuinely listen to the other side, and not make assumptions, and not simply wait for your turn to make a point. It was very important that my mother taught me that we should listen to, understand and respect people, even if we disagree with them.

Generally, people are receptive to this approach. But I think people have difficulty applying it. I think I have an advantage in being autistic, so I don't get as heated with things. It's easier for me to see things objectively. But I do think people appreciate it. When I enter discussions that are heated, I try to help both sides gain some objectivity. Though I may say that I agree more, or completely, with one side, and I will give my reasons. I think people have an easier time to relate and see conversations from a logical point of view where they see that the person they're discussing with isn't angry at them and disrespecting them. But that's just me and how we think at home.

In the movement, we have people who have been campaigning on climate and environment for a long time. People in NGOs for example. We talk to them, and they sometimes help us out with things.

So we have a lot of experience to tap into, but we don't always take their advice. One of the reasons I think Fridays for Future has become so big is because we're doing things our own way, not necessarily the way that it has been done in the past. At least in Sweden, we don't have any specific demands for the government. We have three principles: Listen to the science; follow the Paris agreements and the 1.5-degree goal from the IPCC reports; and climate justice. They encompass all of the specific demands. But if we focus on specific ones, you can easily forget other things and it's less holistic. And you don't realize that there's a big part of the system that needs to change. You would just change certain things within the system, and then, in the end, they won't work together. That is something that a lot of people don't seem to understand. They tell us to formulate specific demands to get more people engaged. Yes, you might get some people to engage in it, but you'll also alienate others who don't agree with us. Or perhaps it's not scientifically-based. Because we always point towards the scientists, it's very difficult for us to formulate specific demands on what laws to enact. I'm sure we could collaborate with scientists on that, but it's a lot more difficult when you don't have all the different perspectives in view, because it's quite complex.

We're trying to steer clear of specifics because we don't want to lose the holistic principle. If the conversation is done together with the scientists and we can collectively say that this is what we need to stay below the 1.5 degrees warming target then yes I think that is really good, because that is what we're pushing for. We want to get our politicians in a room together with our scientists and for the politicians to actually listen to them and then act upon it.

So far the government has not done so. At the end of last year they produced a plan, which wasn't great. It wasn't about active plans to reduce our emissions.

The ministers from several different sectors meet every once in a while to talk about what they are doing for the climate. And they were framing it like it was this really good thing for the climate. But I can't wrap my head around how the ministers meeting each other and talking about it will be very effective unless the scientists are in the room as well. They might be well educated within their areas of expertise, but how educated are they in terms of how their area of expertise affects the climate, and what they can do to help climate change? That confuses me. There is a lack of adequate representation from scientists and science in the parliaments and governments. And there's a lack of understanding of how much it is needed. There's so much talk about, "Oh, we can't do that because of the economy." But they say very little about what will happen if we don't do it.

A lot of our scientists are not allowed to get involved in climate activism, as this is seen as politics, unfortunately. But the scientists in Sweden are trying a lot more now. An organization was created to support us, and it's here in Stockholm. It's called Researcher's Desk. It's a collection of scientists from many different sectors. And they're available to educate people about science. So every week, at least before the strikes were cancelled due to Covid-19, scientists would come to our strike every week and have a street lecture. They would tell us about some different aspect of the climate crisis and the science, and what it actually means.

It was really good because some of the people that come to the strikes only come to support and they don't know a lot, so then they would learn. And now during Covid, we have lectures every Friday and Saturday from climate scientists. So they are teaching us and the public about science. But it is a lot harder to reach the politicians. So we're trying to amplify what the researchers have found out and get politicians and people to act upon it.

How do you ultimately define wisdom?

I think wisdom is a very abstract concept. I don't think it's something that you can fully define. I think it's being able to apply knowledge and life experiences to life, both now and in the future, to benefit yourself and ideally others too. It's something that you can accumulate over time. It's not something that you're born with necessarily. But I do think that wisdom is something that is difficult to define. And it's difficult to see in yourself. It's easier to see it in others. I think wisdom is an accumulation of knowledge and life experiences and being able to apply them to real-life situations.

How can each of us develop wisdom?

As I talked about earlier, listening is crucial to developing wisdom. Listening, and being open to other people is key. Even if you disagree with someone, listen to them. Otherwise, you're both stuck in a little bubble of your opinion and you don't really see and hear other people.

I think it means listening to facts and acting accordingly. You don't necessarily have to respect things that aren't factual. You can still listen to someone that is perhaps arguing against the importance of vaccines. They may say they cause autism, even though the facts say that they don't. You shouldn't just be aggressive and be mean to them, but you should not let them convince you about it.

Most of all it's really important to listen to those who are negatively affected by how the world works. So listen to people that are oppressed and then act and adapt to that, or give them what they need.

Is there anything else you wish to add?

I don't think so. We've talked about a lot of different things today.

How did it feel to discuss wisdom today?

When I was reading the questions, it felt weird because I was looking at them and thinking, 'I have no idea. I am in no way qualified to be talking about any of this stuff.' I don't really look towards the future too much. I see the science, but I take every day as a new day, and just make it up as I go along. So how do I have anything to say about wisdom? But I think while talking about it I have learned a lot, both in how I see things, and how I see myself. It's been educational.

David Bailey

David has been a handmade book maker for the past 16 years. For the first eight years he imported books from India to sell alongside his own; since then he has concentrated exclusively on his own work. Prior to this he had a variety of jobs and experiences, including teaching Creative Sound Production at a Further Education college. For five years he was a professional sculptor, specializing in large-scale cardboard structures.

What comes to mind first when you think about wisdom?

I have come to associate wisdom with clear sight, the ability to perceive what is truly important in any given situation. I see it as taking an aerial, mountaintop view of things. From this high vantage point we have a better chance of identifying patterns and repercussions that it might not be possible to discern from the ground level. When I'm faced with any kind of important decision, I imagine pulling out and looking down on the situation from above. It's a process of getting away from initial emotions and short-term thinking.

I also associate wisdom with age, and a slow accumulation of experience. I suspect lasting wisdom only develops as a result of a certain amount of life on the planet—somewhat like growth rings on a tree.

I have met some wise young people of course, but even then I wonder if we might find, perhaps 20 years later, that those people had undergone periods of challenge and confusion when wisdom was harder to find. None of us escape life's ups and downs.

Do you recall the first time that you witnessed wisdom in action?

This is not my first experience of wisdom, but it's one I recall every now and again, and use as a touchstone. When I was young I had some work experience in a professional gallery. One day I was helping to set up an exhibition in the gallery for a sculptor called Fenwick Lawson, who comes from the north east of England.

Fenwick is a very compassionate sculptor. I love his work. The exhibition featured some large figures made from wood. They were raw and very powerful. I was trying to move one of the figures but it was a bit heavy for me, and I dropped it, causing the base to split. All my breath left me. I gasped Fenwick's name to get his attention so I could show him what had happened. He's a big man, big hands, big beard. He bent down to inspect the sculpture, then looked at me. And he said, "Isn't this great, Dave? Look at the grain on the inside here. Look at what's happened to the wood. Isn't this amazing?"

He probably doesn't even remember the incident. But what he did was see the situation. He could have been angry, but instead he saw the bigger picture. He was so compassionate; so observing of where I was. It was one of those situations that could have been traumatic for me, but I store it as a warm, treasured memory.

There have been a few moments since then when I've been about to react with anger or frustration and the image of Fenwick's face has come to mind. On one occasion, a piece of my own sculpture got destroyed, and I did a kind of Fenwick myself. I'd made a pair of hands in clay. They'd taken ages to do. It was the best sculpture I'd made at that time. They were just ready to be fired. One of the other students picked the hands up and said, "Wow, these are nice," and then dropped them. The hands broke into dozens of pieces. The student was distraught. But I thought of Fenwick and said, "That's okay, I can make them again." I wouldn't have done that had I not had this very moving sense of someone demonstrating what needed to happen in a similar moment.

Who have been your wisdom teachers?

I had a remarkable experience many years ago that has stayed with me. It happened in a Chinese takeaway in Middlesbrough. I went in with my then girlfriend, and there was a guy waiting for his order, and he started asking me questions. I'm normally the person who asks questions, or listens to people's problems, so it was interesting being on the other side of it. This man started asking me about my life. And he did it in a way that made my whole being inflate. The feeling was blissful. My partner at the time felt the same. There was a quality about what he did that has remained with me. And this happened in a takeaway in Middlesbrough! So we don't need to go to India to find enlightened beings.

A friend of mine, Jan, is beautifully wise. Everyone should know her. She is an amazing listener. She's able to pick out the one or two really telling comments from whatever you've said, and reflect them back to you with tremendous clarity and insight. Again, it's this notion of being able to patiently absorb all the information and pick out the signal from the noise. It's a very humble, wonderful skill.

Compassion and nonjudgmental awareness are qualities I strongly associate with wisdom. We know that everyone we meet is hurting; everyone's got a pressing story going on at any given moment. Whenever we're dealing with human beings, that's the basic foundation: we're all broken in some way. It's not a problem, not something to grieve about, it's just the way it is as a human being. Trees get gnarly. Human beings are fragile. It's life.

One thing bookmaking has taught me about wisdom is how important it is to find a good fit between our sensibilities and talents, and how we make our living. It's so important to our happiness. I remember hearing a psychiatrist remark that most of the suffering experienced by the people he worked with arose from them trying to be something they're not.

Over the years I've increasingly noticed that when people start talking about certain subjects, their whole body language changes.

They sit up, speak faster, come to life. A person's whole body changes when they're enthused and energized by what they're saying. If you watched the reaction back on screen you'd see it very clearly. When someone is inspired, their whole being radiates energy. It's magical. It's one of the great joys of my life to meet people who are a good fit for what they do. And of course, meeting anyone sparking like this also serves as an invitation for us to find our own path.

I've come to think of the universe as being filled with an endless multitude of little holes. Our task is to find the one made specially for us, the hole that best fits our unique shape. It takes a lot of discernment. We have to do a lot of sorting the signal from the noise. It's not easy. We've all spent time trying to be something we're not, or doing things that don't suit us.

Bookmaking has been an incredibly good fit for me. I've been doing it for 16 years. It's really been a path of love. I've made thousands of books, and every one of them is different in some way. I don't make them by rote. I've never just knocked them out as quickly as I could, or to a fixed pattern. I've always tried to stand back and be sensitive to what each book wants to be, and I hope I've given every one of them as much as I can bring. So I've come to recognize that for me bookmaking has been a blessed, generous path.

Looking back on your life, what is the wisest thing you ever did?

When I left school I was due to go to art college but I didn't feel ready, so I deferred and took a summer job in a warehouse, counting unsold newspapers all day. I did that hour after hour, day after day. I ended up getting promoted to the management side of the company, and stayed there six years, right into my 20s. It wasn't a good fit for me. I made some good friends, but those years were wasted in a way. These things just happen sometimes, especially when we're young.

One day, when I was about 23, I got offered a big promotion, with lots more money and a company car and so on. That night I had a dream in which I met God. I had died, and was in a hospital waiting room. There was a table with some magazines on it. A nurse popped in and said, "God's not quite ready yet, Mr. Bailey. Just wait there." So I got on with reading a magazine. A few minutes later, I was called, and got taken down the hospital corridor, and into what appeared to be a Victorian drawing room, with a fire, and books filling the walls. There were two red leather armchairs in front of the fire. God was sitting in one, with a glass of port in one hand and a cigar in the other. He gestured to me to sit in the other chair. There was a glass of port and a cigar waiting for me. Nothing was said for a while. We just sipped our port and smoked our cigars. And then God spoke, in a thick northern accent. "So Dave, what did you think of that, then?"

He was referring to my life. I took a puff of my cigar and replied, in the same accent, "Well, thanks very much. I quite enjoyed it."

Then we sat back, drinking our port and smoking our cigars. I thought for a bit, and then said, "But it's a shame I couldn't have done what I really wanted to do."

Then God set aside his port and looked at me very seriously. He leaned into my face and said, "So why didn't you?"

And I realized in that moment that I could have done what I really wanted to do. All that was stopping me was my idea of what my life should be like. It was all my invention.

Then I woke up. So it was a very visceral dream. I went into work and turned down the promotion. I left the company and started working part-time in an art gallery bookshop, then I went back to college and started sculpting. So I consider turning down that promotion to be one of the wisest things I've ever done. I've never done anything since just for money.

I remember that I only had a few hours to write out my application for the art gallery job; it had to be in the day I found out about it. I filled the form out and handed it over, but something made me snatch it back. I had filled it in the way I thought I should. So, recalling the dream with God, I asked for another form and filled it in across the road in a coffee shop. And I wrote an impassioned artistic statement about how if I got the job I'd use it to support me going to college to study sculpture. I hung everything out there, my whole heart. I was the last person to be interviewed for the job. And the people from the gallery said, "Just to let you know, we've had five really good interviewees today. We could employ any of them." And then one of the women doing the interviewing held up my application form and said, "But let's talk about this." And I went for it. I just let it out with complete honesty. After a minute or two she stopped me and said, "The job's yours." It was a really nice moment. I think they liked the romance of it, but it might also have been a reward for being real.

Some years later, in the early 2000s, my partner Adele and I went to do voluntary teaching in an orphanage in India. I'd always wanted to go there. I remember in primary school we were all asked to do a big project on a country, and I immediately chose India. I used to have regular dreams of a little green bridge over a river, and I always associated it with India.

Adele and I had only been together a month when we went to the orphanage. She'd already set up the trip. So I left my job and went with her. It was funny; just weeks after we got together, we found ourselves living in a tiny hut, with mice scurrying around and spiders the size of your hand on the walls. We arrived in the middle of the night, in a little village called Lakshman Jhula. It's about four hours north of Delhi by train, up where the Ganges is still quite clear. We grabbed a few hours' sleep then left the orphanage, which was high up on a hill, and went exploring. We scrambled down a rocky path, turned a corner and we were suddenly facing the Ganges. And the green bridge I'd dreamed about as a child was right there in front of me, exactly as I'd been seeing it all my life.

In the orphanage there were 38 kids, aged from three to 16. We were with them a few hours a day. I got on with all of them, except one. He just rubbed me up the wrong way. He was a six-year-old boy called Oinak. I secretly used to call him Annoy-nak. I remember one day after Adele and I had been there about three months, I had a particularly frustrating morning with Oinak. We went down to the river for a break. And Adele said, "You know, Oinak might be your spiritual teacher."

And I put my head in my hands and moaned, because I couldn't resist the truth of it. Adele left me alone by the river, and over the next half hour I pondered everything. And when I finally headed back up towards the orphanage, Oinak ran out of the compound to meet me and gave me a big hug. That had never happened before. We were thick as thieves afterwards. India is like that, of course. The heart tends to open there. And the wisdom I found that morning was to hear the truth, not resist it.

My journey with making books also began in India. We'd been in the orphanage for a few months and wanted to see a little of India before our visas ran out. We didn't know where to go, but there was a faded old map of India on the orphanage wall. We took it down, Adele spun it round, and I closed my eyes and stuck out a finger. We'd decided to go wherever my finger landed. It ended up being a beautiful place called Udaipur, to the far west of Rajasthan. It was a 30-hour journey by train. And it happened to be a place where they were making books by hand. They cut the leather, made the paper and bound the books together. Sometimes the leather would be left unadorned, sometimes it would be embossed, sometimes decorated with precious stones. The books took my breath away.

I bought one after looking at literally hundreds, did some drawings in it, and went back every day. So I got to know some of the book suppliers really well. They used to call me Dev, instead of Dave. They said, "Dev is being a very good name! It's the name of a God!"

I loved the books, so Adele and I decided to buy some to sell in England. It was a good confluence of things. Udaipur is a beautiful city and I felt completely at home there. At one point some of the Indian guys I'd got to know came over to me and said, "Dev, we are thinking that you are not being a Westerner. You are being an Indian with white skin!" I treasure that as one of the warmest compliments of my life.

I began making my own books a short while later, learning through making repairs and improvements to the Indian books. I loved it straight away. It's easy to read things into events, of course. We can convince ourselves something was meant to be, but it does feel like that sometimes. And special things do seem to happen more often when we get out of the way, and are quiet enough to be guided.

What has been the toughest lesson you have learned?

One of the most enduring lessons that having a business has taught me, is the notion of sustainability. At one point I started wholesaling the books. I made good money, but the sustainability of the business was being eroded.

I like the Zen story where a novice comes to the monastery, and goes completely over the top. Everyone else is meditating five hours a day and he's meditating ten hours. Other people are doing a hundred chants a day and he's doing a thousand. One day he's walking down a corridor at the monastery and meets the old abbot. The novice is full of questions, but the old monk leans towards him and sniffs.

"What are you doing?" the novice says in bewilderment. The old monk nods. "You stink of Zen," he says.

We don't want to be stinking of Zen. It's not sustainable. And although I was making more money when I was wholesaling, my life reeked of business. If I had continued doing it I would have burnt out and quit the whole thing. So I backed off. In the end I pared my whole business down to as simple a model as possible. It increased the sustainability of it by years.

When faced with big business decisions, I like to picture a meeting in a boardroom. Everyone is free to input thoughts concerning any new idea, from the perspective of their department. Finance, manufacturing, etc. The wise elder at the head of the table listens to everything, and when everyone has finished speaking he simply asks one question: "Is this new idea going to make our business more sustainable, or less sustainable?"

In some respects it may be the wisest question we can ask. I use it a lot when making decisions. How will this affect long-term sustainability? We can apply the question to our health and wellbeing, our job choices, everything. It might not always provide an answer, but it'll always provide insight. And we can ask it with reference to many different timescales. How will this course of action impact things over the coming weeks, months, years, even decades? If we think in these longer timescales, we invariably make different decisions.

In the world today, where do you see wisdom, and its lack, being demonstrated?

It's obvious that as a species we are living very unsustainably. It undermines and haunts everything we do. I think it is affecting each and every one of us, emotionally and spiritually, whether we realize it consciously or not.

We are in dire need of thinking in much longer timescales as a species. There is a story about a village that earns its income by selling the produce of its orchards. One year they endure a bitterly cold winter. The villagers go to the elder demanding they should be allowed to chop down the apple trees so they can have firewood to keep warm. But the elder shakes his head, and counsels them that to make such a decision would affect the village's long-term survival. So he urges them to find a different, more sustainable solution, one that doesn't alleviate the immediate problem at the expense of long-term disaster. Once again, it's about taking the mountain-top view of the situation, the long-term view.

How do you apply wisdom to the care of your mind, body and soul?

The phrase, 'As much as possible from as little as possible,' has a lot of meaning for me. I first encountered it via the Spanish composer Federico Mompou. Most of his compositions were short, often simple pieces for the piano. He had that phrase, 'As much as possible from as little as possible,' above his piano.

When you do enough creative things you come to realize that one of the most undervalued tools of the creative process is taking the time to focus things down. Leonardo da Vinci said, "Small rooms discipline the mind, large ones weaken it." That notion of hourglassing, narrowing something down towards a point of creative limitation, can be very fruitful. If you calibrate it right, a huge amount of ideas pour out of the other end. If you squeeze too narrow, ideas become stunted; pull out too wide, and ideas become too diffuse. There's a real skill involved in getting the focus just right. So this notion of as much as possible from as little as possible can be very powerful. If you work with it effectively a huge amount of growth can come from it.

Another example of mind and body care is walking in nature. I do it almost every day. And 95% of the time I walk exactly the same route, because I've learned over the years that it encourages me to get to know individual trees and hollows and rocks. Through them I can track the changes over the seasons. I can notice the first leaf in spring on a particular bush, for instance, or if a tree has been damaged, or the day new fungi appear. By narrowing my field of focus, I can get very aware and sensitive.

But I've also been lucky in never wanting much from life. I've always been like this. I'm a pretty content person by nature. It's not torpor, but a feeling of enough. That feeling is a great litmus test for me in how my life is going. It may also be that if we get our fit right, a lot of our needs and wants fall away.

At one time I did a lot more art than craft. Sculpture, painting and music composition. Not that I'm really sure what the difference is between art and craft. I don't know if anyone's really answered that; there's such a blurry line. But one of the things I treasure about art is that it contains a sense of mystery. Something is trapped in a piece of art that we can't unpick. We'll never know exactly what it's saying. With craft it's different. When I make a book, we can look at it and appreciate something obvious in it, if only a basic craft skill. It's a tactile thing. It's not trying to be something it's not. It's just a book, however nice.

But if I were to do a painting of a book, perhaps sitting closed on a table, that is an enduring mystery. What does the book signify? We will never know. I suspect that art somehow reflects the reality that a fundamental aspect of the world is forever beyond our ken. It's eternally mysterious. We might wish that the world would make sense, but it doesn't, and art somehow points towards that elusive quality in life.

It also offers us a glimpse into someone else's being. Good, or certainly great art, expands us. It enables us to experience something we might not have reached on our own, and allows us to stand at a new vantage point we might never have reached. I think we are enormously grateful for that, whether we'd articulate it that way or not. Craft does something else. We probably stay in our own shoes to appreciate craft.

From a personal point of view, the rewards of being a craftsman have come from giving myself over and surrendering to it. I never pick up my tools and think, 'Oh God, another book to make.' I've always thought it a worthwhile thing to do. I genuinely feel I am carrying on a lineage, albeit in a very tiny, insignificant way. I have great respect for that lineage.

I work with leather and paper, and cut everything by hand. I remember a fellow book-maker came by my stall one day. He inspected the paper in one of the books, and said, "You don't cut your paper by hand, do you?" I said, "Yes. With a ruler and scalpel." "He said, "That must take bloody ages! You can get the paper laser cut by machines." And I said, "But then I wouldn't feel the paper."

When I did a pottery course, half the class would do wheel-throwing, because you can make a pot really quickly that way. The other half, including me, did hand building. Some of us have to feel what we do.

Anyway, this other bookmaker said, "I can't believe what you're doing! You must be cutting paper all the time!" So I said to him, "I only cut paper when I feel in the mood. I clear the room, put on music and it becomes a totally meditative experience. I don't cut paper unless I want to cut paper. But when I do it, I do it with love."

I'm probably in the top 0.001% of people who have cut paper. I've done the same cutting motion hundreds of thousands of times and I still get pleasure from it. Somehow I've found a sustainable method that involves concentration, awareness and enjoyment. The only way you can do this is to be ever new with it, genuinely. You can't kid yourself with a smoke-and-mirrors tactic. The enjoyment is either there or it's not. It's not a technique or an affirmation. I don't brainwash myself into thinking I enjoy it. But if you bring love to it, you can join with the paper, and it can be a dance between the two of you. It is an ever-generous process. But you have to give in to it, surrender to it.

It reminds me of that Confucian saying: "We have two lives. And the second begins when we realize we only have one." With only one life available, it's wise to at least try to do what we do with love. Otherwise, it may be time to find a different path.

Is wisdom a uniquely human concept?

I don't know, is the honest answer. When I look at nature, I see it display the characteristics of wisdom. As I said earlier, I go into the woods almost every day. In this lockdown, I haven't missed going into town at all. But if they'd locked down the woods, I would have been bereft. I feel cradled when I go into the woods, at peace. There's an old saying: 'If you want more questions, go into town. If you want answers, go into the woods.' I find that so true. I always go for a walk when I need to sort through something.

When I was first in Bristol a friend from back home in York asked if I had any friends down here. And I said, "Lots, but my best friend's name is Leigh." I was referring to Leigh Woods. It was true. I wasn't being funny. I went into the woods every day and it kept me in Bristol, when I could easily have left. Being in the woods is being with a presence that I can't meet any other way.

How do you ultimately define wisdom?

Recapping some of the things we touched on earlier, I see it as being founded on understanding and compassion. We're essentially all the same, and all connected. That holds true across the full spectrum, from hard science at one end to mystic spirituality at the other. I'm reminded of that saying: 'If a leaf falls from a tree, the whole wood is changed.' It's that notion that we don't operate in isolation. From that grounding, wisdom can mature.

How can each of us develop wisdom?

The spectrum of human beings is wide, far wider than I once thought. There is such a difference between people, in terms of wellbeing, intelligence—a whole host of things. So in that respect, I don't think there's a 'one size fits all' approach to developing wisdom. We've touched on some things already, but perhaps a starting point might simply be getting to know ourselves really well, in a spirit of inquiry and kindness.

How did it feel to discuss wisdom today?

It's been a really rewarding experience. I love having my thoughts stirred and engaged. So it's been a gift. And I can't remember ever going deeply into what the word wisdom means to me.
By the way, I don't know if anyone else you've interviewed has said this, but to be asked to talk about wisdom does make you question yourself a bit, like: what do I know about wisdom?
It's also nice to spend time with you as a person, Miguel. I find you inspiring. That's a really powerful word for me. I've always loved knowing people who, the next time I see them, might surprise me with what new thing they're into. Thank you again for asking me to participate.

Lyn Buchanan

Lyn Buchanan has a master's degree in psychology, specializing in prison psychology, linguistic psychology and psycholinguistics. He was a guided missile specialist, and for the last 17 years of his professional life, an intelligence agent for the US military. Today, he is best known as a member of the US Military's 'Psychic spying unit'. He was trained in the skill known as Controlled Remote Viewing (CRV), and wound up being the unit trainer before his retirement from the military. After his military retirement, the unit's existence was declassified and became public, and he began using and teaching CRV in the civilian sector, developing civilian applications for the skill, working with police departments, other agencies, businesses, medical research, and speaking and writing about the mental skills involved. He is the author of *The Seventh Sense*, a book about CRV and its use by the military. He now teaches CRV in online classes. crviewer.com

What comes to mind first when you think about wisdom?

What comes to mind first about wisdom is that it's probably different from smart. It entails a whole lot more than intelligence or education. There are a lot of intelligent, educated people who are just not wise at all. And it's not street smarts.

One of the core parts of wisdom is your ability to care about others. I know many of the things that I teach, and that I teach my teachers to teach, is that we're learning CRV in order to see what good we can do with it. The thing that I teach can be done a thousand ways, but I must always remember that I'm not teaching them to do it *my* way, but to do it in the way that's best for them. If you get your ego involved, you're not going to make wise choices. I think wisdom focuses on the end result rather than on the self.

Do you recall the first time you saw wisdom in action?

This is a very simple little thing, but for some reason it stands out in my memory of childhood. My grandmother said with great authority, "*This* is the way you cook oatmeal." And it came out like library paste. My grandfather would make oatmeal and it would come out in very tasty flakes. So one time I asked my grandmother why they made it come out so differently, and she said, "Oh, he makes it a crazy way. This is the way you make it." And my grandfather a little bit later said to me, "Make it like *you* like it." That stood out to me for a long time. There's an old saying in the military: "Nobody messes with the cook." That's very true. There are chefs who pride themselves on their work, their name, their reputation and their expertise. But I'd prefer, at any meal, to eat food prepared by a person who only takes pride in the pleasure people get from eating their cooking. And that's a difference. One is smart, the other is wise.

One of the best Christmas presents I ever got was from my nephew. He had gone out into the river and picked up some rocks and he brought me a box of rocks. I'm personally interested in everything, and he knew about my love for rocks, that from them I could learn about how they got there, the history, geology and geography of the landscape. Somebody else would give me aftershave or a tie. But instead, he asked himself what fascinates me. Next Christmas, if you're having difficulty trying to figure out what to get someone as a present, just ask yourself the same.

Who is the wisest person you know, and why?

I have trouble answering that question, because I think wisdom pops up here and there, and everybody has very wise moments. Who has the most wise moments? I don't know, I don't keep a tally. I've seen wisdom in everybody. I've seen stupidity in everybody. I've seen both in myself. Sometimes I'll look back and be surprised at how something I thought was wise was really stupid, and sometimes the reverse is true.

Looking back on your life, what is the wisest thing you ever did?

Picking the right partner was certainly one of them.

There was a thing I learned which is CRV-oriented. I learned that you can influence the past. So I did a four-year study and kept data on influencing my own past, and developed a successful methodology. And from that study, life, family and everything else has got better. Putting in the effort to document, study and analyze the method was a lot of work, but it made for a better life.

You can't change the past. But in remote viewing, you can not only receive information, you can also pass information. So if I'm making a decision now, and I listen to myself from the future to get hindsight, I'll make a better decision. That means that at a future time, when I know the right answer, I have to sit down and do a CRV session, targeting myself in the past and sending along that hindsight, which effectively becomes foresight. So you make a time loop. The trick is knowing how to listen at the moment the information comes through. When we were looking for a home, we were up in the mountains above here in Alamogordo, New Mexico, and we found a house that we wanted. I was getting ready to sign for the house, and all of a sudden I lifted my hand because I'd just heard myself from the future saying, "No, you don't."

And so I turned to my wife and I said, "No, this is not the house we want. Why don't we look around at other options?" About five days later, we found the home we have down here, which is a hundred times better than what we were about to sign for. And so after we moved in here and got settled, and knew for real that this was the best choice, I sat down and did the session. I targeted the moment when I was about to sign my name for that other house, and kept putting in,

"No, you don't. No, you don't." That doesn't change the past, but by putting hindsight into your decisions, you will change your future. But you have to influence the past to do it.

For people who don't know, remote viewing was originally developed at Stanford Research Institute by a man named Ingo Swann. It was developed for military use, and became known as Controlled Remote Viewing, or CRV. When the public learned about this, psychics of all kinds declared themselves to be remote viewers, so it became associated with the New Age. But it is based on the psychological part of martial arts. Ninjas are trained in what's called 'saki no jutsu', where they become entirely aware of their surroundings, 360 degrees around them, without looking. What controlled remote viewing does is, it makes you aware of things that you can't pick up with your other six senses. The six senses are the five senses and ambiance. We feel ambiance. It's a feeling we get in our bodies. It's real. But the seventh sense is psychic. There's no way we can physically feel what's going on in Moscow right now, yet controlled remote viewing takes the six senses, and lets you apply those to the seventh sense. So if I tasked you with learning what's going on in a certain place in the world, you will feel it. You will smell it, you will hear it, you will sense the ambiance of it. And so the controlled remote viewing is a martial art, which takes your normal six senses and applies it to the seventh sense as a tool to get information.

In terms of ambiance, the sixth sense, I would love to study the mechanics of this, in terms of the role of our nerve endings. Our five senses are physical senses that depend on their nerve endings, that transmit signals from our skin, our ears, eyes, nose and tongue, along our nerves to our brain. Those nerves are extremely thin strands of biological material that act as antennae. And each antenna can broadcast as well as receive, within your immediate surroundings. If you're sat in a room and somebody walks in behind you, and they're angry, your body can feel it. You don't have to turn around and look; you know it, you feel it. The same thing if they're happy. One of my students is an eighth level black belt in ninjutsu. I would never mess with this guy. We were walking down the hallway one time and I was walking behind him, and I thought, 'I wonder if I could reach up and tap him on the back without him knowing?' And without turning his head, he said, "Don't even think about it. I'll break your finger." That is saki no jutsu. He is totally aware of ambiance.

In the CRV training we have an exercise that teaches you to be aware of your ambiance, because if you can't feel your surroundings here, I can't send your mind to halfway around the world to see what you feel there. One of the exercises for the 20th level is to sit in a restaurant, with your back to the door, and no reflecting surfaces in front of you so you're not picking up anything. I then have the student tell me, when somebody walks in, if they are male or female. Describe their clothing. Describe what they're going to order, what they're hungry for. And with this ambiance exercise, you can do it without ever turning or looking. And this is not psychic, it's about developing the sixth sense.

If we are training agents to gather information from a place, if they go in looking all around the space, they're not going to make it out of that place. So ambiance training, developing the sixth sense to gather information, is vital. Given that we have developed these tools, the wisdom is in training and deploying them effectively.

I think that another of the wisest things I've ever done is to learn that, although I'm in a society, and that my actions and morals must be tightly intertwined with others in my society, I also have both the need and right to independence. People often come to me asking me to heal them or do something for them. In CRV, we do not even try to heal them. We try, instead, to help them find the causes for their illness and to heal themselves.

The analogy of teaching a child to ride a bike applies here. You steady a bike to get a child safely on it, but that doesn't teach them to ride one. What teaches them to ride a bike is when you let go and make them realize that they don't need you to hold them anymore. That principle goes for a great many things in life, not just riding a bike, or learning how to be well.

What is the hardest-won wisdom that you have?

I've had to learn a lot of things the hard way. A big part of dating is about learning who you *don't* want to marry. There is a huge difference between getting married and being married. A big part of learning what you want to do with your life is in not just 'working for the man' and depending on 'the man' to keep you safe and financially secure. To find what you want to do in life often means going out and taking risks, sometimes going hungry, sometimes being scared, sometimes being lost until you find your way.

I remember one summer when I was very young and my dad was out of work, my grandparents were taking me for the summer to help out. One of my grandmother's friends was a widow who had been married to a banker and who had developed the hobby of making money in creative ways. When she baked cookies, she would make a double batch and take the second part to the local motel to sell to the people who were lodging there. When she made a garment, she would always make a second one and sell it.

She knew that I was there for the summer because my dad was out of work. I vividly remember her pointing her finger in my face and saying, "Lyn, you remember this and never forget it! There are a million ways to make money in the world, and everyone has a problem finding the second one. People get a job and depend on that as their only way to make a living. But once you find that second way to make money, you won't have to depend on the first one so much anymore. You'll soon find a third, then a fourth, and pretty soon, you don't have to go looking for a job or depend on anyone else to support you." There have been several times when I've been unemployed, but I can't ever remember a time when I've been out of work, or money.

In the world today, where do you see wisdom, and its lack, being demonstrated?

In terms of a lack, that's easy. I have not seen wisdom in

government in decades. Plenty of smarts, no wisdom. And part of that is because of the way we elect people in the US. We will not have wisdom in government if we continue to elect people on the basis of their personality, or their ability to pay for media campaigns, or the heated nature of their rhetoric, or the slyness of their spinning of events, or their ability to throw mud at their opponents, or whatever other thing they do to avoid knowing and discussing the real issues.

How do you apply wisdom to the care of your mind, body and soul?

To be brutally honest, I don't always do that. Smart is knowing that the cinnamon roll is going to make you fat; the lack of wisdom is eating the cinnamon roll because it tastes good. And I do love cinnamon rolls.

In terms of spiritual practice, I pray, I believe in God. As a young man I trained to become a Methodist minister. I believe in morals. Even though there have been times when logic comes up, and I think about the fact that I can't see God, and wonder if the Bible is just fable. But I have lived a life without Christianity and I've lived with Christianity, and even if it winds up that there's not a God, the life with Christianity has given me a better life. It has given me a better family. It has given me happiness and satisfaction. It has given me kids with morals. So even if Christianity is nothing more than a social thing, it works. It's wise to do it. It's unwise to not do it.

In my controlled remote viewing work I had many of what could be called religious experiences. You're always blind to the task, meaning that you never know what it is you're viewing, because then your logical mind would come in and take over the process. We call it AOL, or analytical overlay. During the Gulf War, I was tasked with remote viewing Saddam Hussein and other evil, militant and destructive despots. I had to look at their plans, intentions and strategies for the next day. It was wearing me down emotionally and I asked the director, "Please give me something else." And he said, "You're a soldier—do your damn job." But about a week later, there was a lull in the military requirements and my monitor came in and said, "Okay, we have a personality assessment to do today." I thought, 'Oh great. Another evil potentate.' But as soon as I started out I realized that this is a good guy. I said to the monitor, "Hey, you got the wrong guy." And he replied, "Well I don't know who it is, but it's in the task and we'll just do it." And by the end of the session, I was just glowing internally. I'd never met anyone like that before in a session. And my summary for the session was, "Whatever evil you think this guy did, he didn't do it." Then the monitor opened the envelope, in which the director had handwritten on a sheet of paper: 'Jesus'. That close, individual meeting with Jesus, which was actually real, was a literal religious experience and it changed my life quite a bit. Afterwards, somebody asked me what Jesus had said to me in the session. My answer was that it was not what he said; it was the fact that when I was in his presence there, I could see myself as He did. He said, "Whatever bad you've done, I have seen worse. Whatever good you've done, I have seen better. You are who you are and I accept you." He accepted me, and it was that acceptance that changed my life.

And there were other times when religion came into play. Saddam Hussein never thought he was a bad guy. He never thought he did any evil at all. In his mind, God wanted him to be the ruler of the world and so it was his religious duty to kill anybody who was opposed to God's will. Saddam Hussein was just simply crazy.

In doing that kind of work for the military, it became very important for me to remember the wisdom of staying independent and not allowing the self-justifying thoughts, feelings, motivations and purposes of the target person to affect me. They had had a lifetime of justifying the things they did. They had developed such persuasive reasoning that they could get a whole nation of people to agree and follow them into some of the most horrific things humans do to other humans. Cult leaders do the same. The simple wisdom of knowing that "I am me!" kept me mentally, spiritually, politically and emotionally safe during those times.

Is wisdom a uniquely human concept?

I think probably the origin of wisdom for our species was self-protection. It is often the loss of that type of wisdom that brings us the greatest pain. We know that when a tsunami is going to hit the shore, the animals will head for the hills 12 hours before it hits. But the people often sit there and get washed away. Did we have that wisdom and lose it? Is that what we think of as wisdom? I don't know, but it's pretty wise.

Do you have a favorite parable or anecdote on wisdom?

Intelligence and education is knowing that a tomato is a fruit. Wisdom is not putting it in a fruit salad.

How do you ultimately define wisdom?

Wisdom would probably be your ability to think of the entire result of your action rather than the immediate. Again, it's wise to not *get* married, until you're ready to *be* married. You may want some glitzy, shiny thing, but do you want it enough to spend all of your bankroll on it and not have anything to eat?

The church can focus so much on eternity that it doesn't deal with the immediate need: deny yourself your immediate needs and you will reap rewards in eternity. At other times, it may have a missionary drive and push that to the point of not servicing the needs of the individuals in the congregation or in their own local community. But wisdom is both immediate and eternal. Anti-religion says focus on the immediate and forget about eternity—live only for today.

Wisdom is considering the full picture. In the military, wisdom is necessary, though many military planners are not wise at all. Is it wise to lose the lives of a battalion of soldiers in order to take one hill, which is just going to be taken back by the enemy the next day? Much of both military planning, and the political planning which brings about military crises, is based on the immediate rather than the long term. But to be wise it needs to not only see the battle but the war, and after the war, and the ramifications of even having a war. A lot of wars happened because politicians aren't wise. And a lot of politicians aren't wise because the people who elect them aren't wise enough to elect politicians on the basis of their wisdom.

In the basic introductory class on CRV, everybody wants to describe the target accurately. They want to have 90% accuracy, or higher accuracy than they had before. That is because our educational system has taught us that the score is the thing we should strive for in life. But the fact is that in training, the purpose of the practice target is not to learn about the target. We already know about the target. The purpose of a practice target is for the student to learn about themselves. The purpose of the basic class is to learn the methods, the techniques, the tools. But everybody wants the target. They want that high score. They have been trained to believe that a session is only a good session if they get a high score. But the fact is that if you have a purely 'pig slop' session, and then go back and analyze it to learn about how your mind works and how you can improve, *that* is one of the best practice sessions you can have. I think it was Gandhi that said, "The successful person has failed more times than the failure has ever tried." That was a very wise thing to let people know.

How can each of us develop wisdom?

I think it comes from experience. Many times the world crashes in on you and gives you the experience, and many times you go get the experience. Many people are afraid of experiencing things, without realizing that in the experience, good or bad, there's going to be some wisdom gained.

Is there anything else that you wish to add?

Along the lines of that last thing, wisdom is worth whatever it takes to get it. Many times that means getting hurt. Many times it means experiencing the hurt that you've done to others. Many times it means going out and having a good time, and even being foolish. There is something to learn from that too. I think that if you quit learning, you quit getting wiser.

How did it feel to discuss wisdom today?

It felt good. I'm not sure I've imparted any wisdom to anybody, but it's something I like to talk about. When I was growing up, one of my often-repeated prayers was asking for the ability to get wisdom, not realizing what it was going to take for me to get it. It's like that Chinese curse: 'May you live in interesting times.' Many, many days and nights this old body and this old life has suffered, but I've learned a lot, and I would never trade that for the safety of a boring ignorance.

Rachel Corby

Rachel Corby is a plant whisperer, sacred plant medicine practitioner, permaculture gardener and personal rewilding coach. She has trained with contemporary teachers including Patrick Whitefield, Eliot Cowan and Stephen Harrod Buhner. She has also has spent time with traditional herbalists across Asia, metis from both Cherokee and Mohawk descent, and various indigenous teachers in Central and South America and Kenya. Her greatest teachers have been plants themselves, along with deep wilderness immersion experiences. She loves to share what she has learned from the plants and her own personal rewilding practice, often leading wild medicine walks and plant whispering workshops at festivals and events throughout the summer months in the UK where she lives. Rachel also runs her own retreats, apprenticeships and online courses and mentoring. She is the author of four books, including *Rewilding & The Art Of Plant Whispering*. wildgaiansoul.com

What comes to mind first when you think about wisdom?

   To me wisdom goes beyond knowledge and intelligence. There's another layer to it, which is the benevolence and the kindness that goes with it. It has a generous quality to it. It involves making considered decisions.

Do you recall the first time you witnessed wisdom in action?

   An early memory is of getting stung while out on a walk. And my father immediately found a dock leaf and rubbed it on the sting to heal it. And that has influenced me, as I've become someone who works a lot with plants.

Who is the wisest person you know, and why?

There are three. The first is my dad, who is a very wise man. He made great decisions. He came from a working-class background but he worked and studied really hard, and got his PhD. He brought up a family, and gave us good morals, good direction and good health. He kept us fit and healthy. He's an incredible human who is kind and thoughtful and uses his experience and his intelligence to advise and guide others and himself.

I apprenticed with Stephen Harrod Buhner, who is the second. He writes on nature consciousness, herbal medicine and related topics. When he worked with our group of apprentices he did this thing we called 'the hot seat'. If he felt somebody wasn't quite there, wasn't quite being honest about who they really were, he would call them out on it. He would confront you until you worked through it. It was very uncomfortable, but if you accepted the challenge, instead of becoming defensive, you would grow in the experience. It was transformative, like drawing the butterfly from the caterpillar. He'd made an agreement with all of us that he was going to help us do this work, help us find this different way in life, and the hot seat was part of keeping that commitment. For me that's wisdom because he did something that wasn't comfortable, but it benefited both parties, and all of us. The response at the time could be tears and frustration, but over the next couple of days you would see that it had landed and that they started to respond to it. So for me that was an act of great wisdom. He was very considered in terms of the impact of everything he said and did.

The third person I thought of is Stephen's wife, Trishuwa. Stephen did the more didactic, intellectual work, while she was doing a lot of ceremonial work with us; sweat lodges and things like that. I've done a few vision quests with her. She's in her 70s now and is still going out there into the middle of the desert, leading groups of people. She again is very considered and perceptive. She sees things in people and draws them out. I think that is a very wise quality to have.

Looking back on your life, what is the wisest thing you ever did?

To listen to the whispers calling me back to my wild self. I began paying attention to who I am, and honoring that. I had the realization that I am part of wider nature, and I allowed that to lead me on this path of listening to the voices of nature, which is my wild self. There is no separation. You could call it the wild heart of the world, the source, all that is. It's about allowing myself to be called into communion and communication with something much greater than myself, but that also resides within myself.

I grew up in a small town in Hertfordshire in England, and went through the typical teenage thing, of not being at ease in myself or in the world. These days I'd probably be medicated. But things shifted when I did the Duke of Edinburgh Award through my school, from 1986 to 1990. It's a youth achievement program. We went camping and walking in the hills of North Wales. I was out in the rain with a 15-kilo backpack, and it wasn't comfortable or normal, but I suddenly started to feel more alive. Just splashing my face in a little mountain stream was waking me up inside. I recognized that there was something here that I didn't have when I was in my suburban home with my mum and dad, even though they'd created a safe, comfortable life for me there.

That was the start of a long journey, of following a thread that eventually took me to a place of deep connection with my wild self and the wildness in the world. A journey that took me around the world, to mountains, beaches, jungles and deserts. In these places I learned about growing plants, foraging and plant medicines. I also learned that being surrounded by plants and wild nature made me feel alive and well and at ease; it made me feel really vibrant. I realized that when there's a separation between the wild self and the wild world, you are not going to be at ease in yourself. Each experience was a step on the path, and brought me into deeper connection, and closer to seeing myself as a natural person—as much as you can be in this modern world.

The more I embed myself as this modern hunter-gatherer, the more I feel at ease in myself. Like I'm not alone. If your whole community is just humankind, you can feel really alone. Through following this path, I started to understand that I felt more comfortable and more relaxed in the company of various different beings. Maybe a beautiful stone or tree. It started by just noticing what things made me feel better, understanding the language of the heart, of feeling. And I developed the practice of pausing, paying attention to the feeling I'm having, and understanding what that feeling is telling me.

After school, I worked for a while then went to university to study geography. I had a boyfriend at the time, and some friends had been to a solar eclipse in Peru. It sounded so amazing that we decided to experience one in India. We ended up trekking in the Himalayas and going to lots of other places. Later on I was heading to another eclipse in Venezuela in 1988. That was my intention, but I didn't know any Spanish. So I flew into Guatemala and went to what was called 'Ecoescuela', an eco school. You lived with a local family, and spent half the day doing Spanish and the rest of the day doing basic eco work, like clearing fire corridors in the forest.

I'd already done a bit of traveling in India, Thailand and Japan, but when I got to Central America, that's when I first really got to know some indigenous people, and learn how they lived and worked. And I was absolutely stunned by this one guy at the Ecoescuela. He took us for a walk in the forest, and every third step he was showing us a different plant, and explaining its nature, and role in the ecosystem. I was fascinated, but I was also shocked that I was so completely unconnected to the plants back home. I knew nothing about them.

I spent time in Ecuador working on permaculture projects and eventually was led to an indigenous teacher in the jungle. He was creating a botanical garden to catalogue the local plants as the area was under threat from oil exploration. He was also an ayahuasquero. We did some ceremonies together. I learned a lot from him and his family.

My only other major experience of being fully among indigenous people was in Kenya in 2007. I had a friend who lives out there, and she had another friend who was connected to a lot of local people. Her work focused on honoring their herbal medicine, their plant lineage, because a lot of them were becoming ashamed of that lineage as they turned instead to allopathic pharmaceutical medicine. She made this beautiful picture book which told the story of the native plants and what they offer. She was worried that they were going to lose their plant knowledge in two or three generations because so many were buying into the idea that allopathic medicine is the way to go. She is white, but wanted to give them another view, and regain pride in their knowledge rather than turn their backs on it.

She took me to meet and live within several different tribes. At that point I was already working with plant consciousness. The people showed me their medicine plants: various berries, leaves, roots and so on. One night we were all sitting around talking. This was complex, as in each direction it had to be translated through English, Swahili and the local tribal language. Traditionally the men and women have very different roles and status in that particular tribe, so I had felt that I had not really been seen or accepted by the elder medicine man. However, he asked me how I learn about plants. And I said to him, "I enter the dream of the plant." And as soon as that was translated to him he grabbed both my hands from across the table and looked me deep in the eyes, because I was talking the same language as him. It was the same thing they do; they learn directly from the plants. And he suddenly understood that I wasn't just a foreigner coming to catalogue the plants then go sell them to a pharmaceutical company. I was actually talking the same language.

When I went off on that first trip to India, I had been a raver. I had taken quite a lot of pills, LSD, mushrooms and so on. So I was having that consciousness-expanding experience. For some people it's just about getting out of it, but actually you get into it as well when you're in that situation. So that was an interest for me. When I did ayahuasca in Ecuador I remember thinking at the time that it's not that strong. But the most interesting effect came later, through 'echoes' in time. I moved to Wales and was living on the cliffs. I would suddenly get a ping back to my teacher in Ecuador and everything would be really echoey, and I'd suddenly understand another thing that had come from the ayahuasca ceremony.

So then I started working a lot with what I call 'entheogens'. I don't call them 'teacher plants' because all plants have something to teach. The initial encounter in Ecuador opened my understanding of plants and changed my relationship with them in a big way. I began to find more plants to see what they had to show me, things about myself, what I need to change and update and move on from. They helped me enormously, but I don't work that regularly with them anymore. At this point I just have to think of the question that I was going to go to the mushrooms with and the answer comes in. So you don't get the pretty patterns but you get absolute clarity in the information. It's a psychic communication with someone. That period of serious investigation was probably from around 1999 until 2003. By the end of it I was pretty much talking to everything. I learned that communication can take place at many levels. My awareness expanded dramatically, and I felt a deep connection to the stones and the rivers, to everything.

What is the hardest-won wisdom that you have?

Going all the way back to that distraught teenager that I was, the hardest-won wisdom has been to trust. Trust in the universe that everything's going to be alright in the end, so I need not worry. And to trust in myself, that where I am right now is perfect. It is where I need to be even if it doesn't feel that way in the moment. That I am enough. That it's okay. Whatever I'm going through, there will be something of value in it, a lesson held within every story, a teaching that I can take from any and every experience, whether it felt good or bad in the moment. So it's about trusting the experience. Just trust in the universe.

In the world today, where do you see wisdom, and its lack, being demonstrated?

I think there's some really beautiful things happening in the world. Wisdom for me is being demonstrated in the work on ecocide law. It's about people taking responsibility, taking a duty of care for all of the planet's inhabitants. I think that is true wisdom. You're thinking beyond human life, about the whole connected gaian organism. We can't just be selfish and think of ourselves. Wisdom in action is thinking beyond yourself to the whole planet.

And there are things like permaculture. The philosophy behind it is 'Earth Care, People Care and Fair Share'. So again, it's thinking beyond just yourself. When you plant a permaculture garden, you might plant a walnut tree that you're never going to eat from, but you're planting it because that will feed future generations. Or you will plant not for yourself directly, but for the benefit of local wildlife. Ultimately there is no separation, so by supporting the local ecosystem you are supporting yourself. I love permaculture and ecocide law as they demonstrate joined-up thinking. They're coming from the heart and they're coming from thinking beyond today, the economy and humanity. And I think that that is where we really need to go, if we're going to continue life on this planet.

There are many small initiatives, communities and things like that. Advaya is one example set up by two sisters, Ruby and Christabel Reed. They bring young people together to discuss ecology, economy, spirituality and mental health. In doing so they aim to empower, build community and bring about systems change. There are so many other initiatives and communities like this, feeding people with information and also with wisdom.

Another one close to my heart is the plant consciousness

movement. I'm obviously a massive advocate for it. This movement is growing in the UK for sure, but I see this happening worldwide. It's about turning people on to the fact that the plant world is conscious and that it has something to say, and something to give, more than just the leaf and the fruit. I think incorporating plant consciousness, the awareness of plant consciousness into your life, is wisdom in action.

The other one is rewilding. For me it's a complex term, and some people can be a little misguided on this. It's not simply about reintroducing species from the past. Sometimes things have moved on in such a way that that does not work for any of the species involved. And when we think of invasive species, it is worth considering how and why they are there and thriving. Bear in mind that humans are nature too, so that when we for example brought a rhododendron from Nepal to Southampton and now it has spread throughout the New Forest, maybe we shouldn't simply discount it. Maybe there's another reason underneath it. This planet is changing, the climate is changing, and perhaps those plants or animals need to be in that place. From my perspective, we should ask the land before we decide what it needs. Visit the land, sit on the land, talk to it.

So I use the word 'rewilding' cautiously. What I really mean by it is holistic rewilding. And that starts with yourself. We are nature, we are Gaia. To make the planet healthy and well, we have to become healthy and well. And part of that is taking your shoes off, stepping outside and letting the rain fall on your head. Feeding your wild self. There are lots of people doing this kind of work, bringing people back into connection with nature, which I see as our wild selves. That's wisdom in action, bringing people back to that knowing and that understanding. And I think that will go a long way toward helping solve some of the problems we've got at the moment.

And a lack of wisdom in the world? How many days have we got for this? The first one that came to mind was allopathic medicine. There's a lack of wisdom being demonstrated because it's not joined up. Take for example prescription drugs. There is the intended effect, which is a short list, and the potential side effects, which are actually still the effects of the drug, just not the intended or beneficial ones.

The Bioneers conference is very interesting. They have a book called *Ecological Medicine*, which is a collection of some of their lectures over the years. There is a piece in there about the pollution caused by incinerating medical waste, which goes into the air and water, and gets back into our systems, making us more unwell. It's a negative feedback loop. I also read in that book that human breast milk is the most toxic material on the planet currently. But it's also still the best thing to feed your baby because it's got all the right bacteria and everything in it that they need to build their own immune system. But because we're so polluted, that's one way that your body gets rid of that pollution. It's absolutely horrendous. I was almost in tears as I was reading this. So it's this lack of joined-up thinking. The medical professionals are good people who are trying to help, but the medical system just does not think holistically.

My brother-in-law just had Covid. He was in hospital in intensive care and on drips for six weeks. When he was recovered enough to eat, the first thing they gave him was a yogurt. And then a banana. And then they gave him a piece of cake. That actually makes me angry because something like 80% of our immune system is in our gut health. And when you haven't eaten, your gut is clean. But they'd been feeding him a lot of antibiotics during the process because of other secondary infections that had come up, which had killed off a lot of his gut flora. And then they give him sugar, wheat and dairy, which feeds the bad bacteria. Even when you've had antibiotics from your GP, they never give you a piece of paper with guidance such as: 'After you finish the course of antibiotics, avoid these foods, take these foods. And if you can, get hold of some probiotics, or even better, here's a prescription for some probiotics.' That could be a good idea. Gut health is not a secret, so why isn't it tied into our allopathic medicine? That's where wisdom is definitely not being demonstrated.

I don't really want to get into politics too much, but the general worldwide government policies on environmental concerns are crazy. You have Bolsonaro in Brazil just deciding to cut down the Amazon rainforest, for short-term financial benefit to a few humans. No thought for the living ecosystem whatsoever. And the same with Scott Morrison in Australia. A few little pieces of ancient Australian woodland survive without any wildfire damage and he's now given the green light for them to be cut down. What is this? The general policy of most governments is short-term financial gain over long-term health and wellbeing of the entire planetary system.

And then there is the thoughtless and endless consumerism. It really upsets me when you've got young children who are being given masses of plastic toys because, from what I know of little children, what they really want is for you to get on your hands and knees and pretend to be some animal or something and play with them for hours on end.

When it comes to food, I appreciate that it's often cheaper for people to buy junk food meals, rather than go and buy fresh ingredients and cook a healthy meal. And it may be more convenient in the moment. But it's not that convenient to have type 2 diabetes or heart disease, and once again it is no secret that eating junk foods can leads to such health concerns. That's not wisdom being demonstrated. That's just slow suicide.

How do you apply wisdom to the care of your mind, body and soul?

I feed my mind with things that I think will help me expand my horizons, help me think more, introduce me to different points of view and allow me to have the opportunity to make my own decisions based on that information. So I read books, listen to podcasts, watch YouTube, films and so on. I also journal, and I write, which that gives me an opportunity to process that information. I do a lot of workshops and teaching, and I absolutely love the mix of people I meet. At conferences and events I'm exposed to an array of other people and everybody's got a different take. There's always something else and always more information. So how I apply wisdom to the care of my mind is to keep allowing it to be exposed to new, varied information, so that I can learn and evolve. My creative portal is to journal it out or to write it out. And debate it with people, sit around a fire late at night and discuss these things.

In terms of caring for my body, the first thing is to listen to it, and ask it what it needs. Sometimes I forget to do that, but I always get reminded if I do. If I've got pain, or I'm not feeling full of energy, then I'll stop and ask it, and listen. To maintain it I feed it with good things. Seeing myself as wild nature I give it those things, such as walking barefoot outside, breathing fresh air, foraging for food and medicines. And I take care of my gut health by fermenting foods and so on. It's about using my knowledge and experience to grow that wisdom within my physical body. Obviously there will be exercise and good sleep as well. The wisdom is in staying connected to my body. If you don't exercise your body's ability to tell you something, if you stop listening, you won't be able to hear it.

In terms of caring for my soul, I would say community with both humans and other species. It feeds me with different points of view, different pieces of information, wisdom and intelligence. Also creating space and time to nurture myself, to be myself, and work out who that is! Although I don't use entheogens often these days, they inspire different ways of understanding and existing as part of the universe. And so, if I have a question, I will work with them and learn from them. That feeds my soul more than my mind or my body. That's really soul medicine.

Is wisdom a uniquely human concept?

Definitely not. We have talked about it a lot today. All plants, animals, fungi and bacteria can learn and adapt their behavior. They've got memories, so that if something happens, they can then change their behavior. That implies intelligence, though intelligence doesn't necessarily equate to wisdom. Peter Wohlleben, a German forester, wrote a book called *The Hidden Life of Trees: What They Feel, How They Communicate*. He gives an example. If a leaf on a plant is getting nibbled by a predator, it emits chemicals which other nearby plants pick up. They can then increase certain chemicals in their own leaves so that they become less palatable to the predator. Through the mycorrhizal networks in forests, trees offer benevolent acts to other plants. They take some of their own nutrients and send them across to nurture an old or ailing tree, or a baby tree, not necessarily even of their own species. That is not just intelligence, it's also benevolence. That for me defines wisdom.

When I make a connection with a plant, I often ask, "Do you have any medicine to share with me?" Medicine can be anything, not just something for a cough. It's medicine for my soul really. And when you start learning how to listen to the response, and to interpret what's coming in, they are so generous with what they give you, the wisdom they offer. It's like taking entheogens, but in a much more subtle way. So that's why I say that all plants are teachers. And generally they don't ask for anything in return. Although sometimes they do. Sometimes I have made sacred contracts with certain plants that have asked something of me, and there are other circumstances where I have agreed to do something specific for a plant. But generally it's a benevolence and kindness, giving you something that will help you.

And this goes back to the idea of helping someone else to help yourself, as we are all connected. The plants experience that too. We are part of them. So if the plant gives you something that will help you be a better human being, more balanced, then you will treat the planet better, you will respect plants more, you will be careful about damaging the landscape. And so is it the plants being selfish? No. It's similar to humans upholding the ecocide law; as we help the other we help ourselves, because in the end there is no separation. I think that's the ultimate wisdom.

Do you have a favorite parable or anecdote on wisdom?

I'll share a short anecdote. I was in India about 20 years ago. I was in the Himalayas, going up to a monastery. It was a stunning landscape.

The footpaths were hairpins because it was so steep. And there was this little monk going up, and he was very distinct. He had fairly long white hair and a long white beard, and he was very short. I didn't see anyone else that looked like that. So he overtook me and I gave him a shy smile and he smiled back and carried on his way. And then a few minutes later I slipped and landed on my backside. I took myself quite seriously, so I was mortified. I was looking around to make sure no one had seen this, and saw that the little old guy was suddenly stood below me on the path—even though a couple of minutes earlier he'd gone past me. But there he was, laughing his head off. And I was thinking, 'This is proper weird. What is this? Is this magic?' But I felt it was about not taking myself so seriously. And it helped.

How can each of us develop wisdom?

Tune into your heart. That's the most important one. Learn to slow down and listen to your true self. And through doing so you'll be tuning into the heart of the world. That's where I started. And because it worked for me I think it can develop that way in other people.

Pay attention to your intuition and be brave enough to act on it. You can have these moments of intuition, but it only really works if you are then brave enough to act on it.

And trust. This is my hard-won piece of wisdom. Trust that you have everything you need already, that everything is within you.

If you're looking for support and mentors or guides, I'd say look to the natural world, and develop your ability to listen for a response. Go beyond human mentors. Go to the natural world because it is an extended part of you. Energetically, there's no separation between any of us.

Learn from your mistakes as well. Don't give yourself a hard time. Look for the teachings in everything, whether it's good or bad. If you feel like you've made a mistake, go back to that and see what's there for you, rather than being ashamed and embarrassed. And that can help you not make that same mistake again.

And it's very important to always think ahead for any consequences of your actions. We all act rashly every now and then, but as much as possible, consider what might be the reactions to your actions.

How do you ultimately define wisdom?

Considered actions. Compassion. Having well-rounded knowledge, and acting on that. You don't have to be the most intelligent or well-read person, but with the information that you've got available to you, consider it and to act on that, and have compassion in your heart.

How did it feel to discuss about wisdom today?

I really enjoyed it. Having these questions put to you is a great exercise. It has helped me clarify my thoughts on wisdom. It brought up a lot up and I enjoyed it.

Jane Davidson

Jane Davidson is the author of *#futuregen: Lessons from a Small Country*, the story of why Wales was the first country in the world to introduce legislation to protect future generations. She is Pro Vice-Chancellor Emeritus at the University of Wales Trinity Saint David, patron of the Chartered Institute of Ecology and Environmental Management (CIEEM) and an RSA Fellow. From 2000-2011, Jane was Minister for Education, then Minister for Environment and Sustainability in Wales where she proposed legislation to make sustainability the central organising principle of government; the Wellbeing of Future Generations (Wales) Act came into law in 2015. She introduced the first plastic bag charge in the UK, and her recycling regulations took Wales to third best in the world.

A keen walker, she proposed—and walked—the 870 mile Wales Coast Path. In 2017 she was invited to be guest faculty on the Executive Education for Sustainability Leadership programme at the Harvard University T.H. Chan School of Public Health. janedavidson.wales

What comes to mind first when you think about wisdom?

Complete blankness! I realized I hadn't ever thought deeply about wisdom, which is quite phenomenal in itself. When I started thinking about it, I realized that it's something that I apply to people who think, people who are open to discussion, people who are known or respected for previous good judgment, people who don't want to score points, people who don't want to put other people down. And people who don't come with a fixed position they're prepared to defend at all costs—so their judgment is unbiased. But it also has to be about compassion, because quite often, people who are very knowledgeable or expert can have no compassion and no tolerance of other views. And so wisdom and knowledge are not interchangeable.

I looked up the Wikipedia definition, and I actually really liked it, apart from the notion of experiential self-knowledge or self-transcendence. I felt uncomfortable with that, because I don't necessarily think—in my understanding of the word wisdom—that it is about self-transcendence, because I don't know what the process has been in the context of the person that I consider wise. But I do think it is about being knowledgeable, ethical and kind. It's about using knowledge and experience to make good decisions and judgments to generate the best outcomes. I think it's visible but rare in every mode of life in the world. And I think that we have had it in politics, but it's harder to be wise in politics at the moment because it is so countercultural in terms of trying to deliver outcomes in a very short period of time, and being trapped within an ideology that might be completely inappropriate in terms of the needs of the world.

Another attribute of wisdom is when people do not pretend that they know more than they do. So that old Socratic notion of 'I do not think I know what I do not know', is really important. And oddly enough, that is incredibly positive nowadays as well. In my earlier life, before the worldwide web, it was very difficult to admit you didn't know something, if somebody expected you to know something in the context of your job or role. But now it's perfectly legitimate. There's so much to know. And so much that is beyond our knowing because of the incapacity of our knowing. I think that there's a sort of joy now, that it's possible not to know something. And it's now possible to acknowledge publicly that you don't know something, and yet you can still be deemed competent in what you do and other people can still come to you for advice.

And then I thought really, to some extent, it's about those people who you go to for advice, because they treat you seriously. They think about what you're asking. They won't necessarily give you an easy answer. They might want further discussion. They might do further research. They will want to talk to other people. All those elements. And I realized that actually, when I think about wisdom, it is an absolutely essential characteristic for a healthy world.

Do you recall the first time you witnessed wisdom in action?

   I left Rhodesia in 1973 when I was 15. My father was one of the founders of the medical school there. My parents both had cars because they were doctors. And I still remember that the number plate on my father's was RSD 146, and my mother's was RSD 147. That was the number of cars in Rhodesia at the time. I lived in Salisbury, now Harare, in an area called Mount Pleasant, which was where the university was. During my childhood, there was incredibly safe cycling due to the lack of cars, and I used to cycle to school in Alexandra Park, about three miles away. One day, when I was about nine, a man lost control of his car and hit a tree very hard outside our house. We later learned that he was trying to light a cigarette as he was driving around the corner and hit the accelerator by mistake. I was just coming out of our gate on my bike and I saw this happen, and I went up to ask the man if he was alright. He was in a complete state. He got out of the car and proceeded to try to post me through the half-open window to get his cigarettes. At this point a stranger, who had run over when he saw the accident, began to talk the driver down, and persuade him to stop trying to feed me into a car with a smoking engine. He was determined to not let this man push me through the window, but he was also determined not to antagonize the man.
   The experience was very scary at the time, but when I reflect on it, I think that when people behave in an unexpected way to sort out a problem, they can demonstrate depths of human understanding about people, relationships and behavior, that you just haven't thought about. So I think in that sense, it was a very wise moment.

Who have been your wisdom teachers?

There are two I'll talk about; one of whom is alive, and one of whom is dead. The living example is Satish Kumar. I did an English degree that was very heavy on language. I'm very interested in the component parts of language, in sentence structure. More in semantics than linguistics. And I'm also an avid reader and have been all my life. I was actually nicknamed the 'walking dictionary' at school. It wasn't kind. I certainly wasn't showing any wisdom, I was parading my knowledge. So, I've always been interested in words and although you can be really interested in words, you can still be ignorant as to their meaning, origin or etymology. And it was Satish who brought me back to that. When I was a government minister, I was invited to speak at an event at Schumacher College in Dartington, because of my passion for sustainability. And as part of that, I agreed to stay overnight. It was the first of many visits there. Satish does these fireside chats with the new cohort of students, who come from all over the world. I can still see the room clearly. I can see Satish sitting incredibly calmly, just waiting, and feel the excitement of the students, having come to Schumacher to engage with him and with the other people on the program. I recall the fire being stacked up, and the lovely low light, and candles in the hallway, in the house called 'The Old Postern'. Everybody sits around in a sort of U shape around the speaker, so there's full engagement and no notion of a separation. It's very much about the teacher being among those who want to learn; but the teacher also becomes a learner, and it's that integrated wisdom, which Satish always gifts back at the end of the session.

On this particular night he told the wonderful story of a visit to the London School of Economics. He asked to meet the ecology students and was told they had none. He then pointed out to them that the word 'eco' comes the Greek word 'oikos', meaning our planet home. Ecology is the knowledge of the planet home, because it comes from logos, meaning knowledge. And economy is the management of our planet home because it comes from nomos, meaning management. So he wickedly asked, "How can you possibly teach the management of our planet home without the knowledge of our planet home?" In my book I describe this moment as an epiphany. It was one those shakeups in your life where something just gets into the proper order. And I realized that although I've always been an environmentalist, a nature lover, that I felt that connection more in my soul than through knowledge. So I can't tell you the names of plants necessarily. I don't know a lot about habitats. And therefore I felt almost a fraud when saying I was an environmentalist, because I didn't have the knowledge of an ecologist.

It was an epiphany that was really important because it came around the same time that I was looking to leave politics, and the Chartered Institute of Ecology and Environmental Management (CIEEM) had asked me to become their patron. I was about to say no, because I wasn't an ecologist. And I felt that even though I'd been minister for environment, sustainability and housing, I did not have enough knowledge to be respected well enough as a patron of CIEEM. But after that story from Satish, I decided to accept that role, and I'm still doing a lot of work with them. I think that we all have to become, in a sense, the patron of ecologists. We have to understand that our relationship with nature is the most important relationship we have. And that goes back to the first principles of the Earth Summit, about humans having the right to live in harmony with nature. And so it's that notion about thinking we must get ecology right, because the economy is the successful management of our relationship with the ecology, in a way that helps the universe to thrive.

I thought that was really important. And I think that Satish personally is this wonderful still point in the turning world, because he has this immense calm. And he will ask you the unexpected but perfect question, so he enables you to think your thoughts and discover your own solutions.

He used to scare me because I'm just not spiritual at all, and I didn't know how to deal with somebody who was spiritual. I had rejected religion, and belief systems. But Satish's spirituality is absolutely bound up with his notions of soil, soul and society. At that point he was the only person who was deeply spiritual that I talked to, who brought no conditions to our growing friendship. And that enabled me to drop my prejudices too, in that context. And I think there are few people who can do that.

Somebody else who does that is the previous Archbishop of Canterbury, Rowan Williams. He is deeply spiritual, really interested in wisdom, and really interested in all sectors in a sense contributing towards a thriving world. He has asked me to speak at events though he knows that I'm not spiritual or religious in a traditional Christian sense. People who are able to drop the importance of the belief systems in their own lives, in order to encourage others to find their motivations, are starting to get closer to my idea of wisdom.

The other person who has influenced me as meaningfully as Satish, has been Professor Donella Meadows. She was a great systems thinker, and I'm really interested in systems thinking. I discovered her in the 1990s, but it was her 1972 book *The Limits to Growth* which was the one that inspired me. I didn't read it until 20 years later, but I read that and then the follow up, *The Limits to Growth: The 30-Year Update*, which came out in 2002.

She really brought home to me as a politician, that evidence is not enough. Scientists and politicians often think that evidence is enough, that if people understand the facts they'll make different decisions. But it's not the case, because there's all sorts of ideological factors and other pressures that influence our decision-making. Donella described five tools that she thought were important to add to the scientific evidence base, all of which is absolutely critical. You must have robust mechanisms for developing that evidence base, and it must be open to challenge, etc. It mustn't be for a particular ideological or political purpose. But despite all the open evidence about climate change, and the fact that we were moving beyond the Earth's ability to regenerate, governments were still doing nothing. And she said back in '72 that there were five tools that she thought were important, but she didn't know how important or to what extent they were necessary. And those tools were: visioning, networking, truth-telling, learning and loving. By 2002 she said that without those tools, you cannot deliver a sustainable outcome. At that point in my life, I was known for always saying I was an evidence-based minister. So that was quite a wake-up call to me, to realize that the evidence base was not enough, even in a small country where you could talk to many more people. You can give them evidence, but you won't necessarily persuade them to change behavior. And I think this gets back to the wisdom of what needs to happen to help encourage people to change behavior.

So my key influencers have been a spiritual leader and a scientist, two people who in many ways have had a huge impact on my life. The wisest person who, sadly, I never had a chance to meet, who has had the most impact on my life, is Nelson Mandela. He is also known by his clan name of Madiba, the Xhosa word for father, and a term of endearment. You can take the girl out of Africa, but you can't take Africa out of the girl. I use his quotes all the time and particularly like: "We must use time wisely and forever realize that the time is always ripe to do right."

Looking back on your life, what is the wisest thing you ever did?

I don't think it was an individual action. I think it's when you start understanding who you are on the basis that life makes sense looking backwards. I was trying to find ways for my life to be meaningful, to find things to keep me motivated. And I do understand that partly this is because I had the privilege of an upbringing where I have never been short of food. I've never been short of education. My first job was teaching, and then I moved into youth work, then running an antipoverty organization, and then into politics for the Labour Party, because it was about the many, not the few. I left politics because I believe that no politician should stay in politics for a long time. Politicians need to be in jobs and come into politics and go back into jobs, so that there is an interrelationship between society and its governance. And I think that's particularly important in a small country.

So when I look back at the jobs I've done, I've realized I was always looking for a purpose, to tackle an inherent unfairness. And that has continued. I took on a role at the University of Wales, Trinity Saint David with a specific mission to try and mainstream sustainability in a university. Having recently published *#futuregen*, I hope its publication will encourage more people and governments to take up the idea that we should all be thinking about the interests of future generations, especially in policymaking.

When I was a minister in the Welsh Government, there were only a few countries in the world at the time that had any notion of the interests of future generations in any of their constitutions. The law I proposed, The Wellbeing of Future Generations (Wales) Act, became law in 2015. This made Wales the first country in the world to put the UN Sustainable Development Goals (SDGs) into law. And that's an extraordinarily awful indictment, given that those goals have been agreed in the UN by 192 countries, and they're meant to be delivered by 2030. And yet the only country that has put a mechanism for their delivery into law is the tiny country of Wales, which is only part of a member state.

And if that wasn't bad enough, the next one is even worse. Wales is the only country in the world to put the Brundtland definition of sustainable development into law: 'Development that meets the needs of the present without compromising the ability of future generations to meet their own needs'. The definition was agreed by the UN in 1987, and adopted by the first Earth Summit in 1992. And therefore since 1987, 33 years and counting, all these countries have been talking about action on climate change and sustainability, but they have not put the mechanisms into law in the context of future generations. They might have introduced mechanisms in terms of technology or climate, or more technical aspects, or more punitive aspects, but not philosophically. And I think that philosophical aspect is critically important.

So I think, in my own life, the wisest thing I ever did in leaving politics was to look backwards and see where I'd been trying to go. And when I looked backwards, my life suddenly made more sense. I saw I wanted to engage with young people as a teacher. I wanted to engage with young people—particularly those more disadvantaged—as a youth worker. That led me straight into anti-poverty work, with a notion of education being the route out of poverty, which led me into politics.

And really I'm just a policy wonk! I'm somebody who is passionate about the idea of creating good policy and good decisions for the benefit of as many people as possible. And particularly young people, who have policy done to them, often without benefit. But underlying all of this, I'm still that environmentalist who believes that we have to understand our relationship with nature. And so it became clear to me that everything I'd done had been tiny steps on this journey to understanding that I had a role, as I believe every citizen has a role. I'm not special, it's just that I've worked out that my role is to live as purposeful a life as possible, which is about trying to ensure we leave a world that is habitable for future generations to thrive.

What has been the toughest lesson you have learned?

I think it's this notion that it's always impossible until it's done, which is another Mandela quote. You can be on a mission and know where you want to go, and there might be moments when things are possible, and moments when they're not possible. And you have to learn to seize the moment when something is possible, that sort of 'carpe diem' philosophy.

But if you really want to achieve outcomes, you will be set back time and time again. So there is something about persistence and stubbornness paying off. Regarding my role in taking forward the sustainability agenda in Wales, I remember a civil servant saying of me that I was a force of nature, that I just wouldn't give in. If people tell me I can't do something I believe in, that is my motivation to pursue it. But I may have to find other, perhaps sneaky ways to get it done. It might be about looking around corners and trying to find different ways to deliver the same outcome. And I always find I can do that, which turns out to be a sort of systems thinking philosophy. There's not a linear route. In fact, there's very rarely a linear route for anything really important.

I think that when you get to where you want to go, and then look back, you realize that you've learned an important navigational skill in terms of getting there. In one small example, Wales was the first place in the UK to mandate charges for carrier bags. I was very privileged to lead that initiative. It came about through a democratic process, in the sense that the BBC had conducted a poll in Wales on what action citizens wanted their new national assembly to take when the election was held in 2007. They had two competing propositions. One was a charge for carrier bags, and the other one was banning the smacking of children. The government has now done that too in Wales, but the plastic bag option won the poll.

I came in as minister and was really excited to have this responsibility. The aim was not to ban carrier bags—because we need to carry our shopping—but to ban single-use plastic carry bags. I was interested in how we could take a real sustainability-type approach to this. There was resistance from the big supermarkets, but not from the people of Wales. Only a couple of supermarkets engaged: Marks & Spencer, because they were trying to do create more sustainable proposals through their Plan A agenda; and the Co-op, because they had ethical principles. The other supermarkets generally did not engage. The advantage of government and the civil service is that it does understand processes. We asked all of the various supermarkets to engage with me, but mostly they couldn't be bothered to come to Wales to discuss the proposal with a 'regional' minister. But once we had the legal powers to charge for carrier bags, their first action was to threaten legal action, on the basis that I was trying to take the policy forward without the appropriate consultation. But we could demonstrate years of attempting to engage with them, which they had refused. So I was able to go ahead and introduce the charge.

The only other body who didn't like it, understandably, was a plastic bag manufacturer in Wales. But generally the people of Wales approved, because it reduced litter. Many of the poorest areas, and many of the most beautiful places, are marred by litter. And that's been a big issue recently, where suddenly people have returned to beaches and parks after the Covid lockdown, and left masses of litter behind.

And I thought it was a really interesting notion that yes, people wanted to have bags at supermarkets, but actually a 5p charge changed behavior hugely. On the one hand, you'd see people who didn't want to pay it, buying bags for life, which they use regularly. But you'd also see people coming out to their car with their arms full of shopping because they didn't want to be caught out buying a bag.

And we ensured that all the profits from the bags went to good causes. People therefore didn't need to apologize for buying a bag when they deemed it necessary. But we found plastic bag use dropped 90% in the first year. And the Welsh countryside was greener for it. People's behavior changed and they thought it was an important thing to do. So I think it's really important for politicians to go with the grain of what needs to happen in the context of creating a more sustainable world, and win the debate with people to do so.

I was told at the beginning of this process that it would be impossible, because I would be prevented by the UK government and by the supermarkets. Luckily for me, although the Labour UK government at the time didn't actually agree with the policy, it was prepared to let Wales be the test bed. But within four years, all parts of the UK had charges on carrier bags. It's that idea that it's always impossible until it's done. The narrative is never a straight line. Once you realize that, you can still be purposeful, even if there are more challenges in your way at different times, because of external events that are happening, either in the world or to your country or to you personally.

An important part of my philosophy is that you have to be ready to seize the moment. Wales was the only country in the UK given the duty to promote sustainable development in everything it did when powers were first devolved through the first Government of Wales Act in 1998. I was charged with the responsibility to deliver on the duty to 'promote sustainable development' in everything we did, but I soon realized that it was not enough, because when the Wales audit office told me that we had never failed in our duty to promote sustainable development, I knew it wasn't delivering the kind of change that the people who had put that into our founding constitution were looking for. And therefore, I asked to the cabinet to agree to make sustainable development our central organizing principle. They agreed! We published 'One Wales: One Planet' back in 2009, which was about totally shifting the agenda, including using the ecological footprint as part of the measurement mechanism for delivery. And people really bought into it. The politicians bought into it, at least notionally, but we had no idea really how to deliver. We had the rhetoric, but we didn't know what that meant in our own practice. And therefore it became clear to me that to change minds and behaviors you need both content and a body of understanding. But you cannot deliver without a process that people could easily identify with, and that became really important.

The catalyst which led to Wales becoming the first country in the world to have a Wellbeing for Future Generations Act came in 2010, when the incoming Conservative-Liberal Democrat government summarily got rid of the Sustainable Development Commission. This was extraordinary to me. The body was nonpolitical, and had been providing advice for a decade to politicians of all political persuasions across the whole of the UK. It was giving good, long-term advice based on expertise from across the world, yet it was simply removed overnight. There was no protection to keep that kind of advice in the system. And that was the day, the 10th anniversary of the commission and its final conference, that I wrote the four elements that went into the Welsh law, on the way back from Bristol to Cardiff.

I was particularly fortunate because at that time we were working on the manifesto for the Labour Party for the next election. I was going to the final meeting to discuss the manifesto that Saturday, and managed to get an urgent resolution heard to put the proposal for a new Welsh law to protect future generations into the manifesto. It was agreed, because of course everybody thought it was a good thing. So when Labour got into power again in Wales, it could go into the Programme for Government. So everything aligned. Remember: it's always impossible until it's done. You've got to be stubborn and persistent, because you've got to always be tracking what you want to achieve and how it can be achieved. And when that moment comes, you have to seize it. And I was just lucky with the subsequent alignment. But those three things together enabled Wales to have the first law in the world to protect future generations.

All I can assume is that our alignment in Wales has never fallen to anybody else who happened to have a politician who thought like me in government at the time. But now we need a lot more future-focused politicians, willing to challenge short-termism. There will be a lot more young people who think like that. And if we can get these ideas out through my book and other movements focused on long-term thinking, then I hope this moment will turn into a movement. And of course now there are so many incredible young activists, of which Greta Thunberg is the most famous, but she is one among many, including amazing indigenous activists bringing their wisdom to the world.

How do you apply wisdom to the care of your mind, body and soul?

I think living a more purposeful life is good for all of that. I've certainly found that actively choosing activities that don't harm others or the natural world leads you into different actions. I said a bit earlier that I'm acutely aware that I come from a background in which I have never been short of money or food, so I've been very privileged. I often refer to Maslow's hierarchy of needs because for me—and the reason I went into politics—is that governments should explicitly be looking after the most vulnerable, starting with people's physiological, safety and belonging needs. If you don't have enough money for food and heating, if your daily life is about survival, how do you achieve esteem and self-actualization? I think that most governments have moved too far away from those principles. If we just think about those at the base of the pyramid, about access to food, clean water, clean air, shelter etc, we then look at the safety needs, having a house, a job, being part of a community. It feels to me that what the welfare state did post-war was to recognize that we've been through six years of hell, and we need to keep our future generations safe. As a child of that generation, I have grown up with a welfare state and am therefore part of the most privileged generation that's ever lived, because we had a post-war government that wanted to look after future generations.

Over the last decade, my family has literally changed all aspects of our lives. We use renewable energy at our home. We grow our own food organically, and we mulch with seaweed and horse manure. We grow plants that attract bees. We grow as much of our own food as possible. We don't sell anything, but we swap for other things locally. In leisure we follow the same values. We don't fly for holidays. We haven't done that since my 50th birthday, when we climbed Kilimanjaro. I wanted to see the glacier because I was afraid of how much it was shrinking. And of course it took me back to Africa. We also like to kayak. My husband fishes from a tiny little boat. We're not consumerist. The shirt I'm wearing today I bought 25 years ago. We change things only when they wear out. And this gives us a better quality of life, because we're satisfied, not dissatisfied. And I think that notion about being satisfied, and having an idea of enough, and not being led by stuff, has always been my nature. When I came from Rhodesia as a teenager I was horrified by the consumerism in the UK. I wanted to be a little bit fashionable, but have never a slave to fashion. And as an adult, I've become more interested in making sure that what I buy is fair trade and ethical. So I think that living more purposefully and trying to be part of the solution rather than the problem is actually the way that you take care of your mind, body and soul.

In terms of managing my own sustainability, particularly in politics, I did a pretty bad job. When I was education minister, I was also the minister for work-life balance. And I used to joke that I got it completely wrong, because I used to regularly do up to a dozen meetings a day, in very big portfolios. Being a cabinet minister in Wales carries the responsibilities of about seven ministers in the UK government. You have big portfolios here, with a very small civil service. And because we were in the very early days of the new National Assembly, we wanted to be physically everywhere. I went everywhere I could by train, but the train provision in Wales is dreadful. So there were a lot of car journeys. I wanted to try and visit every school in Wales, so I used to put myself through it. But what sustained me was being supported by my family and friends. When I became a national politician, my husband went down to working four days a week in order to bring up our children, and I was very much the weekend mum.

I used to do my work very late at night. When the children went to bed, I'd start my 'ministerial box'. You'd get a box every night, and I'd finished it at one or two in the morning. But I was somebody then who could survive on very little sleep.

At that time, being a woman in Welsh politics was rare, to say the least. Before Tony Blair won the election in 1997, there had only ever been four female politicians representing Wales in parliament, and only one female Welsh MP from 1984-1997. Interestingly enough, Megan Lloyd George at one point considered standing for the seat that I stood in and said, memorably, "Pontypridd is not ready for a woman." And I'm not sure it was ready for a woman when I came in 1999 either. It's the gateway to the valleys. It was a traditional coal mining area. It was where the big rail yard that distributed coal via trains to the rest of the world was. It was a very male, very trade union area.

So becoming the candidate was in a sense the biggest challenge. But the Labour Party did something really clever, without which I would not have been a candidate. There are 40 constituencies in Wales and it required Labour candidates to twin 20 constituencies with 20 others. My constituency of Pontypridd was twinned with Merthyr, and it required the Labour Party to select one male and one female candidate. And then those candidates went through a process where the two constituencies could vote on who they wanted to be as their candidates. The top woman and the top man were selected as Labour Party candidates, and they then decided between them which constituency they would represent. What generally happens, and what happened to me, is that I was the top candidate for the Pontypridd constituency in which I lived, as a woman, and the top candidate for the Merthyr constituency, in which he lived, was a man. So it was very clear which constituency we would represent on the ballot paper. And Wales achieved global coverage when in 2003, not only was the cabinet composed of more women than men, but Wales was the first legislature in the world to have equal representation of men and women. This was an extraordinary change when you consider the previous history of women's representation. However it's been going backwards ever since, because of course when those incentives aren't in place, there's always a danger that you return to an old normal. And I think politics is particularly brutal for women at the moment, in terms of the hate that they receive through social media. I didn't experience any of that. In that sense, I think I was very lucky to come out of politics when I did. We had discussions about policy. We didn't have personal attacks in the same way.

In the world today, where do you see wisdom, and its lack, being demonstrated?

What's been really interesting about the Covid pandemic has been how decisions have become even more short term and based on less evidence and less wisdom. And there's a sort of ultimate irony that a government can do something like set up a group of wise people who understand epidemiology, and then ride roughshod over them because they're not giving them the political answers they want.

Those countries which have followed the epidemiology and reacted very quickly and with a plan, are often those which have experienced epidemics before, and know how to rise to the challenge. But we've seen many Western countries, particularly liberal ones, completely floundering.

But that hopefully means there's a chance we can actually look towards creating a different politics, and base decisions around future generations. There are traditional wisdoms that are important here. The ancient Iroquois philosophy is that the decisions we make today should result in a sustainable world, seven generations into the future. My political philosophy about looking after the interests of future generations reflects this: How will our choices and behavior affect future generations, to whom we want to leave a thriving world?

A critical part of a thriving world will be to totally rethink land use and agriculture, to move towards living in harmony with nature. I particularly love the idea of the honorable harvest, that you leave something for the soil, so you're always enriching it. We don't take everything off the tree, or take the tree out of the ground, when we harvest. On our own land, we don't use chemicals. We fertilize through seaweed and mulching, and compost from our own vegetables. I don't pick up the windfalls, I let them be part of the mulching for the next year. It's about having rules that govern our taking in the interests of current and future generations. If we shape that relationship, if we reign in our desire to consume, if we restore nature, then the world will be as rich for future generations as it is for our own, not least because we know so much that we can bring into that debate. And that just feels to me a really good philosophy.

Another first for Wales, is that the Wellbeing of Future Generations (Wales) Act also enshrines in law five ways of working: being preventative, being long-term, being collaborative, integrating your goals, and involving people in decisions that affect them. That is a simple way of testing whether your decisions are good ones. It is not just a good act because it integrates the sustainable development goals, it's a good act because it tells you how to do it as well. So you have an outcome and a process. And you must have those, because the problem for Wales previously in terms of the whole #futuregen debate, was actually that the people didn't understand what promoting sustainable development was. And there wasn't a mechanism for delivery, because people had different ideas about what such a mechanism should be. But now there is an act which establishes both the mechanism and the outcome. This offers an interesting model for other countries. They might want to do it differently, but if they can define outcomes and a process that fits with their national characteristics, that will enable people to really understand what to do.

When people say we can build a post-Brexit economy without tackling climate change, this is snake oil in my view. But it is promoted by enough people to enough people who don't understand that these aren't linear issues. When people fear for their job, their livelihood, their family and their family's future, they are tempted by politicians who say, "You can have this today and life will be better." And somehow the politicians, or ex-politicians like me, must say, "Well, if you have that today, then tomorrow, you're actually reducing the chances for your children and their children." Somehow that voice has to become louder, especially from the young people themselves.

How did it feel to discuss wisdom today?

It's been an absolute pleasure. It's really been fun. I think wisdom should be fun, because I think fun is a really important component of learning. I have no pretense about being wise or offering solutions, but I think what I have learned is to separate wise from foolish decisions, to separate long-term from short-term decisions. And what I really want is for more of us to support governments that are wise enough to engage on behalf of the many, rather than pursuing the interests of the few.

So I think that if wisdom is another lens into that, let us spend time reflecting on it. All of us are seeking a lens that enables people to have their own epiphany, to think about behaving differently. A number of people have influenced me, but it's always just been those special moments, those brilliant thoughts that crystallize ideas that become inspirations. And it's really interesting when you have a discussion about something that you think is beyond your ability to understand, and you then find that as a result you are drawn to learn more about it. Thank you.

David Eby

David Eby, founding cellist for the internationally acclaimed band Pink Martini, has an active performing and teaching career on the West Coast.

As a youth, David made his solo debut with the Pittsburgh Symphony at age 16, and studied at the Eastman School of Music. He also had the great privilege of studying under Janos Starker at Indiana University, where he received his MM degree.

In 1996 he began to practice meditation, and completely shifted the focus of his life. Intrigued with the connection between music, meditation and consciousness, he spent years working with choirs and ensembles of meditators in Portland, Oregon, and the Ananda Village in California, where he served as music director for many years.

He was recently featured in the Hollywood film *Finding Happiness*, and continues to explore and share the connections between music and consciousness that become present in inspired performance. davidebymusic.com

What comes to mind first when you think about wisdom?

Wholeness. A sense of being okay. If I am surrounded by manifestations of wisdom, I'm going to be okay; my best interests are being held in consideration by others. And even though I might not like the immediate choices, what's going to come down the road is where I really want to go. So wisdom for me in a nutshell is about getting me where I want to go.

Spiritually I follow the teachings of Paramahansa Yogananda. The beautiful thing about wisdom is that you get to test it out. You get to see and explore and try out the teachings, whether they're teachings for spirituality, or for making money, or in my case for playing the cello. You try them out and see if they work. Do they take you where you want to go? And since many people have many different places they want to go, perhaps wisdom has many different facets to it. But I think I'm going to hold fast to my original statement, that wisdom is that which gets you where you want to go.

Do you recall the first time you witnessed wisdom in action?

It's hard to pinpoint the very first time, but in general it was seeing someone's calm actions solving a problem. I'll give you an example. I was on a swim team growing up. And for one of the practices everybody was supposed to be in six lanes, but we got jammed into three, so it was just too crowded. And the coach said, "Okay, how many people here think it's too crowded?" I raised my hand, and a whole bunch of other people did too. And he said, "Okay, you guys can go home." And it was like, 'Oh, what?' But he handled it so beautifully. It wasn't emotional. It was just: here's what it is. So I love seeing examples of calm, centered wisdom in action.

There's this program called El Sistema, meaning 'the system'. It was founded in 1975 by a Venezuelan educator, musician and activist named José Antonio Abreu. It became focused on music for social change. They brought classical music training into the slums and were able to uplift the lives of so many people through this. And I worked for a number of years up here in Portland with an organization that was associated with it. So I was working in schools where I was the minority and where the behavior is not what I was used to. And I saw how the people in charge were very in control of themselves, and how they would put the responsibility on others to make choices, to contribute their ideas to making a situation better. Oftentimes we get people who would try to control, or punish. But when you place the responsibility on others to help come up with a problem with the solutions to the problems, that's where a lot of change can happen.

And I really wish we had more of that happening in America right now.

So, I don't remember when I first saw it in action, but it's a feeling inside that that just goes 'bing'. You know you've just seen wisdom in action.

Who is the wisest person you know, and why?

For me, Paramahansa Yogananda is the big wisdom teacher in my life. He wrote the spiritual classic *Autobiography of a Yogi*. One hundred years ago he came to America to bring the teachings of Kriya yoga to America. But he brought such a spectrum of teachings with him. His disciple Swami Kriyananda founded the community that I live in, called Ananda. I got to work directly with Kriyananda for a number of years and see him in action. And the philosophy really comes down to two things. Number one: people are more important than things. When trying to make my way in life and get to where I want to go, that's been one of the maxims that has really been helpful.

And number two: where there is adherence to dharma or right action, there is victory. So no matter what, however tempting it might be to take shortcuts, sticking to your principles will ultimately take you to where you want to go.

And of course there are many others. The teachings of meditation have taken me where I want to go. For many years growing up, I had an inner yearning to work under a wise boss. Somebody who I could trust, follow and learn from. And growing up it was really hard to find them. In the musical profession there are a lot of egos that get involved and it's difficult to find those who truly share that essence of wisdom. But there are some that you find. Having experiences with great teachers like Leonard Bernstein, Sir Georg Solti and Janos Starker, there's an aspect of living wisdom that resonates within them. You feel it when you're around them. And it doesn't have to necessarily be expressed in words, it can be expressed through gestures, or through sound, or through the eyes. So when you meet somebody who has this quality of something that you naturally want to honor and respect, you just feel that. I've really enjoyed being in close proximity with people who have that spark in their eye, that sense of quiet centeredness. And again, they don't have to necessarily be lecturing all the time. It's just that you feel something around them that inspires you, that brings out the best in you. So the wisdom teachers that I've met have in some regard transcended ego. They've realized that the ego clings to things, and they found a way to get beyond that, and touch a deeper part of their soul and work from that.

What those great teachers taught me is that it's really the essence behind the notes in music. Music is so mysterious because it's so much more than just sounds put together. And we instinctively know this. You can attend a performance in which all the right notes are there, and you can appreciate their technical ability. But then there are the performances where it might not be perfect, yet you're moved to tears because it was so beautiful. And it could be the same exact piece. What is different about those two performances? You can break it out in the head and relate it to personal taste, and maybe it triggered a memory. But for me, what it comes down to is the inspiration that each musician can feel and bring into their music. So we talk about how energy resonates within us. We say, "That really resonates with me." Or, "That struck a deep chord. I was touched, I was moved." We're talking about an inner experience of awakened energy within us, that is hard to measure, yet we know it's there.

And so for me, the wisest teachers are those who are able to express, through their music, a state of expanded consciousness and expanded awareness. And this is the great mystery. When you hear a great performer play their first note, you're just drawn into that. It's not necessarily the nature of their sonic production, but there's something else. Sound conveys thoughts, feelings and emotions. And we do this all the time with our voices. You may try to be positive, and say, "That's fine." But your voice will betray you. So people in my life would say, "Well, you don't have to take that attitude." And I say, "What? I said it was fine!" So we're betrayed by our voices all the time.

And that's the common thread that I look for in people that I want to work with. Can their sound carry me into a state of upliftment just from their very first note? And we choose people to hang out with that we resonate with. That's where we want to go. We want to go to like-minded frequencies, like-minded vibration.

Looking back on your life, what is the wisest thing you ever did?

One of my wisest decisions was going into music. In high school I was really good at computer programming. And of course there have been years where I've thought, 'If I had followed that in the 80s, just think of how well off I could be right now.' And that was appealing to me. Yet the wisdom of the heart knows. We talk about the intellect of the brain, but there's something about the heart that guides us in ways of wisdom.

So I went into music, I followed my heart, and I am so glad that I did, because I didn't need more intellectual training. I needed to develop that nature of love, that nature of sharing things with the heart that music has to offer. So for me I was just examining the wisdom of playing it safe. Sometimes that is a good thing to do. Going into computer programming would have been playing it safe, but I'm glad I didn't. Music has been a really great opportunity. It has helped me progress in my personal journey, and it's been a reflection of my fundamental nature.

What is the hardest-won wisdom that you have?

To not give myself away. To really stand for who I am and for what I'm looking for. I was in a 27-year marriage that is ending this year. And so for me it's a closure of a life that was lived in looking for security and safety in another. Like, if I subdue myself, I can be accepted. And so for me, that's been a really hard lesson to learn, that the truth is in me, and that I have the keys within me to my own success and my own greater future. I don't have to look for others to give me that.

I've always kind of shied away from going for it. After graduating from college, I lived in a small city in Indiana, and I was a substitute musician in a larger city, Indianapolis, for one of their orchestra concerts. One day I was playing and this guy said, "Dude, what happened?" He meant that I had a lot more to offer. But I had chosen to tuck myself away in someplace safe. And so gradually over time I have these 'aha moments' of realizing that I really do have something to say, something to offer. And so the music itself provides me this opportunity to explore. So every performance is this opportunity, whether it's three people in the audience or 300. It allows me to explore this song of wisdom that I have within myself. It may not have a word to it, but it has vibration. It has resonance. So every performance that I enter into is a way for me to take what I've learned and to express it vibrationally. It's really hard to express in words other than that.

I take the experience that I've had in meditation, in following my spiritual path, and I try to convey that musically. I hold that in my mind and heart, and then I create music with that intention, with that mind. It's amazing. I can just be warming up and somebody will come walking by and say, "What is that gorgeous piece of music?" And I say, "Well, it's the G major scale." So it works. People can really feel it.

To express where I'm at I play, write and improvise, depending on the moment. Improvising is my favorite thing to do right now. Writing music is a different beast because you have to stop the process and make sure you've got it down. And there's a sense of non-attachment that comes from improvisation that I find really helpful. It's this path of trust. It's like, "This is great. I might never have this again." But it might be something beautiful that other people need to hear, so recording is really helpful. I do performances on Facebook Live. So if there's something that comes through, I can always go back and study it.

And I am doing a little bit of composing too. Every great piece of music has within it a seed of inspiration. When Handel was composing the Hallelujah Chorus from *Messiah* in 1741, he was found with tears streaming down his face. He said, "I did think I did see all Heaven before me and the great God Himself." He had a spiritual experience that Yogananda talks about as samadhi. It is an experience of connection, a union with God, a cosmic enlightenment that is universal. And he was able to take that experience and convey it in his compositions.

So this is the great mystery. In the yogic teachings, it's explained that music can hold vibration. It can hold inspiration. Not only that, but it can be added to by the energy with which it's performed, year after year after year. So these pieces are only getting better. And there's this great book, *Talks with Great Composers*, by Alfred M. Abell. And the best part about it is this interview with Brahms, who describes going into the state between dreaming and wakefulness, by meditating on a scriptural passage. And once he is getting close to that state he feels vibrations thrill his body. And he gets into the space that he calls the superconscious, where he connects with something greater than himself. And that's where he says all of his great melodies and harmonies come from. It's not that he's sitting down writing this intellectually, it's that he receives them.

In the world today, where do you see wisdom, and its lack, being demonstrated?

Firstly, New Zealand. Let's just call that for what it is. New Zealand is fantastic. And we have the contrary in America. I just saw something in Canada that somebody posted. They are doing meditation training for the police officers. It's just beautiful.

It's a hard time to be in the States right now. I recently did this call to prayer to bring forth wise leadership. Someone to guide us in the ways that Martin Luther King did. The ways that JFK was able to do, to bring this country together, to bring the racial injustices to a place of healing. So that's my sole call right now, to help bring that about.

How do you apply wisdom to the care of your mind, body and soul?

Meditation, first of all. Doing that which may not be the most rewarding immediately, but which has a greater benefit down the line. Also exercise. And making sure that I'm not inundating myself with media that doesn't take me where I want to go.

There's this great saying by a Kriyananda. You can apply this to anything, but he said, "If your music brings your energy down, avoid it like it's poison." You can think of this in relation to something like Facebook. Often it's a hotbed of anger and frustration. Thankfully I've got good people on my feed, and I appreciate their positive outlooks. Right now we're just clinging to what is positive, and trying to put out as much positivity as we can.

When I'm feeling down, I know I need to put out energy in a positive way. And that's going to help me get to where I want to go. If I'm depressed, if I just want to stay in and watch depressing movies or just complain about everything, I know from past experience that that's not going to get me where I want to go. So I try to see what I can do to help others. Like I'll do an improvisation on Facebook Live, or I will do a class or write an article, to try to inspire.

Is wisdom a uniquely human concept?

No. There's wisdom in horses, in dogs, in animals all over. There's a wisdom in nature. You can see that it's just infused in this entire creation. I heard a quote that went something like, 'If one species were to become extinct, all Earth would perish because everything is connected. If the human species were to become extinct, the Earth would come to its full fruition and allow itself to heal.' So I think there's wisdom all around us that we've ignored for many, many years. We don't live in harmony with our planet.

Do you have a favorite parable or anecdote on wisdom?

There is *The Serenity Prayer*, written by the American theologian Reinhold Niebuhr. It's used a lot in alcoholics anonymous and other 12-step programs.

God, grant me the serenity to accept the things I cannot change,
courage to change the things I can,
and wisdom to know the difference.

How do you ultimately define wisdom?

I'll go back to what I said before. Wisdom is that which helps you get to where you want to go. Wisdom is that which guides your heart and mind into an expansive sense of unity; it is that which connects you to a greater understanding.

When it comes to what makes masters so wise, like Paramahansa Yogananda, we talked about vibration. We talked about resonance. Attunement in music is getting your fingers on the cello to be in tune with whatever you're playing, or even just another string instrument. And what these great souls have done, is tune their lives to that greater understanding, that greater connection. Whether you call it God, whether you call it the universe, they have attuned themselves with that focus. And along with that is receptivity, because attunement involves being receptive. It's not just about forcing something down a path, it's about listening. It's about receiving, it's about feeling, it's about the subtle nuance of trying to sort out what is true wisdom in any decision. The masters are those who have dedicated themselves to attunement, and have put the energy into making that connection and then pursuing that for a lifetime. And some of them come into this life with a highly-developed sense of who they are and are already developed.

How can each of us develop wisdom?

By looking at where you want to go. And by reflecting on those experiences in which you felt that greater connection. For instance, in music I always recommend that we look at the performances that gave us that sense of wow, that sense of connection to each other, to the music, to something higher than ourselves. Use those experiences as springboards for deeper exploration. Allow yourself to become still, to relax your heart and calm your mind.

I've narrowed it down to a four-step process. The hush, creating dynamic stillness; the heart, opening to that receptivity; the lift, engaging the positive energy; and then the flow, stepping into that experience and offering yourself, offering the little ego into something greater. Hush, heart, lift and flow.

Is there anything else you wish to add?

I'm amazed at the answers that came up in this hour, that I didn't have as I prepared for it!

How did it feel to discuss wisdom today?

What I feel is an expansion of my heart, a deep calmness, an upliftment and a clarity.

Michel Ferrari

Dr. Michel Ferrari is Professor in the Department of Applied Psychology and Human Development at the Ontario Institute for Studies in Education (OISE), University of Toronto. As Director of the Wisdom and Identity Lab, he explores the meaning of personal wisdom in people of different ages (from children to the elderly) from different nations.

He has edited or co-edited 12 books and is currently leading a study that explores the relationship between wisdom and acculturation in Islamic immigrants and refugees to Canada. In applied practice, he and his students are studying the experience of wisdom in emerging adults with autism in Canada and Pakistan. wisdomandidentity.com

What comes to mind first when you think about wisdom?

I think of wisdom as a human heritage of the best models, aspirations and insights we have. If you go back to ancient understandings of wisdom, they relate to the natural universe and our place in it; so understandings marked as wisdom are some of the most important things we need to know to live well and most meaningfully, that have been handed down to us.

But also I think of wisdom in terms of needing to bring that understanding to life again in each person, in every new generation, in ways that go beyond the power of words to describe, because they address what is most profound in our experience of ourselves, others and the world.

Do you recall the first time you witnessed wisdom in action?

One approach I've taken to studying wisdom is to ask people whom they consider to be wise. And so my own answer does not surprise me, because it is a really common one: I think that my mother was wise in a lot of ways. She was very astute at figuring out what a situation needed, and she was a great storyteller.

As an adult, Adrien Pinard, my master's thesis advisor at the Université du Québec à Montréal (UQAM), stood out as wise. He could adjust his conversation to anybody who came into the room. A five-year-old would show up and he would talk to them as a five-year-old and they'd laugh. And then a few minutes later he'd be talking to a 30-year-old just as naturally, and they would laugh, too. He could address anybody, but with a sensitivity that I always admired.

One time, our computers were sent in for repair and they weren't giving them back. So after a few days, he said to me (translating loosely from the French): "Call them up. Now they're probably going to tell you, 'Oh, we're very busy and we haven't gotten to it yet.' So then you tell them, 'We really need them because our work is being held up.' They're going to tell you, 'Well there's a long line ahead of you.' So you tell them, 'All our work has stopped. We can't continue without those computers.' And then they'll say, 'Okay, come by this afternoon and you can pick them up.'" So I did this, and it played out exactly as he had described, almost word-for-word. He was like that all the time.

I admired him, because he was also very kind and generous. He was a very caring person. He was about 70 and his wife was maybe 50. She ended up having an affair because they couldn't have children, and she had a child with another man. Of course he was crushed by this. But at one point he said to me, "Well, I've got to rise above this if I want to keep a relationship with all of them. And if I can't be civilized at age 70, then I guess it'll never happen." His whole optic was to try and find the best resolution for even the most difficult things. I have always thought of him as a model scholar and a model person.

My mother was also a great problem solver. She was inventive and resourceful. She had a knack for resource management and logistical challenges. But she also was very generous, like her mother. As a child she would tell me stories about her day that carried a lesson, without being at all didactic. She had risen from conducting door-to-door surveys to being in charge of the Québec operations for three companies. And one day she was offered a raise by her bosses, but she said that her workers needed a raise more than she did, since they were doing all the work. So she negotiated on behalf of everybody, sincerely, and then explained to me that after they agreed to give everyone a raise, they also gave her a raise. But her immediate response was to support all the people working for her. What I took away from that story and others like it, was her generosity and consideration of the bigger picture.

With wisdom, I feel as though you pick it up from all over. I often find that I associate wisdom with people that I take as a model, that I'd like to emulate. In terms of my scholarly work, William James is a model for me because he seems very open-minded. He was really trying to understand what personal psychological experience was for people, and he was very creative. His entire outlook was pragmatic, but at the same time it was honest and expansive, pluralist. It's not about reducing everything to a single answer, but actually looking for the full range of diversity in the answers that you can find about something, and then building bridges between them, connecting them. And we can make this approach even broader today, because we're more easily connected to people from other countries all over the world.

In terms of the arts, I think of someone like Spike Lee. I find him really inspiring. He tells stories that are very simple, but at the heart of it is the same kind of humanity I find in James, and also a clarity about real contemporary issues. One of my favorite films of his is *Get on the Bus*. These African American guys are getting on the bus to the Million Man March in Washington, DC. And the whole movie is about who's going to be allowed on the bus. And they are all such different people. There's a former Marine, who's also gay: should he be allowed on the bus? It's such a great metaphor for who's going to be included in our community. So I feel I've learned a lot from him.

But there are many, many people. Almost too many to name. There is a famous passage from the Analects (7-21) in which Confucius says, 'If I am walking with two men, each of them will serve as my teacher. I will pick out the good points of the one and imitate them, and the bad points of the other and correct them in myself.' That kind of optic is really worth emulating, in terms of gathering wisdom.

Looking back on your life, what is the wisest thing you ever did?

It's hard to say, because the wisest things I have done were not entirely up to me. Getting married was one of them, because my wife has so much insight and is also very sensitive. This helps me because I tend to be in a bit of a bubble and not very observant, very much wrapped up in ideas. And so she connects me to a lot of other things that are happening.

My son was born when I was 53. I didn't think it was going to really happen; that I would ever be a father. And that was transformative. Again, that's not something that I did alone, but it's something that changed my entire outlook on what matters, and so it's been a great source of wisdom.

I think it shows how important relationships are, because you can be proud of your accomplishments, or regret that you didn't get as much done as you wanted to do, but at the end of the journey it's about the people in your life. It's not exactly a wise thing I've done, but it's very enriching and provides a context that helps make greater wisdom possible for me.

What brought you to the study of wisdom?

It started during my Postdoc with Robert Sternberg at Yale University in the late 1990s. He's one of the people who launched the scientific study of wisdom. He'd published an edited book about wisdom in 1990. Although his thinking is very clear and his research is well crafted, it felt narrow to me. And it felt as though there's more to wisdom than what was in that book. Basically, he believes that wisdom is about balance: It's about coordinating perspectives over both the short and the long term, and finding the best benefit for everybody. I think that's true. But at the same time, I thought to myself, 'Is that true internationally? If you went around the world would everybody endorse that? Would people of different ages agree?'

So that's what led me to study wisdom. Wisdom is a very abstract concept, but how would it play out in people's lives? I asked them similar questions to those you are asking me. That's more Jamesian, experiential. What is the quality of what it means either to be wise or to experience the presence of someone who's wise? Of course, I'm not alone or even the first to have this idea; Judith Glück is another researcher who pioneered this way of studying wisdom, and Monika Ardelt was co-principal on that project.

And there's also the issue of whether wisdom can be taught, and if so, how can it be taught? The things that have been said so far about this seem inadequate to me, because they propose a kind of curriculum, a skillset. That is important, but it feels incomplete to me. It seems as though there must be some way to get to something deeper than that. I just discovered recently that Christian scholars like St. Augustine of Hippo and St. Bernard of Clairvaux used the metaphor of 'tasting wisdom', because they believed that taste is more immediate and profound than seeing. That strikes me as right somehow; that's what I feel was maybe missing. The work that I'd seen up to that point had a kind of 'knowledge vision' quality to it. But it misses that tasted or felt aspect. I'm not sure that I have been able to capture it in my work either, but I am trying to find some way to get to that.

What projects did you put together on wisdom?

First of all it is important to say that these projects are collaborative efforts that involve a lot of people. Our first big project started around

2008 and involved looking at younger adults and older adults from different countries, using a contrast of East (China and India) and West (Canada and the USA). I thought that was a bit of a superficial contrast. Canada is certainly different to America. And India is not like China, or like Korea. And people say the Ukraine and Serbia are Eastern-European, classically neither East nor West, so we included all six in our study. Each site had its own principal investigator: Myself in Canada, Monika Ardelt in the USA, Ru-De Liu in China, Ram Mahalingam for India, Elena Ivanova in Ukraine and Aleksandar Baucal in Serbia, with a small army of students and volunteers conducting and transcribing the interviews.

We used standardized questionnaires to measure wisdom, like Monika's Three-Dimensional Wisdom Scale, and life satisfaction and well-being self-report measures that have been developed by other researchers. We then translated them into their languages of each country. We also interviewed people and asked them outright about wisdom, using similar questions to those that you're asking me: 'Think of someone who's wise. Why are they wise?' And, 'What about you, in your own life?' And then we asked them to pick someone historically they consider to be wise, and explain why they chose that person and if they had influenced them in any way. And then we closed by asking for a general definition. 'What is wisdom? What does wisdom mean to you?' We thought that if we asked older and younger adults from different countries these questions we could get a sense of whether there is a difference in the examples they pick.

My biggest trouble was that it was actually very hard to figure out how to analyze all that we found in a way that captured the full scope of what people were saying to us. We were not able to give a really good empirical accounting of it; although we published some of this work, we're still working with these data.

The upshot of it was that you do find big differences between countries, but there were also many similarities. My understanding of this now is that when you boil it down, you actually get two different kinds of questions. You could ask things that are cultural questions, like, 'What does wisdom mean to you?' And then you're going to get something like a dictionary definition, an approximation. I would expect the answers to be closely aligned within countries. It might be a little bit idiosyncratic, but if you think it means something nobody else thinks it means you're either a genius or you don't know the word wisdom means.

And the same thing with historical exemplars. That's actually where we've started now. If you look carefully at which people are nominated, you find iconic exemplars and obscure exemplars. People will pick Madame Curie, for example. She's a good candidate, but very few will pick her. But in our study, 10% of people chose Jesus and another 10% chose Mahatma Gandhi. In a follow up study, it turned out that Mahatma Gandhi was iconic in Canada both for native-born citizens and for immigrants to Canada, as well as for native-born citizens in India. But then if you ask why he is wise, you get a different portrait of Gandhi in these different populations. Which makes sense really, but it was worth showing that. First of all, in India we interviewed people from Gujarati province, which is Gandhi's home province. They had learned about him in school, so they know a lot of specific things about Gandhi. They have very precise stories. In North America, Canadians still put Gandhi on the list, but when you ask why, many couldn't tell you; they just have this idea that he is someone you should name, or they point to a single idea like non-violent protest.

That seems like a kind of understanding of wisdom, almost an ultimate cultural aspiration. But then if you scale it back to people you know, like my mother and my supervisor, Adrian Pinard, then it's really more about people that you could actually emulate, in different ways. So I think there's a range of ways to be wise.

One of my favorite stories came from the Ukraine. Although the participant was older now, she remembered a time when her 19-year-old self was a conductor on a train, and suddenly a passenger went into labor. So she found a doctor, and towels and hot water, and radioed ahead for an ambulance: She orchestrated the entire thing in minutes so that by the time they reached the next stop the ambulance was waiting to take the woman to the hospital and everybody was fine. She said that this was a moment of wisdom, because five minutes before if you'd asked her if she thought she could handle such a situation she would have said, "Absolutely not!"

That was actually part of their way of thinking about wisdom in Ukraine: It's the ability to access some deeper aspect of yourself, some capacity you have, that's always available potentially. It reminded me of the Eastern Orthodox view of a kind of access to mystical or transcendent power that's in the Christian faith. It's a power of God, but it doesn't have to be religious, and most participants did not frame it this way at all. In psychology, people like William James and Carl Jung have the idea of a collective unconscious, a vast reservoir of potential that we have, that we don't usually use. That seemed to be an important part of the Ukrainian definition of wisdom that you don't often find mentioned in Canada. I suspect that people wouldn't deny its importance if you put the questions to them directly, but it doesn't spontaneously come up in their accounts of wisdom.

Likewise in China. It's a myth to say that people are not interested in, or don't recognize individuality. One of my favorite stories was from one of the Chinese participants. When asked to think of someone who is wise, they picked their boss. Why? Because he was able to access his entire network of contacts and draw on them to set up this company. And with that, he's able to hire many people and contribute to the community. When we asked if this participant could be wise in that way, he said something like, "No, all my friends are lazy, and I'm not that skilled at coordinating things in the same way." So we do find an element here that speaks to a more collectivist culture, but at the same time recognizes the special contribution of the individual. It's about what a particular person can do for everybody, by drawing on their social network. That kind of answer also doesn't tend to come up in the North American examples.

We didn't find much difference between younger and older people, although it's true that the older people can look back at their lives and see how they've learned over time. Sometimes they could see that as a younger person they made a lot of big mistakes, and were too wrapped up in themselves, for example. They were able to take a broader view and understand that about themselves and accept it.

In another study, we looked at what other things could matter to understanding wisdom and acting wisely, through the lens of religion. We got a grant to do an interdisciplinary study. We had a political scientist (Ricca Edmondson), a sociologist (Monika Ardelt), a philosopher and cognitive scientist (John Vervaeke), a theologian (Gilles Mongeau) and two psychologists (myself and Hyeyoung Bang). So there were six of us who got together to look at what we should be asking people. The great thing about the project was that my colleagues from other disciplines took me out of the psychological mindset. Especially working with Ricca, a political scientist, she took me out of my psychological mindset focused on individuals, and into social structures, like the Christian church and the Buddhist sangha. They exist as their own organizations, and they require certain things of people in order to remain within them. So one of our questions became: What keeps you virtuous? And we looked at how belonging to different communities, whether religious or national, affected one's understanding of virtue and wisdom. As Ricca reminded us, some people would not want to be caught not being virtuous, because of the social embarrassment or shame it would bring. We put these questions to older and younger adults who were Christian, Muslim, Buddhist and atheist, living in South Korea and Canada (although we didn't find enough Muslim citizens in South Korea).

As we had an interdisciplinary team, we were sometimes working with conflicting conventions, as to what should have given us quality work. Picking the number of subjects was one area of contention.

A variety of things came out of that. One older person said that she had learned a lot, but if she tried to tell her younger self those things, she probably would not listen to her. That seemed really insightful and true. There are things you figure out over time, but you would not want to hear them as a younger version of yourself.

There weren't large differences between the religious traditions, as

I had expected. But we again gave them Monika's wisdom questionnaire, the Three-dimensional Wisdom Scale. The theory behind it is that wisdom involves three things that need to be integrated: Cognitive depth in pursuing the truth; reflection that takes you out of your own biases and perspective and coordinates with other people; and compassion—that you care for other people and want to help them. If you have those three things together, you're predisposed to be wise in any situation.

And it turns out that people who scored high on this measure absorb and use these religious traditions differently than do those who scored lower. And that made a lot of sense to me. It also says something about the tradition itself. They give you a toolkit for dealing with situations in life, but how you use those tools is going to reflect the kind of person you are.

A follow-up from that study is that we asked participants to nominate people in Ontario who they thought were wise. And then we went to interview them. We ended up choosing those who had a community impact, and some kind of presence, say through a website. They needed to have some kind of name recognition.

We chose four of these people so far in Canada (one for each religious orientation). They did a few more in South Korea. And all of these people seem to be making a unique use of their religious tradition. For example we spoke to Gretta Vosper, who is a atheist minister at West Hill United, a Christian church within the United Church of Canada. The radical perspective she takes is in response to the fundamentalist view of God, which people often appeal to as some ultimate power who grants wishes. It's something that people use in fundamentalist Islam and Christianity to attack other people. They use it to justify bombing abortion clinics or in launching jihads, and killing a lot of innocent people. So Gretta believes we should jettison this idea of God and not give them this ammunition, not let them use it as a rationale for what they're going to do. And Christianity should really be about building communities and helping people, as Jesus did. That's my view also.

And when you talk to Gretta, you realize she's actually got a very well-articulated understanding of what Christianity means for her, but also the way you cultivate this type of community. How wisdom relates to that is that this community is grounded in love—you're trying to love and care for other people. But what if people have different ideas about what it means to love somebody? So then you need wisdom to deal with that, because wisdom is going to give you the insight to both get outside of your own perspective, and coordinate with others so that your compassion is able to really be effective. This allows the communities to be more inclusive and avoid problems that come from a naïve attempt to care. And that struck me as something you don't hear in the scientific literature, but is very profound.

Another person that we're talking to is El-Farouk Khaki. With Laury Silvers and Troy Jackson he co-founded the el-Tawhid Juma Circle, The Toronto Unity Mosque, a mosque for gay and transgender Muslims. This already shows you the kind of person he is. He doesn't feel he's stepping outside of Islam to do that at all. He says that Islam is a religion of peace and is inclusive. He's also a practicing Sufi, and a political activist. He's doing all of these various things, so is not just giving a sermon, but is really engaging other people. He also sets up simulcasts, so he's able to reach people in far-flung communities. They can link in. They might be very isolated, like somewhere in Nebraska, but they can link into this mosque and meet a community of people who can acknowledge and support them.

They really inspire me in terms of work they're doing, and their effort to really extend beyond just their immediate circle in ways that are really savvy and effective. They have a clear message that's caring and inclusive. And if you're open-minded, it's very hard to deny it. You can't really say "You're wrong about that." It's very hard not to support them however you can.

You can find some values that cut through Islam and say, Christianity. And you can find people whose message is not bound by their religious tradition, but they make use of it in ways that are interesting, innovative and insightful. As you can probably tell, I'm trying to promote their message. I really think that it's remarkable what El-Farouk is doing. And Gretta Vosper too. When you hear somebody is an atheist and a minister, my first thought is almost to dismiss them out of hand. Like it must be a stunt or whatever. But when you really hear what she's trying to say, you realize that it's actually a very deep message, that I think is probably a better way to proceed.

Even if people are lower on the 3D scale of wisdom, it doesn't mean that they don't have things to offer that have an internal wisdom. Like being supportive to friends and colleagues. For example, one participant admired a friend who showed up to and sat through a mutual friend's play, despite not finding it interesting. For some people they wouldn't find much meaning or wisdom in that, but for others, they may find that affecting, meaningful and wise.

And so if you ask a Gretta Vosper or an El-Farouk who they think is wise, it possibly gives us insight into a rarer or more articulate understanding of wisdom. And they might be closer to being able to achieve it for themselves. They wouldn't necessarily want to claim that for themselves, but they can recognize it in other people. They know what qualities are important to cultivate and look for in other people. They can more easily describe it.

But the other interesting thing about the interview with Gretta Vosper, was that we asked her a set of standardized questionnaires, as I mentioned before. One of them was the Quality of Life Inventory. This includes questions such as: How important is work for your happiness (Not important, important, or extremely important)? And then: How satisfied are you with your work (from −3 to +3)? By taking their scores you multiply them together to get a sense of whether things affect their lives, regardless of how they feel about them.

They set the scale up with 16 different dimensions. And one of the last questions was on family. Things were not going well with some members of Gretta's family, but she accepted that, so it was not impacting her quality of life as deeply as if she were unable to come to terms with it. This arose in discussion. We do not just have people circle a number on a questionnaire; we discuss their answers with them, to get more richness. It was an important lesson that despite the impact that she's having in the community and the clarity of her message, there are still areas of her life where she has to persevere in the face of difficulties. We interviewed her at a time when the United Church was actually considering whether they should just kick her out entirely, because is it even possible to have a minister who doesn't believe in God? But interestingly enough, her entire church community rallied behind her and she is still a minister there today.

So that also seems an important part of the story for these wisdom exemplars. It's not to pretend that you hit some magic threshold and all your problems disappear, but it's more about how skillfully you navigate difficulties, and what perspective you take on how you approach or deal with them, or accept the consequences of your beliefs and actions. And all of that becomes clearer when people are doing grander things and harder things.

What is the hardest-won wisdom that you have?

The hardest lesson I've learned is that, early on, and maybe even up till today, I focus too much on what I'm trying to do, and not enough on this Chinese sense of the social context within which I do them, or that I could cultivate or drawn on. And I think that's really limited what I've been able to do, compared to people who have that appreciation and can do more. Including the people that I've just been talking about. It's a skill set that I feel I don't have. But I'm coming to the wisdom that it's something that I should have been cultivating a long time ago. I'm realizing that it's not actually about any one of us, but it's about what we can achieve together. This seems especially true in activist areas. When you read these Chinese transcripts you appreciate the power of what they're saying. You can find these ideas in say, Taoism, but when somebody says it to you, it, it strikes you much more strongly.

Wisdom

Is wisdom a uniquely human concept?

Not to me. Some people, like Fengyan Wang in China, have wondered whether we can develop 'artificial wisdom' analogous to the development of 'artificial intelligence', and that seems potentially possible to me.

But more to the point, I think indigenous wisdom traditions are right to say that the natural world has a deep wisdom we can learn from if we care to listen. I have been profoundly struck by the Inuit understanding of Sila, which one Inuit scholar said has been translated both as the God of wisdom by anthropologists, and as the weather by climatologists, but then goes on to say that it is not that we personify the environment as Sila, but rather Sila—the environment—personifies us. I love that, and think it is profoundly true. And there must surely be other cosmic personifications of Sila/wisdom, even if they are too far to meet them with our current technology. Or maybe Gandhi was right to say that the highest wisdom is truth, and that truth transcends us.

Do you have a favorite parable or anecdote on wisdom?

I interviewed a 90-year-old gentleman who told me an interesting story about a moment when he was wise. He said that getting on a bus a year or so before the interview he slipped and missed the step and broke his hip. Not really following him, I asked, "So, missing the step was somehow wise?" "No," he answered, "that was really foolish. But my life changed entirely in that moment. I was in the hospital for months. And to realize that every moment of your life is like that, I think that is wise." That our life can completely change at any moment, strikes me as profound. You hear stories in Taoism and Buddhism of moments that are both mundane and yet offer profound insight. I find it both a cautionary tale and a hopeful message wrapped up together. And it is authentically true in his and my lived experience.

In my 20s I studied karate up to black belt. Our Shotokan tradition, led by Master Oshima, emphasized learning to respond creatively and skillfully, without getting hurt or hurting others, especially in our practice. This required a good reading of your immediate circumstances and an ability to respond to it; it meant figuring out the right thing to do in any situation. There is also kind of subtlety to it. You need to be in a certain frame of mind that's open and uncommitted, but engaged and ready to move in any direction, and also physically relaxed enough to do that. If your mind is fixed, the other person can see that and use it against you. There is a very practical wisdom in that.

Later I studied Tai Chi. Our Tai Chi teacher, Master Wong, had an uncanny ability to calibrate his lessons to each person at each moment. He would make tiny adjustments to your position—I'm talking about say shifting one elbow by a centimeter—and the move would suddenly work effortlessly. As he said, memorably: "The difference between getting it right and getting it wrong is very small." That really stuck with me. I think there's a profound truth to that. You can't achieve the same success through force. The greatest effect is felt to be effortless; but you have to be mentally and physically relaxed and accurate to be able to make it work.

And this is reflected in my understanding of wisdom studies and how to teach for wisdom. It can't be just intellectual. Because a large part of wisdom is the entire attitude you bring to bear on whatever you're doing. The martial arts are better at cultivating that, as it's 100% proof of concept. There is no fooling yourself or anyone else about who understands something and can use it.

How do you ultimately define wisdom?

I define wisdom as our way of signaling what is most important about human experience and human existence. The people who embody or channel that understanding are called wise. Wisdom often requires overcoming obstacles, and in that sense wisdom is heroic. But while classical heroes are typically heroic on the landscape of action, wisdom involves heroism on the landscape of experience or consciousness, to use a distinction championed by the psychologist Jerome Bruner. In other words, they show us how to conquer deep human problems like suffering. Thought of in this way, wisdom includes both the everyday heroism of people we know and admire, and the epic wisdom that founds religious movements and makes it into the history books. But in saying that, I don't mean to limit this perspective to the human world, although it includes it. Because I think the truth and power of what we know as wisdom is woven into the ultimate nature of reality itself. It may go deeper than we can grasp, and we are just waiting for someone or something to reveal it to us more clearly than we saw or tasted it before.

How can each of us develop wisdom?

In trying to teach for wisdom, I've used the design of experiments approach, which comes out of engineering. An experiment is run repeatedly, and each time you try to learn from errors to refine the process. For example, for a few years now, I've been teaching a class about wisdom traditions, and my hope is that it can also give students the tools they need to live more wisely. An assignment I've tried is to ask students to take an aspect of one of the wisdom traditions we cover and try to live that way for two weeks, and then write about their experience. I took this idea from Stephen Grimm, who taught a similar course in New York.

Another approach was to write about what wisdom means for you, and do this iteratively, so as students go through the course, they can see how their thinking—and that of other students—develops as they encounter new perspectives about wisdom. This is an open online forum for the entire class, so people can read the experiences and perspectives of others. But they are told to also keep a private diary that is self-marked, about their experience with exercises that explore the different wisdom traditions we encounter each week.

So those are a few ways that I've been trying to bring this to life for students in the course, adjusting each year to try to improve the process, based on how students responded to the previous year. That's been challenging. The issue is that you really have to model these things yourself, and engage students at a deeply personal level. It's not enough just to say, "Read what Confucius said and try that." If the aim is to be open-minded and not bothered by things that happen, and then you're bothered by something, that's what people are going to pick up on, more than whatever they just read. Trying things out is a better, more interesting way to explore wisdom than reading about it. Several students have said that it's vastly different to live for a while as a Stoic, for example, than simply to read about the experiences and worldviews of the Stoics in ancient Greece. It's been fascinating to read the accounts of students who are trying to live out traditional advice on how to live wisely. Sometimes approaches that seem very different on paper, like say Taoist principle of wu wei (action in non-action) and the Stoic one of apatheia (equanimity), can end up being lived in very similar ways by students in early 21st century Toronto.

Is there anything else you wish to add?

Yes. Although everything I have said so far may not be wrong, I worry it might not get to the heart of what it really means to be wise. I once passed someone on the street who asked, "Can you spare a dollar?" I didn't have any change on me, so I simply said, "Sorry, I can't." Encounters like that have happened to me many times before and since, but that time I experienced a profound sadness for this person, and for what might have led him to be standing there, and for what his prospects were now. And somehow he received my feeling as part of my answer, because he replied, "Thank you." I don't usually frame this story as an example of wisdom, but maybe I should.

How did it feel to discuss wisdom today?

I find it humbling and a little unsettling to discuss wisdom, even if

I have been asking other people to do so for years. If wisdom is so rare, how can anything I say about it be worthwhile? But I take comfort in the great educator, Comenius, who called his work an invitation for, 'A General Consultation Concerning the Improvement of Human Affairs.' That's how I see my contribution to this discussion about wisdom. It is part of a general consultation about an important topic that should concern everyone, and to which others might have more import things to add, correcting or improving my ideas. Honestly, I just feel honored to be part of this conversation and this book.

Herbert Girardet

Professor Herbert Girardet is an author, filmmaker and international consultant specializing in 'regenerative development'. A recipient of a UN Global 500 Award for outstanding environmental services, he has been a consultant to UNEP, UN-Habitat, and cities such as London, Vienna, Riyadh and Bristol. He has authored many TV documentaries, including *Far from Paradise*, *Jungle Pharmacy* and *Halting the Fires*, as well as 13 books, including *Cities, People, Planet* and *Creating Regenerative Cities*.

Herbert is co-founder, former program director and honorary member of the World Future Council, and an executive committee member of the Club of Rome. In 2003 he was the inaugural 'Thinker in Residence' in Adelaide, defining eco-development strategies for South Australia, most of which have been implemented. He is a former chairman of the Schumacher Society, UK. He is an honorary fellow of the Royal Institute of British Architects, a patron of the Soil Association, UK, and a visiting professor at the University of the West of England.

What comes to mind first when you think about wisdom?

Well, first and foremost, the desperate need for it. We are called *Homo sapiens sapiens*, implying that we are these incredibly wise creatures. But are we? We are quite intelligent and have a lot of information and experiences of various kinds, an accumulation of knowledge. But there is not much evidence of wisdom. This current age, called the Anthropocene, is defined by our unprecedented technological power to dominate life on Earth. We are forced to think that we need deep wisdom to create checks and balances against this power and the impacts we are causing. But we are probably less wise today than we've been at any time in human history. So that is a frightening situation that we have barely begun to address.

What also comes to mind when thinking about wisdom, is Jesus's Sermon on the Mount. Like most of us at school I had religious lessons, and the Sermon on the Mount has stayed with me as a profound antidote to the all-embracing materialism in the aftermath of the post-war years:

> Blessed are the poor in spirit,
> For theirs is the kingdom of heaven.
> Blessed are those who mourn,
> For they shall be comforted.
> Blessed are the meek,
> For they shall inherit the earth.
> Blessed are those who hunger and thirst for righteousness,
> For they shall be filled.
> Blessed are the merciful,
> For they shall obtain mercy.
> Blessed are the pure in heart,
> For they shall see God.
> Blessed are the peacemakers,
> For they shall be called sons of God.
> Blessed are those who are persecuted for righteousness' sake,
> For theirs is the kingdom of heaven.

I was born in 1943 in Germany, and even though I was too young to experience the war directly, its repercussions were very apparent. So learning about the Sermon on the Mount was a profound experience for me, not so much in a religious sense, but in terms of its ethical message. Christianity has this very powerful and important statement embedded within it, but I have problems with the realities of Christianity as it established itself historically. For me the Sermon on the Mount is linked deeply to the thinking of ethical teachers such as

Socrates and the Buddha, and many other messages of wisdom that come to us from history. So the Sermon on the Mount was not there in isolation, but it has an important provenance, of we should remind ourselves.

Do you recall the first time you witnessed wisdom in action?

Germany's Chancellor from 1969 to 1974 was Willy Brandt. In 1970 his government signed a treaty formalizing the border between Germany and Poland. Brandt went to Poland and visited the memorial for the Warsaw ghetto where the Nazis had brutally put down an uprising in 1944. Instead of making a long speech he knelt before the memorial in a gesture of seeking forgiveness. This was an extraordinary gesture that was deeply admired by many people, and could be called an act of wisdom. But some Germans were furious with Brandt because he was admitting that Germany had done terrible things to Poland and the Jews. But for me this was a very powerful act of wisdom that I witnessed on a television newsreel. It was a political statement, but I think it was also a statement of wisdom.

Who is the wisest person you know, and why?

I have met quite a number, but many have since passed. When I was a student in Germany, I was strongly influenced by a philosopher named Ernst Bloch. During the Second World War, in exile in the US, he wrote a three-volume series of books called *The Principle of Hope*. This became important to those of us who were trying to wrestle with this history of Germany as a country that was so hated for what it had done to the world. He was an important person in my student life because he instilled in me a philosophy of hope, but also a deep concern about how we needed to make peace with ourselves, with history, and with nature.

Another person who I knew well, more recently, and who is no longer with us, was Professor Wangari Maathai. In the late 1970s she started an organization called the Green Belt Movement, which conveyed a powerful message of the need to make peace with nature. She used to talk about growing up in a forest village in Kenya. There was shade from the tree canopy, there were streams where people could take drinking water and irrigate their fields. It was a life of abundance. Then she left Kenya to study in America, and years later, when she came back home, the trees had gone and the streams had dried up. She urged the people to respond to this environmental crisis by replanting the trees, and to restore the environment in a holistic way. The Green Belt movement, led by women, has brought forest cover back to many regions in East Africa. Wangari radiated wisdom. She was awarded a Nobel Peace Prize for being an environmentalist, because she taught that we can create peace in the world by restoring and making peace with nature. Wangari said, "We are called to assist the Earth to heal her wounds and in the process heal our own—indeed to embrace the whole of creation in all its diversity, beauty and wonder."

Another truly wise person I met was an Amazonian Indian shaman and plant doctor called Beptopup. In 1988 I produced a Channel 4 documentary called *Jungle Pharmacy* with the Kayapo Indians, and other tribal communities in the Amazon. There was this man who looked like a professor who had spent his life using inherited knowledge of plant remedies to deal with health problems in his community. His radiant face reflected millennia of knowledge. We couldn't speak each other's languages, but we had interpreters to tell us what he said. It was evident that he had deep, profound wisdom. Walking with him through one of the world's most diverse ecosystems, it was evident that he had a name for every living being around him. One of the really powerful moments came when we filmed in an area where the rainforest had been razed to the ground by cattle ranchers. Thin grassland had taken the place of deep forest shade. He faced the camera and said, "Why does the white man burn everything, why does he have to destroy everything? The forest is gone and what will my children eat? How will they live?" That was how we ended the film.

Beptopup was a truly powerful, wise presence.

I would also add Vandana Shiva and Satish Kumar to this list of wise people I have been close to, and both are thankfully still alive. Vandana, among many other books, wrote *Earth Democracy*, a book about a culture of non-violence, creative peace, and life on Earth as a basis for a just and sustainable future. Satish recently wrote a wonderful book called *Elegant Simplicity: The Art of Living Well*. He often cites Mahatma Gandhi's statement: "The world has enough for everyone's need, but not enough for everyone's greed."

When I think of wisdom, I also think of images from old master paintings. For instance, Rembrandt's portraits and self-portraits come to mind, particularly those he painted towards the end of his life. They are extraordinary images of deep wisdom, reflecting a lifetime of his experiences of the world around him.

Wisdom is not the sole preserve of old people, or people from the past. Every so often young people come along who express a profound understanding of the world and its problems. Thinking of today, there are people like Greta Thunberg, trying to challenge short-term, selfish recklessness, particularly in the context of climate change. She rightly asks what sort of world we are leaving to future generations. And there are others like her, bringing youth into the equation in important ways. And often one can also see in very young children's faces a sense of wide-open wisdom that comes from somewhere we don't really understand.

Looking back on your life, what is the wisest thing you ever did?

I think it was moving to a cottage on the edge of Tintern Forest, where my wife and I have lived since 1976. I had been working in London as a community activist and journalist for several years. We had young kids and were living in rather stressful places. Our flat in Kentish Town had been broken into several times, and that kind of thing. So we looked for somewhere to bring up our children in a peaceful, rural environment. We found a run-down cottage in South

Wales, and decided to put down roots here. I could say that's the wisest thing we ever did. Not only in terms of where we are, but also in terms of what we've made of it. And I would like to particularly stress my wife's wisdom in this context. Barbara has created the most beautiful shrub garden all around us. It reflects a women's wisdom in a wonderful way. It's just extraordinary right now, as spring is turning into summer, with blossoms everywhere. So beauty and wisdom relate to each other too, as do love and wisdom. Barbara's love of nature is a direct interaction with the living world, and this is certainly reflected in the place where we live.

Moving to be close to nature has been professionally relevant for me as well. From our base in Tintern I have done a lot of work internationally as a filmmaker for the BBC, Channel 4 and other broadcasters. Much of this work has involved trying to draw attention to what we're doing to nature, and how we can try and stop wrecking the world's ecosystems. In addition to making documentaries I have written quite a few books. So being close to nature on a daily basis helps me to reflect on the global actions of humanity as well.

What is the hardest-won wisdom that you have?

This probably relates to attitude. I used to be quite an abrasive, even aggressive, and sometimes angry sort of guy. Seeing the world, and what we are doing to it, elicits anger. Whether it was the memory of the horrors of the Second World War or the Vietnam War, or encounters with hungry, desperate people across the world while making documentaries, I would sometimes aggressively confront those who prefer to ignore these issues, including my father. But then I gradually came to realize that it may be better to be kind, or at least to be kind of kind. It's better to love than to hate. It's better to try and heal than to cause more damage. And to be humble, to apologize sometimes. Like Willy Brandt did in Warsaw. So I increasingly found that this is important, and is a hard-won wisdom in my life. We must do more than join demonstrations and scream at the bastards who are destroying the world. We must be aware that the actions we take may lead to reactions that can cause even more conflict and anger, and ultimately do not resolve the deep-seated issues we need to address. So being kind, trying to be loving, trying to be healing, is probably one of the hardest-won wisdoms in my life.

In the world today, where do you see wisdom, and its lack, being demonstrated?

Unfortunately we are surrounded by a lack of wisdom everywhere we look. Short-termism, greed, selfishness, all of that kind of stuff—which is also within each one of us—defines so much of the world around us. I was a co-founder of the World Future Council, and we focused on long-term thinking, trying to be a voice of future generations, trying to deal with the horrendous legacies we are burdening them with. So much of what we are doing reflects an appalling lack of wisdom. So in my own work I've been trying to find ways to be of service.

Right now, in May 2020, we are being faced with a global, viral pandemic. We see wisdom in the actions of doctors, nurses, carers and teachers, people involved every day in caring service. I think it's important to realize that this is happening quietly all around us. And even though people don't talk about this as wisdom, it is profound in its meaning. And so I wish we had a lot more of that happening in our daily world, particularly from politicians and business leaders.

In this context we might reflect on the history of the industrial revolution. This allowed us to extract resources that had not been available to humanity before, buried within the earth's crust. The incredible power of fossil fuel energy that makes our current lifestyles possible could be described as a departure from wisdom because there was little concern about potential consequences. This power came to define the human presence on this planet for the last 200 years, and set in motion many of the huge environmental and social problems that we're facing.

It's frightening to see the greed and selfishness that has come to dominate so much of what we do today, and materialism is at the heart of it. One of the profound problems in the world today is the almost non-negotiable insistence on material advancement, regardless of the consequences. The quest for affluence has spread across the globe. Across the world people are seeing the seeming abundance of Western lifestyles on their TV screens and are asking why they can't have some of that for themselves. You can't blame poor people in Asia or Africa for wanting more affluent lives. We are faced with an unrelenting global quest for economic growth, yet there can't be infinite growth on a finite planet, and in 2020 we are now hitting planetary boundaries everywhere. So in the rich countries we are setting an agenda for people all over the world that cannot be fulfilled without dire consequences.

How did green politics arise?

The rise of green politics has been something of a reaction to these dynamics. Since the Second World War, the realization has grown that this era of affluence has brought about a conflict with nature on a global scale in terms of pollution, deforestation and climate change. This eventually led to the rise of the green movement, and green politics, which has become ever more influential, particularly in countries with voting systems that allowed dissenting voices to make themselves heard. In Germany and other European countries, proportional representation allowed green parties to emerge as a powerful political force. Initially it was a kind of wide-eyed response by young people concerned about pollution and the destruction of nature. They realized that we have to do things differently: we must learn to be wise in how we relate to the natural world.

Green politics developed out of the green culture that emerged within the hippie movement. 'Make love, not war' attitudes acquired a political dimension. At the start of the new millennium in Germany the first opportunities opened up for a green party to join a national coalition government. And soon the question arose of how to maintain an holistic, long-term perspective, while also being politically effective. What could be done to effectively challenge the political realities that the green movement was created for?

Within the new green parties in Europe, a chasm soon opened up between 'Fundis' and 'Realos'. The Fundis are the fundamentalist 'deep green' types, who believe in grassroots action and 'deep change'. The Realos, the 'realists', argue that it is important to work within existing political frameworks toward achieving practical change. This difference in approaches has never really been resolved. For the time being, the Realos have won the day. Wherever you see green politics in action now you see minor changes being initiated, like preventing construction of new motorways, or reducing the use of fossil fuels in energy systems, or cleaning up polluting factories. Realos, in coalition with conventional parties, tend to make compromises in one way or another, which doesn't truly resolve the profound conflicts between modern humanity and nature. All of that is important, of course, but in terms of the bigger picture, the Fundis are still the 'real deal'.

When faced with the choice between a little bit more sustainability, rather than full-fledged sustainability, many will say, "Okay, let's have a little bit more of that." With an eye also on their children. But the kids are now saying to parents, "That is not good enough; we want a different world." But how do we bring about such fundamental change? This is a difficult problem to resolve. Greta Thunberg does it in quite an effective way, by always emphasizing the need for acting on the basis of scientific evidence, when it comes to climate change, pollution and so on.

We are faced with the stark reality that every year we currently burn a quantity of fossil fuels that took a million years to form naturally. We consume around eleven billion tons of oil equivalent annually. If we say that clearly this cannot continue, we are in a safer place than those who remain in the realms of realpolitik. That is why the voices of young people like Thunberg's are so important. She is trying to bridge the gap between realism and fundamentalism by pointing to the primacy of science. I would say that there is wisdom at work here.

Is wisdom a uniquely human concept?

My response would be: look in the eyes of an elephant. I think you can see profound wisdom there, acquired and shared over millennia of life experiences. The unconditional love elephants extend to their young is shared right across the animal world. Nature is oozing love, especially in spring time as life everywhere renews itself. And I feel that is wisdom of a sort. But then there is also the other side, where young animals struggle for survival against rivals within and between species. And predators are always ready to put an end to life as they have to feed themselves and their own young. So there is love as well as fear and conflict in nature. But the continuation of life as a whole in all its incredible diversity seems to be a paramount principle. I would say that there is wisdom to be found deeply embedded in nature. In my view it is not an exclusively human concept.

How do you apply wisdom to the care of your mind, body and soul?

I try to be out in nature as much as possible. I'm not much of an introvert, so I'm not deeply involved in yoga and other such practices. I try taking care of mind, body and soul by being immersed in nature, by gardening, by looking after our bit of land and forest walking, or 'forest bathing' as some call it now. Almost every day I'm out there, trying to understand the abundance, the diversity and the incredibly interactive ways in which nature operates. It's extraordinary when you are out in a forest, reflecting on the complex interaction between fungi, root systems and the soil, or looking up to the canopy and seeing light being absorbed by the leaves of the trees. And then the leaves fall eventually, forming leaf litter as the basis for more growth next year in a seemingly endless circle of life. There is an incredible range of interactions in nature, involving light, soil, rain and a myriad of living beings. Forests exist indefinitely without the need for any outside interference. In fact, they'd probably prefer no human activity of any kind. I guess that they don't like humans very much as we have become rather good at using tools such as chainsaws.

So for me, learning from nature is very important. Understanding its intricate, complex systems of interaction and its astonishing variety of species. This is not just about Darwinist principles of competition and adaptation; nature is not just about eating and being eaten. It is also about creativity and even eccentricity. Watching nature documentaries, we can see the sheer variety of lifeforms and behavior patterns: yes, there is functionality, but also exuberance and weird creativity that we don't really understand. For example, look at an insect that disguises itself a leaf, or at the courtship behavior of birds of paradise, or the feather fan of a peacock. Where does that creativity and exuberance come from? Through being immersed in nature, we can try to develop insight and a bit of wisdom.

My fascination with nature goes back to my childhood in many ways. I was lucky to grow up in a similar setting to where I live now, which is a small farm with a large vegetable garden and orchard, and a forest nearby. So I had close encounters with nature from an early age; pottering around and lying in the grass, smelling the moss, watching birds feeding their young, climbing trees and munching fruit.

But then I remember going down to the river where I used to swim, and seeing chemical froth on the surface. Chemical detergents at the time were found to cause terrible pollution. Dead fish were washing up on the riverbanks. I started asking questions about this. And I also remember my father buying his first car after the war, a VW, and proudly bringing it home to take us for a ride. He then parked the car and left the engine running. I went around the back and saw the exhaust fumes rising and asked him where they went, and he had no answer. So things like that were little triggers in my mind as a young kid.

Another thing that left a deep impression was seeing the remnants of the war. I was born near Essen in western Germany in 1943, and recall driving into that city and seeing the ruined buildings everywhere.

People were sitting there, knocking the lime plaster off bricks in order to reuse them to rebuild the ruined houses.

And then I saw a book called *The Second World War in Pictures*, which my father had on his bookshelf, but he always stopped me from looking at it. But one day when no one else was around I opened this book and saw the horrendous images of the war for the first time. How could a world like this be possible? Who was responsible for this? Later, in secondary school, two of my teachers came from families that had been involved in the resistance against Hitler. When I first heard about Nazi terror, and about the Holocaust, it left a deep mark within me. And when I began to see and hear about the destruction of nature as I was growing up, it became a continuation of the information about the horrors of war. Here another holocaust was under way. These things soon became joined up in my mind, and I began to try and search for ways in which we could be wiser in our relationship to each other, and to the natural world.

Then, when stories about the destruction of rainforests first appeared in the press in the late 70s, I started a campaign called World Forest Action, one of the first efforts to try and address these issues. Later, in 1989, I filmed forest fires the size of a city like Bristol which had been set to create cattle ranches in the Amazon, for a Channel 4 documentary called *Halting the Fires*, and this left another deep mark. These are issues I have tried to address in my working life since then.

Do you have a favorite parable or anecdote on wisdom?

The one that springs to mind is the story of the 'blind people and the elephant'. There's a group of blind people and they are asked to examine a large object and say what they think it might be. One of them feels the legs of the elephant and says this must be a tree. Another feels the trunk and says this must be a snake. The next one feels the side of the animal and says it must be a wall. The next feels the tail and thinks it must be rope. The last one feels a tusk and says it's a spear.

This is a nice anecdote about holism: unless we join up all the parts of reality into one whole, all the forces at work, we are not going to get to grips with the multitude of problems that we need to address. As never before, there is a need to understand that we are engaged in processes that will ultimately destroy the future, unless we see what we're doing in a big-picture way. But from our school years on, we are usually forced to compartmentalize. We are not encouraged to see the big picture. It is difficult to make a living as a holistic thinker and doer. Very few people get the chance to make big-picture thinking the basis of their work. Most of us have to specialize increasingly throughout our education and career. But the need for having an overview, distilling information into knowledge, and knowledge into wisdom, is more important than ever before. And so the parable of the blind people and the elephant explains this point quite well.

How do you ultimately define wisdom?

Again, the idea of distillation comes to mind. You can harvest grapes and make nice, tasty juice out of it. And you can ferment that juice into wine. But ultimately the issue is to make brandy. It is really important for us to learn to distil information, and our experiences.

Another image that comes to mind is getting to the nugget of the issues we are dealing with in the world today. We need to deeply understand, and that is a definition of wisdom for me. But also doing things out of a deep sense of purpose, and beyond that, out of a sense of love for the world around us.

Knowing what is right and wrong is also part of the ethical decision-making process. Simplicity is important. Also being free of fear, anger, ego and greed. All of these things need to be involved in the development of wisdom.

But the concept of distillation also brings us to the need for purity in how we need to relate to the world. Yet that is harder than ever before. To be pure, to be unselfish, to be loving, has become a difficult enterprise, yet we can't not do it, because we must confront the question of what world we are leaving to future generations, and what we are doing to nature. So the ecological dimension is always central in my thinking.

That is in some ways different from wisdom as defined in previous centuries, because wisdom in the past—certainly in the Western tradition—tended to be very human-centered. Whereas I think today, it is crucially important to be deeply Earth-centered in our ideas. We are forced to be ecological in our thinking, as never before. Never before in history has the need to protect and restore life on Earth been central to the quest for wisdom. And that, of course, requires a deep understanding of life in all its complexity.

How can each of us develop wisdom?

By being open, by listening, by understanding reciprocity, by being humble. And the golden rule comes to mind: do unto others as you would have them do onto you. It's an ancient wisdom that is very relevant today.

And this is not just about human-to-human relationships, it's a human-to nature relationships as well. Because we are beginning to experience nature's boomerangs, like the climate emergency we face. James Lovelock wrote a book on this in 2006 titled *The Revenge of Gaia*. As we burn fossil fuels, and as CO_2 accumulates in the atmosphere, nature's boomerangs will hit us, sooner or later. This is not 'conscious revenge' by nature, but an autonomous process, resulting from our activities. The consequences of this are actually being experienced in the here and now, particularly in countries that have done little to contribute to the climate crisis.

Is there anything else you wish to add?

I want to mention my wife Barbara. We've been together since 1965. She doesn't spout about wisdom, but she is certainly a wise woman. I think women, more often than not, tend to be wiser than men. The time has come to learn more from their sense of prioritizing continuity of life, and love for life, as a critical part of doing things. This raises the issue of the overwhelming historical dominance of patriarchy. Male aggressiveness has created many of the issues we face today, and it is time for more balance in the way we make decisions. If we look at the way governments have dealt with Covid-19, we tend to see that ones led by women have done somewhat better than those run by brash individuals like those leading the governments of Britain and the United States. The tragedy that we are facing is that wisdom is sorely lacking in how decisions tend to be made. This book will hopefully be an antidote to some degree. I think it's a pioneering initiative, and I hope it will have some impact.

How did it feel to discuss wisdom today?

Really good actually, because the need for wisdom is obviously there in the back of your minds, but it is not often present other than in our discussions. I've really tried hard to think about this important matter and I'm grateful that you have initiated this within me. It has been a very positive and rewarding experience. It is nudging me to do more of this, more deeply. I try to be fairly deep in what I do, and certainly a conversation like this is a great help in that process.

To end with, I would like to share a poem. Some years ago I had a dream that I wrote down when I woke up. It is called 'Compelled to be Wise.'

COMPELLED TO BE WISE

We are the earth's own creatures,
Children of her living body,
Born onto her to cherish
Her glorious beauty and her fruitfulness,
And to have our needs fulfilled.
We've listened to the voices of the earth,

Wisdom

In all their calm exuberance,
And since the ancient days
We've followed them across its
Verdant plains and forests, and desert sands.

We have seen the mountains
Standing silent in the wind,
Clouds draped around their icy summits,
Rain descending into streams and rivers
To rise up again into the sky.

We have nourished ourselves
Off the earth's sun lit abundance,
and built our nests of cosy human life.
We have used life's power to create more life,
And we have lived, and lived again.

But we have also acquired the powers of death.
We plough oceans and soils with furious force,
We've built unprecedented machines,
We've made our own relentless, toxic world,
A city of man lost to the wisdom of life.

We rush across the faces of the earth
But have lost the sense to know it well.
We no longer understand
The ancient languages of birds and whales,
We are indifferent to the murmur of the forest stream.

We ignore the flower by the side the road,
Or the whispering wind in the canopy.
We have become lonely in a deadened world.
But as we find ourselves in the darkness of despair,
We're opening up again to what we've nearly lost.

We are starting to remember
That we are only mortal beings
Who will die one day like flowers
That drop their tired petals and
That shed their seedpods as they wilt.

And we're beginning again
To sing the praises of forests and rivers,
The great lakes and the mighty oceans
Like the ancients did before us,
All that time ago.

And our hearts are telling us
That we can sow new life.
We can yet restore the worlds we've damaged,
We can resow the pastures we've stripped bare,
We can replant the forests we have cut.

In the end we'll be compelled to be wise.
We'll open our eyes again
To the glory of our native earth,
And our ears will hear once more
The pulse of life out there and deep within.

And as we've caused suffering and pain
So we will feel compelled to bring joy.
And as we touch the earth again
We will remember she is our sacred body
Onto which we were born.

And as the heron stands watching by the riverside,
As the eagle gazes down from the sky
We'll feel compelled once more
To cherish the glory of life,

Wisdom

Eternal in its rebirth from year to year.

The sun greets the morning,
And the morning is made of song and light,
And as the day rises again so night also falls.
There is no light without the night from which it came.
To live again is to renew the ancient bonds,

The song of life learned in birth,
Again and again.

Randy Hayes

Randy Hayes is Executive Director at Foundation Earth, a non-profit organization rethinking a human order that works within the planet's life support systems. As a former filmmaker and Rainforest Action Network founder, he is a veteran of many high-visibility corporate accountability campaigns and has advocated for the rights of indigenous peoples. He served seven years as President of The City of San Francisco Commission on the Environment, and as Director of Sustainability in the office of Oakland Mayor Jerry Brown (four-term governor).

As a wilderness lover, Hayes has explored the High Sierras, Canadian Rockies and the rainforests of the Amazon, Central America, Congo, Southeast Asia, Borneo and Australia. He is a special advisor to the World Future Council and the training group Green Corps. He has been described in the Wall Street Journal as "an environmental pit bull." fdnearth.org

What comes to mind first when you think about wisdom?

Wisdom is good thinking applied in action. Good judgement. But also around a set of values of consequence. Values such as love of life matter. Wisdom is also about the result of that thinking.

And I think of time thresholds as important to wisdom. If you've got an immediate threat, you better be thinking in the short term. But it's the long-term thinking where people these days tend to screw up. The long-term perspective is part of the wisdom combination.

Do you recall the first time you witnessed wisdom in action?

Probably as a little kid with my dad. I was born in 1950 in Northern West Virginia, along the Ohio River near a little town called Chester. It was hillbilly country, but beautiful, with many kindly people. You get four seasons, including wonderful, hot muggy summers and snowy winters. I had lots of woods to play in as a kid. My dad was many things, but most of his work was as a truck driver. His nickname was 'Ace' Hayes. Everybody knew him as Ace. In fact, in the phone book he was just listed as 'Ace Hayes'. His wisdom in action was sort of a simple thing, with trucks and truck driving. If I was out on the road with him and the truck broke down, this was pre-cellphone, there was no AAA to call. He had to think about the problem, and sometimes crawl under the truck and fix it. And he was a good teacher, so I would watch him and he would talk it out with me, as he thought his way through the problem to a solution.

And I learned to think a little bit in terms of a truck driver. If something's broken, there's some common sense and logic to the solution. And you've got to just figure it out, crawl under there, fix it and drive on. That's what comes to mind as an early, simple, pragmatic lesson in wisdom.

Who have been your wisdom teachers?

My great grandmother in West Virginia was half Blackfoot Indian. I knew my great grandparents on my mother's side in West Virginia. The Blackfoot tribe come from the border area around Alberta, Canada, and Montana. My great, great grandfather was a trapper from West Virginia. He went up to that area and met this native woman, fell in love and married her. They settled in West Virginia. I always knew that I had that connection and I embraced it. As little kids we would play Cowboys and Indians, and I wanted to be an Indian. They were cool. They were out in the forest, tracking deer. It just resonated with me.

I went to college across the river in Bowling Green, Ohio, and in my senior year of college, the beatnik nature poet Gary Snyder came to our university to read poetry. He was part of the cohort which included Jack Kerouac and Neil Cassady. He was a nature poet, but he had that sort of bacchanalian energy of the beatniks. When I graduated from college, I moved to California where people like Snyder lived. I was around 22 years old. My best buddy from college jumped in my hippie van with me and we took off across the country. It had green and yellow shag carpet on the inside, and an 8-track playing Jethro Tull tunes. It was a great adventure. I wanted to go where I liked the way people thought. Snyder seemed to combine a mystical nature spirit worldview, with a sensible and exciting way to live one's life. I was just attracted to that beat energy.

So I moved across the country, and circumstantially, I ended up taking a yoga class and meeting another student who was doing his senior thesis at the University of California, Davis on cross-cultural prophecies. And one day he said, "I've got to do some research for my paper, and I'm going down near the Grand Canyon to see the oldest tribe in North America, the Hopi. Do you want to come along?" I was interested in native people and the Gary Snyder connection was linked to that, because he was quite a student of native peoples and their way of thinking, being and living. Snyder had wanted to study the Hopi, but they were so secretive that he decided to go to Japan and study Zen. Both are a wise way of being in many respects; that low-impact lifestyle, a connection with the real world, the web of life itself.

And so I went down to the desert in 1973 and we met some of the Hopi elders. This started a 10-year odyssey from 1973 to 1983, where I informally became kind of secretary and chauffeur to the Hopi elders. So my real graduate school training in wisdom, so to speak, was that time period, living on and off over 10 years with the Hopi. I stay in touch with them to this day. In fact, I was helping them during the pandemic crisis to get some protective gear for their nation.

Looking back on your life, what is the wisest thing you ever did?

   Probably spending that time outside of the industrial, modern-world culture, outside of the milieu that most of us grew up in. Up to around age eight, I was living in West Virginia as a kid near the forest. And then from eight to 16, I lived on a dirt road in the swamps of Florida, because my dad started a trucking business down there. I had pet alligators, the whole thing. And so the first 16 years of my life, I was in a wonderfully rare situation to enjoy and hike through the forest and navigate the swamps. But the most important thing for me was the 10 years with the Hopi. It was training in what I would call deep, long-term thinking and sustainability. Hopi means 'peaceful people'.

   On the heels of those 10 years, along with two good friends I made an hour-long documentary film about the coal and uranium mining in synthetic fuels—what's called oil shale, down in that area. I had gone back to graduate school at San Francisco State University in environmental planning. That film was my master's thesis. It was a film titled: *The Four Corners: A National Sacrifice Area?*

   Having completed my 10-year stint in the desert, I wanted an ecosystem shift to something else exotic. But I really honored the fact that I got to hang out with and learn from these indigenous peoples and the elders. And I didn't want to give that up. So I shifted from the painted deserts of the Grand Canyon to the grandeur of the tropical rainforest. There I could still fight the evil empire, in the sense of transnational corporations, and their insensitive industrial worldview. I could work with peoples who embrace a nature-worshiping way of life. And so I started and ran Rainforest Action Network from 1985 to around 2000. That was the next phase of my life, and it was extremely rewarding. Mike Roselle, Herb Chao Gunther, Catherine Caufield and David Brower were indispensable to that shift.

   In going back to how it started, I was a graduating senior at Bowling Green State University in Ohio. And one day I was with one of my buddies, sitting around and having a talk about heavy things. In the era of the hippies, that's what you did sometimes, you'd smoke some pot and sit around thinking heavy thoughts about society and life. I remember saying something to the effect of, "I don't want to be a cog in the wheel of a machine going nowhere." I was referring to the idea of graduating and getting a job in what was then called 'the real world' —the human industrial world. My wise friend said, "Well, it's not really a machine going nowhere. It's a machine going somewhere bad. I'm just not gonna take that path."

We were reading the *Whole Earth Catalog*, which Stewart Brand published originally between '68 and '72. And that was about holistic thinking. Stewart Brand and the poet Gary Snyder were friends. And there was some of that energy in the book. At college I was beginning to understand general systems theory and systems thinking. And my friend said, "I'm gonna work for the *Whole Earth Catalog* or something like that." And he said it with such confidence. And that inspired me.

I ended up having to start my own organization to be gainfully employed. So my dad, good old Ace Hayes, he used to joke and say, "You're kind of like the John D. Rockefeller of the nonprofit world. You've got a lot of innovative energy." And so I built Rainforest Action Network up from nothing to a multimillion dollar operation employing 50 or so people. I don't run it anymore. I've turned it over to other people so I can do other things. But it all goes back to that one seminal conversation, where my friend just declared, "I'm not going to be a cog in the wheel of the machine going somewhere bad. I'm going to do something constructive with my life." Snyder told me that Buddhists call it 'right livelihood'.

Running the organization was exciting and difficult. It was a lot of work to take on multinational corporations and dictatorships that were destroying tropical rainforests.

In the course of things I had met Edward Abbey, author of *The Monkey Wrench Gang*. We were interviewing him for that film that was my master's thesis. And during that time we met some of the leaders of the new radical environmental group called Earth First! It's tagline was 'No Compromise in Defense of Mother Earth.' These were not quite Black Panthers in the sense of brandishing weapons, but they were very tough-minded wilderness lovers. And they were friends, interestingly, also of Gary Snyder, who advised them. So Gary and I got to be friends, and he joined Rainforest Action Network's board of advisors. Gary's about 90 years old now and still living in the forests of Northern California.

I used to ponder definitions quite a bit and if I didn't fully understand something, I would just think about it and write it down. I even keep a glossary of terms that I've defined for myself. But one of the simplest ones was: what does it mean to be political? Sometimes the simplest definitions are the more meaningful. And I boiled it down finally to: Being political means trying to get what you want. It can be selfish or it can be good for the whole. That outcome depends on your deeper value system.

A lesson I learned in part with Rainforest Action Network, was related to the old cliché: don't throw the baby out with the bathwater. At the time, it was the era of Ronald Reagan and George Bush, Sr. We knew the federal government was not going to be on our side to help save the rainforest. So I threw the baby out with the bathwater, so to speak. I didn't set Rainforest Action Network up to be political in the sense of electoral politics. And in this era of late-stage industrial civilization, the politics and the public governance of things does matter. If I had to do it over again, I wouldn't have just taken on the transnational corporations, the McDonalds, Burger Kings and Home Depots of the world.

The largest public bank in the world was the World Bank, and we took them on. The largest private bank at the time Citibank, and we took them on. We also took on the World Trade Organization. And in some of those campaigns, we brought them down to one bended knee, and then we extracted some level of change in their behavior that would save rainforests and support native rights. And I think we had more victories back then than some of the bigger, better-known organizations like Greenpeace US. I'm quite proud of that. I learned how to fight those fights and sometimes win.

But you also have to pay attention to what it is you're not paying attention to. It's tricky. Know what you know, and know something about what you don't know. Look into the shadows, or look between the spaces. I remember reading the Carlos Castaneda books about Don Juan, because they were starting to come out when I was graduating college. And it was a lot about looking between the spaces of things, instead of the 'things' of things. And really, what is ecology? Ecology is the study of relationships. It's not about this or that, it's about the relationship between this and that. The space in between, so to speak. It's about the ecological system, and the interactions of a system, of a whole. And so the word ecology to me is synonymous with wisdom. It's a study of interrelationships of the whole. You can't imagine yourself to be wise if you're not a holistic thinker, if you're not thinking about all that you need to be thinking about. And so giving lectures about the Rainforest Action Network, I would often tell the audiences, using a simple, dogmatic statement, "There's two things you need to care about. That which you do care about, and that which you damn well should care about." And then one could construct a simple example. If a hungry tiger is on the other side of a big boulder that you're hiding behind, you damn well better find out about and care about that. But even if a threat is far off, you better care about that, too. And certainly the short-term thinking of the industrial economy and financial mindsets, doesn't seem to care very much about the loss of life on planet Earth. The loss of the web of life, a loss of the conditions that support life, the biospheric conditions, the planetary boundaries and those sorts of fundamental things. And so, to be wise, you need to care about that which you do care about, but you also need to care about that which you better care about, or life itself will not carry on.

What has been the toughest lesson you have learned?

I suppose it is that sometimes you have to turn around and go a fundamentally different direction. I go back to the Hopi. The Hopi are a different kind of tribe; they have a different kind of worldview. They lived near the Grand Canyon for easily 7,000 years that archeologists have no trouble documenting. But the Hopi think it was really much longer than that. And in their worldview, their cosmology, this is not the first time that humans have had a highly technological civilization. You can take that figuratively as a cosmological story, or you can take it literally, but it's interesting to think about. The symbol of the Hopi is a circle with a cross inside the circle. And we think of that often as the four directions. And yes it is, but it's also the ability to divide and rearrange within a cycle. Like technology is dividing and rearranging. And if your technologies are in sync with the great cycles, you're okay. That's appropriate technology. And they told me a story that illustrates this, because they still have that oral tradition. Five hundred years ago, when the conquistadores came up from Mexico across the Painted Desert, near the Grand Canyon where the Hopi lived, they went down to see them. And they looked to see what the symbol of their society is. They saw a cross with no circle. And to the Hopi elders that meant that this culture seemed to have lost sight of the importance of the great cycles, of the holism of things. So they felt they may be in for a dark era. And indeed, that is what has transpired. The age of industrial technology is just shredding the fabric of the web of life itself.

And it's really quite advanced. We don't know if it's too late or not. My wise friend David Suzuki from Canada gave a lecture once on the question of: Is it too late? And his bottom line was that we humans aren't smart enough to know if it's too late. And so we better keep working meaningfully towards the deeper solutions.

Another teacher of mine was David Brower, who built the Sierra Club into the largest, most powerful wilderness-loving group in the United States, and then started Friends of the Earth. Friends of the Earth UK is an important group over there in your neck of the woods. David and I logged a lot of time together, and he had some simple, clear ways to express wise thinking. And one day I was complaining about corporations. So he said, "Randy, sometimes if you're standing on the edge of a precipice and you're about to fall to certain annihilation, the simplest thing is to turn around and go a fundamentally different direction." He thought of that as the great ecological or societal U-turn to a better world. Industrial society is shredding the fabric of life, and with a population projected to reach at least nine billion by 2100, and most seeking to consume more and more of Earth's resources, it's madness. We have got to turn around and go in a different direction.

In the course of hanging out with Hopi, I was in the desert camping with Edward Abbey. He said, "Growth for the sake of growth is the ideology of the cancer cell." That's not living within the great cycles of nature, as the Hopi would put it. So the circle and the cross, and what that means in terms of the relationship of technology and nature's ways, is part of my wisdom compass. It guides me in terms of my action and the kind of work that I have been doing for the last five decades and hope to do for a few more decades. We need a new direction and just maybe the pandemic will help force a meaningful rethink. Ponder the old adage: 'To stop a stampede, change the direction of the lead steers.' Bottom-up change is fundamental to eventually get top-down authorities and institutions to support the shift.

In the world today, where do you see wisdom, and its lack, being demonstrated?

At the nation-state level, I've been keeping my eye on New Zealand, and Jacinda Ardern, their prime minister. It's an island nation, so it's got those natural boundaries that give it a distinct definition, but also a bit of clarity in terms of policy and governance. You've got the international ins and outs in terms of air traffic, but their goal is not just damage control, but to eradicate the pandemic. And they're close to that in mid-2020.

But you rarely find wisdom at the nation-state level. So that's not where I tend to find it, looking around the world. I took a trip down to the Amazon last year, to reconnect with a couple of the tribes on the Ecuadorian and Peruvian border. Years ago I met some of their elders and warriors and became involved in working with them to drive the oil companies out of that part of the Amazon. Conoco was a major oil company trying to extract oil there at the time. Together we were able to drive them out. I'm just amazed at the level of wisdom and strategy that's embodied by some of these tribal groups. Right now there's over five major tribes that are working together to set up a protected area called Sacred Headwaters. It's a protected area where extractive industries like cattle ranching, logging, industrial agriculture and mining would not be allowed to expand. They don't think they're powerful enough right now to just shut down all of that activity. But they are powerful enough to stop it from expanding. And then they're looking at long-term sustainable lifestyles as they interact with the outside world. They're not isolated tribes with very little contact anymore. But they still embody and embrace a quite ancient worldview and deep connection to nature. And I have a lot of respect for the nature-based wisdom in these tribes. I don't seek or pretend to understudy their particular approaches. But because I lived with the Hopi, I began to at least have my understanding of their version of what might be called sacred.

In defining the word 'sacred', I boiled it down to one word, which doesn't please most people when they hear it: functional. Why is a sacred site sacred? Why is a sacred spring sacred? Why is a mountaintop sacred, when there are lots of mountaintops around? Well, there's a function going on there. And we may or may not understand the nature of that function. But they have their understanding of that functional relationship. And the interaction of things. That shadow space we need to sometimes see in the foreground. Energy currents around the Earth were of great concern to the Hopi. And in some of the villages they didn't want underground pipes and water brought in, because they said it upset the whole of that particular area in some way that modern science may not really understand yet, but they understand. The world view of industrial nation states simply dismisses such notions. People used to think the world was flat as well. I don't know the validity of all of this, but I do have a deep respect and want to honor their ability to live as they choose to live in relationship to nature.

In my mind, a wise path for a person is trying to get humanity in sync with the ways of nature. Through my work with the Native American elders, I met an author by the name of Doug Boyd, who wrote a book called *Rolling Thunder*. Rolling Thunder was a Cherokee medicine man. He lived out in the desert in the West of Nevada, because he was married to a Shoshone woman. Doug Boyd and I were two non-Indians who had the rare opportunity to spend years and years with these often hundred-year-old elders. In our experience these women and men embodied a great deal of wisdom. We could sit at their feet as sort of secretary and chauffeur and try to be helpful to them as they educated many.

Doug and I would sometimes give talks, and we put together a talk we titled, 'The Natives, the Newcomers, and the Natural Way.' Because you and I may not be indigenous or native to the place we reside in the sense of the Hopi and the deserts, or the Amazonian Indians. So we're newcomers, but that is not the point anymore. The point is that we all need to live in the natural way. So there's the natives that we can learn from, there are the newcomers that we are, but the natural way is what we all have to embrace and embody. And so that's the great societal shift that's needed.

And it doesn't look too pretty right now, if you look at the data of the planetary boundaries—the biosphere and the cycles that support life. They're all in trouble and they're virtually all getting worse. So will this pandemic teach us any kind of important lesson to shift the way in which we relate to nature? Well, I've been counseling with some of the elders that I stay in touch with. And they essentially say, "No, not yet. It's not bad enough. It will probably have to get worse before we're ready to make that level of change." But they'll also say they don't really know. And so really the only thing to do is to keep working for the kind of systemic change that's necessary to take that great societal U-turn.

In simple terms, what does that shift involve? Of course we need

100% renewable energy for post-industrial life. But we also desperately need 100% ecological farming. We need low-impact lifestyles. We need to be humble in terms of our numbers. We need to humanistically get back to under three billion and then reevaluate the carrying capacity of this much-damaged planet at that point in time.

All of these things and more have to be done in unison. I boil it down into a seven-point plan, and have a document where I can keep all of that in one place, a framework for that new direction. And yet, like you, I have no magic wand. I don't have the political or financial power to move it very much. But knowing what needs to be done is an important starting point. And a window of opportunity could be just around the corner. A long time ago I started an informal little document called '20 Windows.' What are 20 big ideas that, if the window of opportunity opens up, we can jam through? Those windows haven't opened up yet. But perhaps it's the darkness before the dawn in terms of the pandemic. Though I'm in accord with the elders: we're not quite there yet.

How do you apply wisdom to the care of your mind, body and soul?

A combination of things can get you through quite well. At Rainforest Action our motto was to work hard and party hard. And we did. But one also has to study hard, think, and be aware of what the deeper solutions are all about. Simple 'happy talk' solutions are seductive, but not helpful. Tell the truth about the deeper change that is needed, as best you can. We built a grassroots fighting force: Rainforest Action Network. We had 150 RAGs (Rainforest Action Groups) across the country. The London RAG was run by George Marshall. I worked with John Seed in Australia, and there was the Melbourne RAG, and there was one in Sydney, one in Alberta, and others in Calgary and Vancouver. And we had a lot of them in the US. Mostly I was focused on North America and trying to get our foot off the throat of the rainforest, and support the rights of indigenous peoples back then.

I think of that David and Goliath campaigning as heroic, but insufficient. We didn't save the rainforest. We saved a lot of cathedral areas and we're proud of that. Such victories are not unimportant. But it was insufficient. Things are getting worse in terms of industrial society shredding the fabric of life itself. Tell that greater truth even along with your interim victory press releases.

And so for personal health purposes, work to understand, at least conceptually, what the deeper, more permanent solutions are that we must achieve. If I understand conceptually what needs to be done, that gives me an important level of comfort. Tell that truth loudly and keep refining the message over time.

In the early Rainforest Action Network days, when we were parting with wilderness-wild Earth Firsters and the Edward Abbeys and the Gary Snyders and such, we had a good time and enjoyed our activist life, hand in hand with fighting the evil empire. And there's some evil out there. We had our death threats, and we lost some of our activists in different parts of the world. But we also saved a lot. And we were able to put meaning into our lives for a number of decades in that way. There's internal solace and comfort from knowing that you've used a number of your years decently well, even if we haven't been able to complete the great U-turn.

At some point, I think something like the framework in that seven-point plan that I laid out could be enacted. It leads with calling for major structural changes in the economic model of global capitalism toward a steady-state, truly circular economy. Conceptually, a circular economy, which does not focus on endless growth, honors the great cycles of nature. It encircles innovative technology and delimits what is appropriate. It's still a market economy. So I don't think of it as a solution for the long-term, but perhaps it buys us a couple of decades. We can buy time to look at other economic models and solutions. But we've got to change the rules of the global economy. We've got to internalize those pesky externalities that economists talk about.

Pollution and damage to nature is called an economic externality. I thought about that and a better definition of the word 'externality'.

Those of us in this field understand internalizing externalities in economic speak. But my definition of externality is: definitely not external. Even if toxic pollution and extractive industrial damage is external to the cost that you pay for a good or service, it's not external to the biosphere. So economic externalities can be properly defined as: definitely not external. That is an ecological truth that needs to be told by every *Financial Times* reporter and every other journalist. Journalism leads the discussion and they need to tell a more holistic truth clearly in their reporting.

We humans are not just isolated individuals. We function as a set of imbedded systems. We have our circulatory system and our respiratory system, our digestive system; we're systems within systems. And each so-called individual, as well as our economy, are embedded in the larger system of the biological region that you live in, and that region is embedded in the biosphere of the planet as a whole. That's the day-to-day kind of understanding that I embraced with the Hopi elders and the warriors in the Amazon. That's what Doug Boyd and I embraced when we would give our talks to people about The Natives, the Newcomers and the Natural Way. Campaign hard. Tell the ecological truth. And enjoy life. It is calming to the soul. It is the natural way.

Is wisdom a uniquely human concept?

Consider that we may be the only species that is not wise. Quite recently I've been pondering the word 'human'. I don't like it. What does it mean when people use it? When we say we are humans do we forget that we're animals? We think we're a unique category. It's not that we're not special. Obviously, with the opposable thumb and the brain power and such we have done things other species haven't. Remember that for 99.9% of our human species' existence, we lived as hunter-gatherers embedded in the natural world. And so that's shifted. I think we need to decrease thinking of ourselves as humans. We're in the great ape family. We have some damned unique properties, but I think we need to remember that "we're just a strand in the web of life," as the great John Muir would put it. Everything is hitched to everything else.

We're the only species that does this level of planetary damage. We need to understand carrying capacity, and how sustainable our lifestyles are. We have been moving from sustainable to unsustainable ever since the birth of agriculture. This terrible trend accelerated with the last 200 years of the industrial revolution, beginning in Britain.

Considering those time perspectives, a friend of mine once said, "Randy, we were born in dark times." This was said in the late 70s, and I was hanging out with Fritjof Capra, the physicist who wrote *The Tao of Physics* and *The Turning Point*. A great systems thinker. But the person we were talking to was Ernest Callenbach, who wrote the book *Ecotopia*, about an ecological utopia. It's a wonderful little book. I didn't quite understand or agree with what he said about being born in dark times. I was in my 20s and feeling my warrior energy. But he meant the last 200 years of the industrial revolution. The industro-agricultural, overpopulating world had already steamrolled through much of the precious natural systems.

And subsequently, there was another wise ecological thinker named Wes Jackson who started the Land Institute here in North America. He's probably the best friend of Wendell Berry, a writer that many people know. Wendell Berry once told me, "Wes Jackson: he's half my brain!" Wes helped me understand that the use of iron in the plow could have been our real demise. As we became settled through agriculture we became sedentary. Hierarchy and patriarchy all began to emerge. Employing some of those lessons learned, I wrote an essay around 1992 called 'The 500-Year Plan.' And the subtitle is 'Short-term Thinking.' We've got to expand our time horizons. In geologic time we've got to use some short-term thinking in the next few decades. We damn well better orchestrate a change of direction or we'll see not just the collapse of industrial civilization and maybe the extinction of the human species, but possibly the collapse of the livability of this planet.

I would say what appears to be uniquely human is our societal lack of wisdom. That we have let things get so out of control decries much claim to active wisdom. When I look at the humpback whales working in teams bubble fishing, I see wisdom. When I see the salmon jumping up the stream to get to the spawning grounds to carry on life, I see wisdom. David Brower used to remind me that a simple walk through the forest is like a visit to the library to read a book, if you're aware and absorbing that which is there to learn. And so the forest is wisdom. I was in the Amazon last year with this remote tribe sitting with some of their elders next to a lagoon. One of them was telling a story about a nature spirit that used to embrace this lagoon as its friendly overseer. Then an oil company damaged the area and that particular spirit disappeared. The area is part of the newly formed Sacred Headwaters. In the last couple of years, that spirit is back again. And there's a sense of rebuilding the natural way. So nature has the capacity, the wisdom, to rebuild. Shouldn't we ask: is it nature that is wise?

The problem is that we humans like to think there's something in an engineering sense that we need to do. The primary action we need to take is an act of not doing. We need to get our foot off the throat of the natural systems that support life. And so that is not happening fast enough or far enough in terms of global outreach. And the pandemic is likely not to be a sufficient lesson to force a change of direction. But it may be not too far in the future where we experience the great wake up, and we get our foot off the throat of nature as an act of un-doing. At which point we would be embodying a greater level of wisdom.

How do you ultimately define wisdom?

I thought about that a little bit. Some time ago I wrote in my dictionary: "Wisdom is that which comes from wildness." But for us so-called humans let's say it's about good judgment, and an understanding of holistic thinking. And you've got to incorporate the time horizon that's of consequence. Wisdom embodies a deep love of life. All of these aspects come into play, and wisdom is synthesizing them into the appropriate actions to take to get humanity in sync with the ways of nature and treating each other with dignity and love.

How can each of us develop wisdom?

It's important to do your homework. When the young and impressive native leader Winona LaDuke was introducing my film partner, Toby McLeod, and myself to a new set of elders, she prefaced the intro by saying "Don't worry grandfathers, they have done their homework." It meant we knew enough to not waste these people's time with dumb tourist questions, and that we knew about the corporate and government threats to their land and life.

If you haven't already, do some homework in general systems theory and holistic thinking. I was able to study ecology and the basic life support systems of the biosphere, which helps you understand systems thinking.

If I had a magic wand, every graduate doing a master's in business administration, and every graduate in economics would have to graduate with a dual degree in ecology and business, or ecology and economics. But really all of humanity needs to be literate in ecological thinking, because ecological thinking is systems thinking. It's the study of relationships. And that's all that really does exist that promotes life. It's that interactive relationship, those spaces between things.

So people need to do that educational work to embody wisdom, but it's also wonderful sometimes to get out of your cultural milieu into wild nature. Read recommended books. I read some of the early books of Don Juan by Carlos Castaneda. Living in Northern California, I met Castaneda twice. And I never could quite figure out whether he was full of bullshit and made a lot of that stuff up, but did I learn lessons from his writings? Yes. They're wonderful books and wonderful stories. The second book was *A Separate Reality*. And it's really a 'way of the warrior' book. I recommend it. Be a warrior, from that kind of nature, mystic, Earth-loving perspective. It soothes the soul.

Is there anything else you wish to add?

Maybe one little David Brower story that relates to having an alternative to the current deeply troubling economy. Again, I was pissing and moaning about irresponsible giant corporations and the executives who run them. And David said, "Randy, sometimes you'll get where you want to go a little faster if you employ a different approach. Think about it like this: there's a boat out in the middle of a lake, and it's on fire. There's 10 or 20 people on that boat and they don't know how to swim. You're on shore and you're screaming at them: 'Get out of the boat!' But if you pulled up next to them with a barge that they could jump onto, you're going to get a lot more cooperation."

So hand-in-hand with screaming about the insanity of what is being done wrong, we've got to lay out a vision in which we can live and be, in terms of feeding their family, paying their bills, putting braces on the kids' teeth, and maybe saving a bit for college and retirement. We need that coherent alternative economic vision that radically reduces harm to the planet Earth, but is attractive enough to build some wind in its sail.

Degrowth, coming out of France and now spreading throughout Europe, and to some extent Canada and parts of North America, has a lot to offer in terms of simplifying and reducing our footprint. But degrowth is a step towards something. Herman Daly writes about the steady state economy, which also addresses the endless growth issue. A steady state is the dynamic balance of an ecological system. It's energy, nutrient cycling, and all of that is in relative harmony. The balance shifts somewhat from time to time, but that's still a healthy ecosystem. And that's what the human economy needs to be. It's a bold level of change that's needed.

Every individual action matters. We've got to continue to be bold thinkers, to be thinking in terms of that great societal U-turn, as we're not seeing it at all yet. Post-pandemic, the attitude of most people, including those in positions of power, will be to get back to businesses as usual. Remember it's industrial business as usual that's really killing us. Remember as well, if the truck is broken down in the middle of nowhere, crawl under it and figure it out. That's a wise lesson that Ace taught me.

Is it too late? Again, as David Suzuki said, we're not smart enough to know if it's too late. And at the very least, we want to go down swinging. We're going to see great societal change and episodes of collapse in the next couple of decades. And somewhere in there, the elders tell me, will be that darkness before the dawn. We need that attractive, alternative economic system that allows us to step out of the burning boat onto the platform of our future. Be it now or post-collapse, there is still a chance that we can make that shift, and rebuild a humanity in sync with the ways of nature. At that point, we will have shown that we know at least the basics of wisdom—our return to wildness.

How did it feel to discuss with them today?

It was refreshing. I thought about the interview a little bit just a day before. I'm isolated in this pandemic, and watching too much TV, not getting enough truly useful things done and feeling bad about that. Kicking myself around a bit. I hope I've been able to convey a couple of important points today, from my lessons learned over 70 years, including those from some of the rare opportunities that I've had, meeting people like Gary Snyder, David Brower, Winona LaDuke, David Suzuki, many Amazonian warriors, and elders like Thomas Banyacya and Oren Lyons.

I've never thought of myself as any kind of an original thinker like many of those people are, but I think I'm not a bad synthesizer from time to time. And that's really what I tried to do with Rainforest Action Network: synthesize a lot of the problems into action steps that people could take, to help stop Burger King from buying rainforest beef, stop Home Depot from retailing mahogany stolen from the ancestral lands of the Amazonian tribes, stop Citibank from funding illegal logging in Southeast Asia, Stop the World Bank from funding giant hydro dams in the rainforest, and other such things. But there's lots more to be done and there is a wonderful team out there to work with. And yes, don't forget to celebrate with a wild party.

David Krieger

David Krieger is president emeritus of the Nuclear Age Peace Foundation (NAPF). He was a founder of the Foundation and served as its president from 1982 through 2019. He is the author or editor of more than 25 books, including ten books of peace poetry. He was a founder of Abolition 2000, the International Network of Engineers and Scientists for Global Responsibility, and the Middle Powers Initiative. He has received many awards for his work for peace and the abolition of nuclear weapons, including NAPF's 2019 Distinguished Peace Leadership Award. He has been nominated many times for the Nobel Peace Prize. wagingpeace.org

What comes to mind first when you think about wisdom?

The first thing that comes to mind is how rare wisdom is. And yet I think there is a paradox there, because when you begin looking into it and thinking about wisdom you find there's a lot of it in a lot of places. Wisdom often has more to do with questions than answers.

I find that wisdom is rather simple, not complex. It has to do with knowing yourself.

Do you recall the first time you witnessed wisdom in action?

I witnessed wisdom in action when I was a young child, maybe six or seven years old, when our dog died. I was very upset by the dog's death, and my mother had me write something about the dog that I was missing so much. When I say write, she actually had me tell her how I was feeling about the dog's death. Looking back on it, her wisdom was in having me express my sorrowful feelings about the dog, and to dig deep into my feelings. I think that was for me the first time I experienced wisdom.

Who have been your wisdom teachers?

I think immediately of Joseph Rotblat. He was a scientist who worked on the Manhattan Project, which was the secret American project during World War II to develop the atomic bomb. The only reason he thought the allies should develop an atomic bomb was for deterrence, so when he realized that the Germans were not going to be successful in developing an atomic bomb, he left the project as a matter of conscience. He was the only scientist to leave the project due to conscience. I think that demonstrated great wisdom and also courage. And 50 years later, in 1995, he received the Nobel Peace Prize, not only for what he did in leaving the Manhattan Project, but in dedicating his life, from that day forward, to abolishing nuclear weapons.

Socrates was extremely wise. His basic message was to recognize how little you actually know. That is wisdom. And Lao Tzu, accredited as being the writer of the *Tao Te Ching*, I think was a very wise individual.

And jumping to more recent times, I think of Muhammad Ali. For me he was a very wise man. He refused to go to Vietnam, and stood his ground. I remember being impressed by it at the time. I did something similar myself. I was in the army reserves and was called to active duty in the Vietnam War and then ordered to Vietnam. But I decided I couldn't in good faith accept those orders. So I filed for conscientious objector status. Most of my friends and family were supportive of my decision. My wife was strongly supportive, but my wife's parents were aghast. My wife's father had been in the Navy in World War II. He just didn't think it was the right thing to do. But I knew myself that it was the right thing to do because that war was based on lies to start with. It was immoral and illegal. So I chose to not participate in it. I had been a graduate student at the University of Hawai'i in political science, and I was in strong opposition to the war. As I went into the process of filing for conscientious objector status, and then suing the Army on a writ of habeas corpus when they denied me conscientious objector status, I was helped by some church people who opposed the Vietnam War. I also had a very fine young attorney in my lawsuit against the Army. He helped me tremendously. I did not go to Vietnam and eventually I was released from the Army with an honorable discharge.

Looking back on your life, what is the wisest thing you ever did?

I think that refusing to participate in an illegal and immoral war was the wisest thing I ever did.

Starting the Nuclear Age Peace Foundation (NAPF) also ranks among the wisest things I have done. I was able to spend 37 years working for peace and a nuclear weapons-free world. For me it was a way of balancing the scales, by not just refusing to participate in the Vietnam War, but working for peace instead. I feel very fortunate that I was able to do that. I had the good fortune of getting the organization off the ground and keeping it involved in working for peace and the abolition of nuclear weapons for nearly four decades.

I had worked for two think tanks prior to starting the NAPF. And I was also an assistant professor at first the University of Hawai'i and then San Francisco State University. The think tanks were the Center for the Study of Democratic Institutions, and the Foundation Reshaping the International Order. When the latter lost its funding I was suddenly without a job, at the age of 40. And my dream was to create a new institution that would work for peace and a world free of nuclear weapons. I was fortunate to have some friends that joined me in that effort. There were five founders of the Foundation. We started with no resources, only the belief that what we were doing was essential for the future of humanity. Somehow we had the good fortune to grow and remain viable for four decades. I retired from the

Foundation at the end of 2019, but its work still continues and I remain involved.

One of our major achievements was our role in creating the International Network of Engineers and Scientists for Global Responsibility. Another was working with the Republic of the Marshall Islands in their lawsuits against the nine nuclear weapons states. The lawsuits concerned their failure to comply with their obligations under the Non-Proliferation Treaty, and under customary international law to pursue negotiations in good faith for nuclear disarmament. The lawsuits eventually were not heard on their merits by the International Court of Justice or by the US Federal Court. But it was a valiant effort. I must say that the former foreign minister of the Marshall Islands, Tony deBrum, was one of the wisest, most courageous people I have known. No other country would join the Marshall Islands in their lawsuits, although we tried hard to persuade other countries to come in behind them. Only the Marshall Islands had the wisdom and commitment to pursue it.

What has been the toughest lesson you have learned?

I'd say the toughest lesson was realizing that you can't succeed in doing all the things you want to by yourself. You have to build teams and networks, and work together with others over a long period of time, in most things that are important. That was a very important lesson. I think we were able to do that, in my work with the NAPF.

In the world today, where do you see wisdom, and its lack, being demonstrated?

A lack of wisdom is being demonstrated by Trump in almost everything he does. He is probably the worst and most foolish national leader I have experienced in my lifetime. He is doing his best to damage democracy not only in the United States, but far beyond as well.

Wisdom is being demonstrated by various civil society organizations that work for a more just world, based on human rights for all, or for more specific goals, such as Black Lives Matter.

How do you apply wisdom to the care of your mind, body and soul?

I try to practice moderation. I try to take care of what I eat, what I read, what I think about. I've been very involved with writing poetry for many years. I've written seven poetry books and edited three others. In many ways poetry has been my best means of expression as I've focused on building a safer and saner world.

Is wisdom a uniquely human concept?

Not at all. I think there is great wisdom in nature. I think the challenge for humans is to learn from the wisdom of nature. Animals don't necessarily think things through, as far as I know. They just do. They live their lives as what they are. A tree knows how to grow from a seed to a tree. That is a kind of natural wisdom.

How do you ultimately define wisdom?

I would define wisdom as knowing oneself. And I think one element of wisdom that is very important is perseverance. Going back to Joseph Rotblat, I happened to be at a conference with him when he was celebrating his 90th birthday. In thanking people for their birthday wishes, he said, "My short-term goal is the abolition of nuclear weapons. My long-term goal is the abolition of war." So coming from a 90-year-old man, I thought that was pretty wise. He was definitely making clear that he was not giving up.

I first learned about perseverance when I lived in Japan. I was fairly young and studied karate. My teacher (sensei) always emphasized perseverance. He said that when things get tough we must continue on and not give up. There is a Japanese proverb I really like that says,

'Seven times down, eight times up.' If you get knocked down, you must always get up.

How can each of us develop wisdom?

It's important to remember that there's more to be learned from so-called failures than from successes. That's one way to develop wisdom.

I think another is to read great philosophers, such as Socrates (as described by Plato), Lao Tzu, Marcus Aurelius and others.

Ultimately, I think wisdom is about how you live your life. We make choices in everything we do, and wise choices are those that benefit others, even more than they benefit ourselves.

One of the wisest things that's ever been said is called the Golden Rule: treat others as you wish to be treated. It's so simple and clear, and such a great guide to living a wise and decent life.

My wife has been deeply involved in water issues for the last three decades. She founded the California Water Impact Network. The wisdom I've learned from her work is how important water is to humanity, and that it has to be distributed fairly. It's such a critical element in our wellbeing. She focuses on water issues in California, and she's discovered that the state water agency promises five and a half times more water than exists. She calls it 'paper water'. It's not available when it's actually needed. So she's been trying to straighten that out for decades. They do a lot of their work by way of lawsuits. I believe they've had quite a bit of success, in keeping water out of the hands of the most greedy water users. But there's still a long way to go. She is particularly interested now in applying the public trust doctrine, which means that a certain amount of a resource, in this case water, has to go to the environment.

She says, "Water follows the path of least resistance. Water wears down stone. I care deeply about the environment and fairness. What I discovered is that if water is managed for personal greed, the consequences are devastating to the environment and all of us who depend on it. Greed is powerful but standing up to it and fighting for something beyond oneself is even more powerful. Ultimately, we each have to live with ourselves, and fighting for something I believe in is the ultimate reward."

Is there anything else you wish to add?

Wisdom is based in values. Kindness and compassion are at the heart of wisdom. What I call 'the three Cs' are important: compassion, commitment and courage. If you live by them, and add perseverance, I think you can live a wise life.

And I think it's important to have Socratic dialogues. I've had the good fortune to have had a couple of dialogues that have resulted in books. The first one was with Daisaku Ikeda, the Japanese Buddhist leader, philosopher and educator. The dialogue was called *Choose Hope: Your Role in Waging Peace in the Nuclear Age*. I really enjoy the experience of going back and forth in dialogue. It was a growing experience for me.

Another dialogue resulted in the book titled *The Path to Zero: Dialogues on Nuclear Dangers*. This was with Richard Falk, a professor emeritus of international law and practice. The dialogues were broken into sections, such as nuclear deterrence, nuclear weapons and international law, and nuclear weapons and morality.

It was a wonderful experience to engage colleagues in dialogues on what I felt were incredibly important issues.

In working with these men, I learned about their perspectives. And they challenged my perspectives. I learned that even though we have much in common, we still had areas of dissonance and disagreement on areas in which we were seemingly both strongly committed. I gained new insights about how to approach the challenges of waging peace in the nuclear age. And also the challenges of abolishing nuclear weapons.

One wise thing that I've heard on nuclear abolition, is that it's like building a cathedral; it may have to go on for many generations. But hopefully that won't be the case. Perhaps it will, but you can't lose heart in the meantime. You have to keep striving for any worthwhile goals.

I also think of lines from *Hamlet*. Polonius says to his son Laertes:

This above all: to thine own self be true,
And it must follow, as the night the day,
Thou canst not then be false to any man.

I think of that because we live in a time when truth has become as rare as wisdom, or rarer in some cases. Integrity is so important, as is truth. I don't see how you can have wisdom if it's not rooted in truth. You may aspire to change the world for the better, and change yourself for the better, but it has to be rooted in truth.

How did it feel to discuss wisdom today?

I feel very inadequate in discussing wisdom. It feels like there's so much that's important about wisdom, and I feel like I'm just scratching the surface of the subject. But I'm glad that you asked me to do this because it gave me the opportunity to focus on wisdom. And I think that I'll be more attentive to it moving forward.

There are certain wisdoms that I learned long ago that come back to me, such as the Delphic maxim: 'Know thyself.' Or Lao Tzu: 'We begin as uncarved blocks.' What we do demonstrates our wisdom, or lack of it.

I'd like to share a poem that captures some of the spirit of the subject as I see it. It is from December 2014.

A POEM FOR THE CROSSROADS

I would like to write a poem and nail it
to a stake at humanity's crossroads.
It would say: choose your path wisely.

It would say: this path we are on is far
too treacherous, a trap for the unwary
and complacent.

It would say: take down the gun pointed
at humanity's heart – enough of war,
enough of nuclear weapons, enough
of stumbling toward collective suicide.

It would say: enough homage to death –
choose life and be a citizen of the world.

It would say: be kinder than necessary.
It would certainly say: when it rains, the water
sinks into the Earth and the grass grows
toward the sun.

It would say: when the winds blow, the leaves
will flutter from the trees like butterflies.
It would remind us to stop and look at
the beauty around us.

It would say: this is Eden, but it needs care.
It would say: before you choose a path, think
about the people of the future.

It would say: make each moment of your time
on Earth matter.

It would say: choose the path of peace.

Satish Kumar

A former Jain monk, Satish Kumar campaigned for land reform in India and working to turn Gandhi's vision of a renewed India and a peaceful world into reality. Inspired in his early 20s by the example of the British peace activist Bertrand Russell, Satish embarked on an 8,000-mile peace pilgrimage together with E.P. Menon.

In 1973 Satish settled in the United Kingdom, taking up the post of editor of *Resurgence* magazine. During this time, he has been the guiding spirit behind a number of now internationally-respected ecological and educational ventures including Schumacher College in South Devon, where he is a Visiting Fellow.

His autobiography, *No Destination*, first published by Green Books in 1978, has sold over 50,000 copies. He is also the author of *You Are, Therefore I Am: A Declaration of Dependence* and *The Buddha and the Terrorist*.

What comes to mind first when you think about wisdom?

The first thing comes to my mind is that one has to be humble. Humility is the first quality of wisdom. When you are wise, you are not arrogant. You don't think, 'I know everything and I have all the answers and everybody should listen to me.' The words humility and humanity come from the same root: hum. The word hum is related with humus, which means soil. So humility is connected with the soil and with humans. And the soil is humble because it's always under your feet. And over the years it is always yielding, always giving. So if you trample on it, if you dig it, still, when you plant the seed, it will give you food. If you dig a well, it will give you water. So: yielding, giving, fruitful and abundant—all those qualities come from humility. And so, wisdom is to be humble.

And when you are humble, you are likeable. When you are arrogant, you are not liked by other people. So, being humble is very useful, because then people will listen to you. And so for me, humility is the first principle of wisdom.

Do you recall the first time you witnessed wisdom in action?

In India I worked for a couple of years with a wonderful wise man called Vinoba Bhave. He was a follower and friend of Mahatma Gandhi. And he had a dream that as India became independent by nonviolent means, it should become economically and socially independent, again through nonviolent means. So political independence is not enough. And so in his humility and wisdom, he went to the landlords and said that India is very poor, and we have a few landlords owning many thousands of acres of land. We had millions of poor, landless workers who are employed only seasonally, at sowing time and harvest time. When there is no farming they have no work. So he would like the landlords to give land to the poor. And he was able to persuade hundreds of thousands of landlords throughout India to donate land for the poor.

And he walked, in his wisdom. He said, I don't want to go by car, train, airplane or any other means. I will walk from village to village. Over 12 years, from the mid-1950s to the mid-1960s he walked 100,000 miles, throughout India. And he collected four million acres of land. He had no power, no political or party affiliation, no money. He himself was very poor. And he did not want any money. It is a supreme example of a wise, humble man, who was able to bring land reform on a scale that no government could do. With no legislative power, he persuaded many landlords. He said, "If you have five children, consider the poor as your sixth child, and share one sixth of your land with them." And in this way he distributed four million acres of land. And that land was given to untouchables, the poorest of the poor, the lowest caste. He said there should be no caste discrimination. We are all humans, so this discrimination in the name of caste, race, color, religion or nationality should be abolished. That is pure wisdom. In our narrowness, in our meanness, we think one class is better than another. This shows a lack of wisdom. When you are wise, you say we are members of one Earth community, with one future.

There are many other examples you can take. I met Martin Luther King when I was walking around the world. He was also a wise man. His civil rights movement was very similar to Vinoba's movement for land reform in India. Dr. King said that discrimination in the name of color is a lack of wisdom. If you are wise you respect every human being equally. And you respect the value and dignity of all life. And the unity of all life. So Dr. King's civil rights movement and Vinoba Bhave's movement for land reform are two great examples of wisdom and action coming together.

I was very inspired and influenced by Dr. King. He had an aura, a very special presence. And you feel that you are sitting with somebody who has something special. But at the same time, as I said in the beginning, humility was also his mark. He was more interested in my ideas than in telling me what to do. So that was very impressive. He was asking me about India, about Mahatma Gandhi, about peace and nonviolence, and about my ideas. And I said, "But Dr. King, you are the great leader. I've come to hear you." He said, "No, no. I have learned from India, from Mahatma Gandhi." And there was Mahatma Gandhi's photograph on the wall behind his desk. And he said, "I am very interested in India and Indian philosophy, culture and values, and particularly Mahatma Gandhi's nonviolence. So I want to learn from you." He had great charisma, but also humility and wisdom. It was a great pleasure to meet him. I've met many people, but Dr. King left me with the most outstanding memory I have of any one meeting.

There have been other wisdom teachers. Wendell Berry comes to mind immediately. He is a great American poet and writer. I had the opportunity to meet him a few times, which was a great pleasure. He also came to teach at Schumacher College. His wisdom was mainly that however much intellect you have, this is not enough. We are not just the head, we need to use our hands. And we used to be connected with the land, not just with ideas. He was a professor and a great writer and poet, and he also had a 150-acre farm in Kentucky. And he plowed the land with horses. He said, "I will not use any machinery. I will use horses. And I use my hands." He showed me around his farm. He grew all his food, including fruits and vegetables. Half the time he was a writer. He had a nice hut by the river, and there he would write. And half the day he would farm. He said that everybody must do something with their body, whether it is to work on the land and produce food, or build a house, or do pottery, or do some woodwork. So wisdom is to use your whole body rather than just to be sitting in front of a computer all day.

When you are a wise person, you say those who are growing food are as important as those who are writing books. If we don't have food on our table, how are we going to do all the intellectual work? So why should somebody working at a bank get a thousand dollars a day, whereas somebody working on a farm gets only a hundred dollars a day? Why should there be this discrimination? Wendell Berry, as an example of combining intellectual and physical work, and giving equal dignity and value to both, was another great example of a wise man that I met.

Looking back on your life, what is the wisest thing you ever did?

I would like to be humble and not call myself a wise man, but I walked around the world for peace, and I would say there is wisdom in that. And that was an opportunity for me to meet many great people. I began that journey in 1962, at the height of Cold War. There were four nuclear powers at that time: The United States, Great Britain, France and the Soviet Union. I was 26 years old, and with my friend E. P. Menon, we decided to walk to these four nuclear capitals and protest against nuclear weapons. And, if you can call it wisdom, we decided not to take any money with us.

So for two and a half years, my friend and I walked 8,000 miles, through India, Pakistan, Afghanistan, Iran, Azerbaijan, Armenia, Georgia and Russia to Moscow. And from Moscow, we went through Belorussia, Poland, Germany, Belgium and France, then into Paris. We took a boat from Calais to Dover, then walked from Dover to London, then London to Southampton. We took a boat to New York. Our boat tickets were paid by peace campaigners in Britain mainly. And from New York we walked to Washington, and that was 8,000 miles.

All our walking was supported by ordinary people everywhere. They gave us food, clothes, shoes and shelter. If we had gone by airplane, it would have cost us lots of money and nobody would have taken any notice of us. It would have been uninteresting. But because we were walking, thousands and thousands of people became very interested in our human story. "Oh, you're walking from India to Washington? Amazing! How can we help you?"

And we got tremendous publicity in newspapers, radio and television. We had coverage in *Pravda*, *Izvestia*, *The Guardian*, *The Times*, *The Washington Post*, *New York Times*, *Asahi Shimbun*, all the newspapers from Japan, America, Europe, Russia and India, and on the BBC. And we wrote a book, called *No Destination: Autobiography of a Pilgrim*. It has sold 50,000 copies.

All that happened because we decided to walk without money for peace. So I would say it was an action of humility. Walking is a very humble act. When you are walking you are touching the earth. And when you're walking, you are going from village to village, and meeting ordinary people, encountering everyday life. And we encountered every season. You can see the bounty of the earth and the miracle and the majesty of the environment and nature, the majesty of the forest and the mountains, and the miracle of the seasons. And you are in the mountains and the desert, and you're in the snow. That rich experience was, I would say, the wisest decision I have made.

What has been the toughest lesson you have learned?

The most important lesson I learned is not to judge, and to accept without expectations. Things don't work out as you expect, and therefore you get disappointed. So wherever you go, whatever you do, whoever you meet, you must accept the situation, accept the people as they are, and without expectation. So drop the expectation, and live with acceptance. And after having acceptance, you participate in dialogue, in living, in gardening, farming, writing, teaching, in whatever work you are doing. And through participation, you transform yourself and others, and in this way, you transform society.

Vinoba Bhave's action for land reform and Martin Luther King's action for reform of racial integration, were achieved through participation, and persuasion. If somebody did not give Vinoba Bhave any land, he did not complain. If somebody did not give me food or shelter while I was walking, I did not complain. I say, "If you give me food, it's up to you. I'm walking for peace in the world, and this is in the interest of everybody." So if people give something to you, accept it, and if they don't, still accept it. If they like you or don't like you, accept it. So this is the key for me, acceptance without expectations. And you can say that wise idea took me through my life.

I walked without expectations. I had a vision. I had values and ideas. I wanted peace and equality in the world. But I don't expect individuals to do what I want them to do, to act how I want them to act. This is not my personal expectation. I am working for the environment, for sustainability, for organic farming, because it is good work, it is worth doing, it has intrinsic value, but I don't expect that things must change today or tomorrow. I do it because I have love for the Earth, for humanity, and therefore all my actions are acts of love. And this is how I have no disappointment. I have no burnout. I'm an activist, but my activism comes out of my love for Earth, and love for people, and not an idea that I know better than somebody else, and therefore they must do as I want them to do.

In the world today, where do you see wisdom, and its lack, being demonstrated?

A lack of wisdom is clear in the climate change issue, because we are focusing on short-term economic growth at the expense of ruining the source of life, which is nature. To think that money is true wealth, and nature is only a resource for the economy, is a total lack of wisdom. Money is only a means of exchange. The real wealth is nature. It is the source of life. If we destroy nature, then we are cutting the branch on which we are sitting. We are creating global warming, destroying rainforests, poisoning our soil with chemical fertilizers and pesticides. We are poisoning the oceans with plastics, and poisoning our rivers with industrial waste. With so much damage to nature, how are we going to live a good life? So this is a total lack of wisdom. Particularly the Western world has spread the idea that economic growth is the new God. You have to worship money. So economy has become the master and humanity has become its servant.

I would say wisdom is shown by people doing things to mitigate the effects of climate change, and coming to recognize the importance of agroecology, permaculture, forest gardening, and of growing food and making things locally, without pollution and carbon emissions. And that is now spreading around the world. In many countries, people are looking at ways to create a regenerative economy. So when you are farming and gardening, soil should be regenerated. And people are talking about a cyclical economy. So the economy should not be linear, where you take from nature, use it and throw it away in a landfill site. Everything that comes from nature should go back to nature. So the cyclical, regenerative economy, is a wisdom that I see. But these are more grassroots movements, and at a smaller scale, although there are maybe a few million people engaged in this. So this is still a minority. The mainstream economy is still wedded to more and more production and consumption. What should be a means has become the end. So now, whether you need it or not, you have to produce and consume in order for the economy to function.

How do you apply wisdom to the care of your mind, body and soul?

You have to start by loving yourself. Every day you need to take some time for yourself. Spend at least 20 minutes alone. In a kind of meditation, you can take deep breaths, and think of your life: Who am I? What is the purpose of my life? What kind of day do I want to have? How am I going to be, rather than: what am I going to have?

There is a beautiful book by Erich Fromm called *To Have or to Be*. At the moment we live in a society of having, and we have forgotten about being. And therefore, we want to have friends and lovers, and a house and possessions, but we have forgotten how to be. So in order to have a healthy mind, body and spirit, you need to be who you are, and recognize yourself. Self-awareness is the key to the care of mind, body and spirit. And that self-awareness comes when every day, like you have breakfast for your body, you have breakfast for your mind, soul and spirit. That morning meditation, thinking about the deeper meaning of your life, your purpose, the purpose of the day, and how you are going to be with yourself and with other people, is one important tool in self-care.

The other thing I would say is that we are very 'boxed' human beings. We live in boxed houses, like high-rise buildings, apartments, then we come out of those and sit in a box to travel to work in an office, and sit in front of the computer, another box. And then we come home to our box in the evening, and sit in front of the television, which in Britain we call 'the box'.

Therefore I would say that to take care of your mind, body and spirit you need to take your time out of the box. Go walking in nature, be with the trees, go along the river, or by the sea, looking at the flowers or the birds. When you are in touch with nature, then you know nature. When you know nature, you love nature. And when you love nature, you protect nature. But if you are not in nature, you don't know what nature is. You don't know about the forest, or the land. You don't know about animals, about the birds, about butterflies and insects. You don't know about rivers and oceans and mountains. You don't have any experience. So experiencing nature is a very healthy way to nourish your mind, body and soul. I would advocate that everybody take some time off from being in the house, in the office, in the car and instead be on your two feet in nature, enjoying nature and nourishing your soul.

Of course, we have to earn our living, but don't devote all your life to just earning money and then shopping and consuming and producing and consuming. Life is more than consumption and production. Life is about living and being, and that comes when you are with yourself and in nature.

And also, I would say it is very good to have a community relationship. Helping other people is very satisfying. When you are kind and compassionate to someone else, you will be happy. You will be healthy. We all need each other's help. Without mutual aid, humanity cannot survive. But we have become very disconnected. We have no sense of belonging. And when we don't belong and have connection, we suffer. So in order to mitigate that, we need to meet other people, make friends and look after other people's needs. Mutual aid can nourish your mind, body and spirit. So meditation, being in nature, and being with other people, these are the three ideas that we should consider.

Is wisdom a uniquely human concept?

No. There is wisdom in trees, in the rivers. In their wisdom, animals are living in harmony with the natural world. Wisdom is a kind of intrinsic value of all living beings. So I do not see humans as somehow special and something different, something separate from nature. I think humans are made of the same elements that trees are made of. The trees and animals are made of air, fire, water, earth and consciousness. Consciousness is primary. We are all united by consciousness. Humans are one species among millions of other species. And all those species have their own kind of wisdom. Every human has their own wisdom. Satish's wisdom is not the same as

Miguel's wisdom. So wisdom has a diversity to it.

Trees are intelligent, they have imagination. William Blake said that nature is imagination itself. Nature does not lack imagination, and therefore it does not lack wisdom. So we must not think of nature as something inanimate, something below us that has no intelligence, wisdom or consciousness. Earth is not a dead rock, it is a living organism. It is Gaia, a goddess, Mother Earth, Mother Nature. How can you have Mother Earth without that mother having wisdom? So wisdom is not a unique human attribute. Wisdom is intrinsic to life itself, in every form of life.

Do you have a favorite parable or anecdote on wisdom?

When we were walking around the world, we came to Georgia, which is very famous for its tea. During our walk we were distributing leaflets about why we were walking for peace, walking without money and so on. And I gave this leaflet to some workers at a tea factory. Two women took a leaflet, and were amazed that we were doing this journey without money. They asked how we survived. So I said, "People give us food." So one of the women said, "Can we offer you food? Are you hungry? It is lunchtime, would you like some tea and some bread? And would you tell us some stories about your journey?" So I said, "Alright, any time is tea time."

So we went in and they brought out tea, bread and cheese, and so on. Then suddenly one of these women had a brainwave and she got up, went out, and came back with four packets of tea. She said, "I want to give you these four packets of tea, but not for you. You are going to Moscow, Paris, London and Washington. I am poor and I can't go there. But if you are going to these countries, please meet the leaders of the four nuclear powers and give them each a packet of 'peace tea'. And please give them a message from me. My message to them is: 'If you ever get a mad thought of pressing the nuclear button, please stop for a moment and have a fresh cup of tea. And that will give you a moment to realize that your bombs will kill not only your enemies, but will kill everything. Men, women, children, farmers, workers, animals, forests, birds, lakes, rivers—everything will be destroyed. So this cup of tea will be a cup of peace, and do not drop the bomb.'"

That was a real pearl of wisdom. From an ordinary woman, working in a tea factory in a small village in the Caucasus Mountains near the Black Sea. This ordinary woman had an extraordinary piece of wisdom. And that was so inspiring to me that I said, "Alright, now I have a mission. I will carry your packets of peace tea, and I will deliver them to the Kremlin, to the Élysée Palace, to 10 Downing Street, and to the White House." And I did. So nobody is ordinary. Everybody is extraordinary in their own way, if they use their own wisdom. And this was spontaneous. It came in a flash. So wisdom is not fixed. It's spontaneous. When you are free in your mind, it comes, fresh.

So wisdom is not complicated. It can be elegantly simple. Life can be simple, and wise. An elegant simplicity of thought, speech and living spontaneously. Freedom is a prerequisite for wisdom. If you are fixed with ideologies, with nationality, with superiority, then you cannot have the openness that is necessary for wisdom to arise. Wisdom is emergent.

How do you ultimately define wisdom?

Wisdom is more intuitive than rational. It cannot be analyzed. You feel what is it right and good in your consciousness. Wisdom is a quality of the heart, whereas thinking and analyzing is a quality of the mind. So we need thinking and analyzing, but we also need intuition and feeling. And so wisdom comes from intuition. You somehow feel it in your heart, your gut, your whole body. You can be in touch with wisdom if you allow yourself to be free of prejudices, concepts, opinions, fixed ideas and ideologies. Be fresh, be open, be prepared to look and listen. When we are married to amazement and wedded to surprise, then wisdom is available to us.

So a unique quality of wisdom is that you are not fixed. Wisdom is not fixed. Wisdom is fluid, it is an emergent property. It's not a fixed idea or philosophy. It's not an intellectual theory. It's not an opinion, it is something which emerges intuitively. And wisdom is always fresh. When a situation arises, in your feeling and your wisdom, you make a spontaneous decision. So that spontaneity is a quality of wisdom.

How can each of us can develop wisdom?

We can develop wisdom by being aware that we should not be fixed with ideas and labels. When you imprison yourself in a fixed idea, ideology and philosophy, or any group, then you cannot be free. So freshness come from freedom. When I went around the world, I did not go as a Hindu or Indian. If I go as a Hindu, I look at the people and see them as Muslims or Christians. If I go as an Indian, I see them as Europeans or Americans or Japanese. But if I go as a human being, I see human beings everywhere. So being free of fixed ideology, being free of labels, being free of fixed prejudices, that is a quality that we need to develop. Freedom is a prerequisite for wisdom. The moment you lose your freedom of thinking, freedom of being yourself, freedom of being spontaneous and open, you cannot have wisdom. So freedom is a prerequisite; freedom of thinking, of mind, of being.

We have got this wonderful possibility to be ourselves and create our own kind of wisdom, but we lose our own true self. We become imprisoned in a religion, or a political philosophy; socialism, communism, capitalism, Hinduism, Buddhism. All isms are detrimental to wisdom. In order to cultivate wisdom, you have to be a free spirit.

Is there anything else you wish to add?

I think to be wise, you have to have an ideal view of life, because reality is what you measure. The word real comes from the same root as rule, and ruler. And rules and reality are measured. That's a material aspect. Matter can be measured. Wisdom cannot be measured, and therefore wisdom goes beyond reality and into idealism, an ideal view of life. Of course we have to have food, clothing, a home and work. We have to measure and quantify things. But wisdom cannot be quantified. Wisdom is a sphere of qualitative living, it is about quality of life. So when you move from quantity to quality, you are moving from measurement to meaning. And so wisdom is related to the meaning of life, not the measurement of life. Measurement is that you live for 80 or 90 years. But what about the quality of your life? You don't know. So meaning and measurement must be combined; realism and idealism must be combined. Then you can have quality and quantity in balance, in harmony. They can dance beautifully together.

When people say that you are not being realistic, I say: but what have the realists achieved? All the problems we have today, including climate change, global warming, racial discrimination, poverty, hunger, wars, conflicts, all come from a lack of wisdom, a lack of meaning, policies that only think about measurement and money.

So unless you are an idealist, and meaning-oriented, quality-oriented, you cannot be complete. Those who are only realists, are only half of the truth of life. And those who are only idealists have the other half of truth. The wisdom is to bring realism and idealism together, bring meaning and measurement together, bring quality and quantity together. That is wisdom. When you can bring these two together, there's no dualism. There's no separation. At the moment, the world is very much a world of separation. We are separating, disconnecting ourselves, but we are not separate. We are all one. We are interconnected, interdependent, interrelated. So this separation should end; separation of blacks and whites; of Hindus and Muslims; of communists and capitalists; of humans and nature; of Americans and Chinese, of British and Europeans.

The wisdom we need is the transcendence of divisions. And when you transcend divisions, then you see difference and diversity is a good thing. And so we can celebrate and enjoy diversity. It is wonderful to have so many religions in the world, and so many languages. So biodiversity, cultural diversity, religious diversity, linguistic diversity, truth diversity; all kinds of diversities are a wonderful thing, and we should celebrate them. Evolution favors diversity. In the beginning of the Earth, there was no diversity, but over billions of years, nature and evolution has evolved and created a diversity of life. And of languages and philosophies. And when you can have that combination of unity and diversity, then I think we can share a more creative and effective society.

How did it feel to discuss wisdom today?

It feels good. I feel very enthusiastic and I'm delighted that somebody is interested in wisdom. Mostly people are interested in external things, like how to fix and organize things. People are mostly spending time thinking about external organization and administration. But very few people talk about something so refined, delicate, subtle, but so profound, meaningful and fundamental, as wisdom. And so I feel very enthusiastic, inspired and grateful that somebody is interested in the idea of wisdom. I feel very good about it.

Kim Langbecker

Kim is a 20+ year veteran working in the social sector and is Executive Director of Sacred Fire Foundation, an international social profit organization that supports indigenous wisdom, teachings and knowledge systems through programs, events and offerings. These are transformational experiences meant to give people the guidance they need to understand how to apply these teachings in their own lives. These instructions, accumulated over thousands of years, provide a roadmap on how to reconnect with the living world, empowering us to move toward a heart-centered way of living, and a global society that re-awakens to balance, community and connection, working together for a more sustainable world for all.

Kim lives in Santa Fe, NM, the land of the Tewa, with her partner and a veritable plethora of wild creatures. All opinions expressed are her own. sacredfirefoundation.org

What comes to mind first when you think about wisdom?

There's an assumption that wisdom is gained over the years, and as you become an elder, you automatically join a club where you've gained wisdom. The nature of that wisdom obviously depends on who the person is, and your life experiences. I've just started doing this course with the Pachamama Alliance called Game Changer Intensive. It's about leadership, how we need to show up in the world, but it's on a different level. It's much more heart-based. And there was a woman that was talking about how our bodies hold the sum total of our conditioning. We have three billion years of evolutionary wisdom, and it really comes back to that interdependence, that cooperation and that empathy. And that really struck me, because I think that when you talk about what our bodies hold, for a lot of us, there is a varying level of generational, historical and ancestral trauma that we don't necessarily know that we have. So if we are carrying all this wisdom, how do we access it, when we may be carrying some of these things that are preventing us from actually getting to it?

I had a conversation a couple of weeks ago with a friend of mine who didn't grow up in India, but she's Indian. We were discussing the question of whether you can only have wisdom if you're of a certain age, or is it possible to have wisdom if you're younger? And she said, "When my brother and I were about five years old we went to India with our parents, and we got lost in Mumbai. We got separated from our parents, but we figured out how to make our way back to where we needed to go. And we were only four or five years old. So what was that? Just blind luck? We have some wisdom that allowed us to tap into something that we shouldn't have had when we were that age. And we didn't ask anybody, we just figured it out."

I've worked for a long time with indigenous communities where the elders are revered for their wisdom. They are the keepers of all of the pieces of the culture. In most of these traditions, the teachings are passed down orally. There's nothing written. And once the language is lost, the knowledge is lost, if there's no one else to carry it on.

But then there's also the other piece of it where all the community members have a certain level of wisdom that allows for them to work cooperatively, to have that interdependence and to be able to understand how to caretake their environment, and how to identify, for example, the medicine that comes from trees and plants. So, wisdom is a bit of a soup for me.

I was told by a dear friend of mine, Grandmother Flordemayo, that when I turned 54 I became an elder. It was intimidating. It felt like, wow, now I'm supposed to have all this wisdom and knowledge and then be able to somehow impart this to somebody who needs it. But I didn't feel like that. So all these things converge around this idea of wisdom and knowledge.

Do you recall the first time you witnessed wisdom in action?

It was probably in my grandmother. I'm adopted, and my adopted parents were second-generation German immigrants. They were in their 50s when I came along, and my adopted mother's mother lived with us until she passed when I was around 10 years old. And 48 years later, I still miss her presence in my life. She wasn't highly educated, but she had this understanding, in a simplistic yet profound way, of looking at the world and being able to talk to me about it in a way that my parents couldn't. Or maybe I didn't think they could.

When I was little, my adopted mother used to make this joke about dragging me home from the hospital tied to the bumper of the car. I don't know why she thought that was so funny, but she did. And I got to a point, when I was about three or four years old, where I stopped talking to her for about a year. I would talk to her via my grandmother. We'd be sitting at the kitchen table and I would only address my mother this way, so my grandmother would have to relay messages to her. My grandmother would not take sides, and had the intuition—which I think is part of her wisdom—to understand that I needed to be seen. And even though it was meant to be funny, it wasn't funny to me, it was hurtful. She had a simple yet important understanding of how to meet people.

Who have been your other wisdom teachers?

Right now, I'm reading a book called *Sacred Instructions* by Native American author Sherry Mitchell. She is an attorney and activist. While this book was published in 2018, so much of what she talks about is even more relevant now. The challenges we're facing, including environmental catastrophe, human rights abuses, inequality and racism, can be confronted and healed, when we remember the sacred instructions that indigenous people offer. Indigenous wisdom gives us a road map on how to live a life of meaning and purpose, and what our responsibilities are to future generations. And so that for me is hitting home right down, along with this program that I'm doing with the Pachamama Alliance. My first experience with indigenous communities was traveling with John Perkins and a group of people to Ecuador. It was the first time that I had been in the Amazon and really had the experience of being with these people who, from the Western perspective, had 'nothing'. They didn't have cars or fancy jewelry, they lived very simply in cooperation with the natural world. Connecting with that indigenous wisdom and that understanding of how to be in stewardship of nature, rather than dominance over it, was really profound to me. Indigenous peoples are the caretakers of the natural world; they are not separate from but a part of the living world. We've forgotten that.

I remember Maori elder Pauline Tangiora responding to the statement that we are all one. In a stern, yet kind and gentle way she said that no, actually we're not all one. We are all human beings, but we are diverse. We all have unique languages, ceremonies and teachings. That really was eye-opening for me, to hear somebody who I deeply respect and love say that actually we're not all one because that's the common response when talking about spirituality. I'm sure that if you put 10 people in a room and ask them the same question, they'd have a different response. But it was a great learning opportunity.

I have had a couple of opportunities to be in the audience, and then with a small group of people, with the Dalai Lama. I experienced in person what I had seen while sitting in an audience of 2,000 people. It was his humor first and foremost. He does not take himself seriously. He says, "I'm just a man. I don't have anything that anyone else doesn't have." And then the last thing that he did was, he wanted to take a picture with all of us. He made sure we were all holding his hand. And I just remember his hand was so warm. It was like his love, compassion and empathy was literally in every cell of his being. That was such a gift.

I have been blessed to spend time with many tribal leaders, wisdom keepers and indigenous elders, but being with a community of bushman friends in the Kalahari is one of my most treasured experiences. They talked about how when we sit around the fire, if we are not speaking truth, our words will be burned by the fire. By contrast, in the western world, we sit around a table. Words can travel under the table and what we say or hear may not be truthful.

Music has always been important to me. There's been so many artists, and some of them people wouldn't know. Fink is a great artist. He's English. Prince always impacted me, because he could say things with his lyrics that nobody else could. And Tori Amos. I worked with her on her first record. And she was saying things that no one was talking about, and getting into people's souls. They all gave me these little pieces of wisdom, by looking at the world through a different perspective.

Looking back on your life, what is the wisest thing you ever did?

Leaving California. I lived in LA for 20 years and I had great friends and experiences. I lived in places that I absolutely loved. They weren't fancy, they weren't big, but they were my sanctuary. And that's something I really value. And I know that people that came to my home valued that as well. In 1999 I founded Journey to the Heart (JTTH), and then in 2004, I co-founded The Indigenous Land Rights Fund. They both worked with indigenous people in different ways.

I was still in the music business at the time I started JTTH and I had money that I could put into these organizations. Most people that start organizations, they are the first funders until they coerce their friends and family into helping them, and then they go out to raise money and either it lasts or it doesn't. My last job in the music business was in September, 2003. I decided that I was going to focus on the organizations full time. And somehow, I didn't realize that I was going from a six-figure salary to a lowish five-figure salary. But I still had the same bills, and it basically snowballed. At Christmas, 2008, I drove from LA to Dallas to see my brother and sister-in-law. And I literally felt like I was the only person on the planet that was struggling financially. Because when you're in that place where you are trying literally everything you can to get out and get above it, it is debilitating. And even though I let my organizations go, I still wasn't able to do it. Nothing was working. I just couldn't figure it out. Before leaving Dallas, I stopped for gas. For some reason, I was listening to talk radio, which I never do. They were talking about the financial crisis and how people were losing their homes and their mortgages. And that was the first time where I thought, 'Oh my God, I'm not alone. I'm actually in better shape than half of the world right now, because I don't own a home. I don't have a big overhead.' But fast forward a few months, and the home that I was living in ended up being occupied by the landlords, who were remodeling their home. And in my head, I believed I would be able, in a few months, to come back.

But I was still not even remotely financially stable. And as it turned out, for over four years, from October of 2009, I was essentially homeless. I didn't live on the street. I still had my two cats with me. Some of my things were in storage. Some of them I had gifted to people. But I spent four years living in nine different places, sometimes sleeping on couches. I had to ask for help and then I had to have the grace to actually accept it when it was given. It was humbling.

However, I had amazing experiences during that time. I worked with an organization called Children Mending Hearts. At the time they were using art to connect children in conflict and disaster zones with kids in the United States that were homeless or at risk. I was producing these events where homeless kids were coming with their parents, in New York, Los Angeles and Las Vegas. About a year after the earthquake, we traveled to Haiti and held an art exchange at an IDP (internally displaced person) camp. It was so visceral for me, even though I didn't experience that level of homelessness. But I was in essence going through the experience while I was doing these events. Even though it's something I never want to experience again, and I wouldn't wish it on anyone, it gave me a perspective and a new level of empathy. It gave me a level of understanding, compassion and wisdom about how to be a human being, and to see people in a different way, to meet them in a loving and kind way, and to be grateful for every single moment. And I'm human. I forget that gratitude sometimes, but that experience was extraordinary. And it's also what brought me here to Santa Fe, New Mexico, a place that I always wanted to live, at least part time. And that wise choice in me leaving LA was the thing that shook everything up. Because I couldn't see how to get out. And if I hadn't had the opportunity to come here, I might not have left LA.

What has been the toughest lesson you have learned?

I'm a second-generation adoptee, and the same people that adopted me had adopted my birth mother when she was a baby, which is a whole different story. I think every adoptee has a different level of feeling about what it is to be an adoptee. And there are different levels of abandonment issues. I don't know what my mother's level of abandonment was, but I think that her inability to be compassionate toward me stemmed from that. I knew her growing up, but she was out of the house by the time she had me. She took my birth as the reason why her life went to shit, and told me so on many occasions. She was beautiful and funny and always seemed to attract a large number of admirers. And she had a beautiful singing voice, but she didn't follow any of her dreams. She blamed me for that, but I never believed it. Whatever contract I signed when I came onto the planet this time around was a contract that allowed me to not take those things that she said personally.

She lived with me for six months when I lived in Phoenix, because she was going to lose her house. She was actually the age I am right now when she came to live with me, but she came off the plane looking like she was 80 years old. And this was a woman who was always beautifully put together—hair, nails, clothes. But she showed up in a wheelchair, a 58-year-old woman who really should not have been in a wheelchair. I don't know exactly what was going on health-wise for her. I found out that she was an alcoholic while she was living with me. And she had some mental health issues. She was likely chronically depressed.

In my younger self, I saw I wasn't angry at her for the things that she said to me. I was actually grateful because she was the vehicle that brought me onto this planet. I knew I was here for a very specific purpose. But then there was the other part of me that had this unfounded fear, that whatever genes were laying latent in me that came from her were somehow going to wake up one day and I was going to turn into this bitter, angry, sad person, like her. But when she lived with me, it somehow fixed that. I finally got to the other side, where I could actually look at my mother and not feel pity for her. I could be sad in a way that was kind, like 'I'm sorry that you did not have the life that you wanted. I'm sorry that you were not able to experience the things that you dreamed about when you were a little girl. I'm sorry that you weren't able to enjoy life to the fullest, because it is beautiful.'

It was hard to get there, but it was important. And to also get through some of my own issues around feeling abandoned by her. I didn't have physical reference points in blood relatives like uncles and aunts, grandmothers and grandfathers, to draw on. So, I did not know who I was carrying forth. Who are my ancestors? And so there was a part of me that felt really sad about that—a bit untethered. Journey to the Heart was actually very healing. All of these grandmothers, grandfathers, aunts and uncles that would come to The Gathering—Grandmother Pauline being one of them—became my family, and these connector points that I had not had before. And I became able to acknowledge my mother in a completely new way, that was kinder and more loving. Because if I'm being kind and loving to my mother, whether she's here or someplace else, then I'm being kind and loving to myself. And whether I have kids or not, I'm stopping that cycle of feeling inadequate, and not truly honoring the gifts that I've been given, and using them in this lifetime.

In the world today, where do you see wisdom, and its lack, being demonstrated?

I think what is probably the most disappointing to me is our leadership. Maybe I shouldn't be disappointed. Maybe it's because we tend to put more onto our leaders than they deserve. We're starting to realize that those in power are not necessarily using that power for the good of the many. If we want things to change, we can't wait for our leaders to 'do the right thing'. We're seeing the results of a haphazard response to the pandemic in the economy and our healthcare system, in disproportionate rates of infection of under-resourced communities of color, and in a refusal to sacrifice a little in the short-term for a better outcome in the long-term.

In terms of the climate crisis, the racial reckoning and the inequalities that have permeated our society for decades, we can't expect change to happen unless we bring everyone to the table. The people closest to the issues are closest to the solutions. Without their wisdom and insight, we will not be able to create lasting solutions. But you can't just stop, even though it's exhausting! That change is coming. To me it's like the caterpillar turning into the butterfly. There's a disruption and there's an awakening happening at the same time. So that's where I see wisdom not being exercised.

The flip side of that coin is in the youth. You recently talked about interviewing a young woman who was part of the climate movement in Sweden. Aside from Greta Thunberg, there are so many other young people working hard for change. You might say they don't have wisdom because they don't have experience, but these are kids who have grown up in a completely different time, where they are exposed to so many different experiences that we didn't grow up with. We didn't grow up with active shooter drills happening in our schools. We didn't grow up in a climate crisis. And in some ways, I feel like we lived this Pollyanna life where we just were blissfully ignorant, floating around, then all of a sudden we went, 'Whoa, what just happened?' I remember having this conversation with a 14-year-old girl a few years ago. I was on the board of a youth arts organization. And I said to her, "I can't imagine what it must be like to go to school and wonder if somebody is going to show up with a gun." And she looked at me like I had two heads. Her mom said, "She's grown up with this. She doesn't know anything different."

I love the thing that just happened in Tulsa, Oklahoma, where the Trump rally people were bragging how they had almost a million people sign up. It turned out it was kids on TikTok. Again, is that wisdom? I don't know. But to me, it's like these kids are finding ways to tap into who they are, and really be out there using their resources. So maybe that's not wisdom, but they're wise enough to understand that if they go out and be a part of a movement they care about, they're using their voices for change, whether they can vote or not. So, they have to be wise enough to educate themselves, to learn, to understand how to work the system. These kids are out in front, dragging our asses along with them, going, 'This is how you make change. This is how you have to keep going.' And to me there is a level of wisdom that they've gained, just because they've had to. We're learning from each other.

How do you apply wisdom to the care of your mind, body and soul?

We live five minutes from downtown Santa Fe, up in the foothills of the Sangre de Cristo Mountains. We have deer, foxes, bobcats, bears on occasion, hummingbirds and all sorts of other birds up here. I've been here now for seven years, observing the changing of the seasons, new life, the migration patterns. I watch how the animals navigate this land. There's this rhythm, and if you are quiet enough and you pay attention and you allow yourself even five minutes to be with that rhythm, you can step back from everything that's happening right now. Humanity has created a real shit show. We are out of balance with the planet. We have no one to blame but ourselves. The pandemic is likely caused by human interventions with the natural world. I need to stop and to be in that rhythm, because Earth is a living, breathing being. We're so busy doing whatever it is that we're doing, that when the pandemic hit, we had to stop. We've essentially been given a time out by Mother Earth. And for some people, I understand that it's very difficult to be self-isolated because they may live alone or may have health issues. But being privileged enough to be able to go out and be quiet and take five minutes to center myself, that has kept me sane. If I had been living in LA, I don't know that I would've had that same experience, because it's a different beast.

I had this conversation yesterday with someone who had been dealing with a lot of anxiety. And part of it is that she's in a place where she doesn't normally live, and she hasn't been home since before March. A download came through me. It wasn't me imparting this wisdom to her. It was from source: "You're in a place where you can go outside and you can spend time being quiet and just walking. There is no ceremony that you have to do there. There's no ritual. There's nothing to do except breathe and be. And this is what you're being asked to do. And you're also being asked to do this because it honors what you're carrying for your ancestors."

For me being here, the ancestors are very close. If you're quiet enough and pay attention, you can hear them. They may not be my direct ancestors, but they're the ancestors of this land. And if I'm open enough to hear them, then it gives me a sense of being on the right path. I'm fulfilling my mission and purpose. There is a wisdom in being able to find that quiet, because the noise is what keeps that wisdom from coming in. This land, the gift that I've been given, just being here in this beautiful place is my self-care. And a pedicure, a manicure and a facial, here and there. And of course, wine on occasion. That's self-care too, but not necessarily wisdom!

Is wisdom a uniquely human concept?

I don't think so. When the world shut down during the pandemic, we saw all of these photographs of animals showing up on a beach in Oregon, a coyote sitting on a park bench in San Francisco with the

Golden Gate Bridge in the background, turtles coming back en masse on beaches. When we stepped back, they could come forward.

People say, "Oh my God, aren't you afraid of the bear?" I'm like, "Well, yes, I prefer to not be bear lunch, but I'm living in his home or her home. I'm a guest here." So when I think about the animal kingdom and even the plant kingdom, they have figured out ways to adapt, to thrive, despite our best efforts to obliterate them.

Fire has always been a natural way of regenerating things. After the wildfires in Australia, literally a couple of weeks later, plants were starting to come up and green was coming back, life was coming back. We're a part of nature. We're not always the wisest or most intelligent part of nature. But down to the smallest microorganism, we are all interdependent and interconnected. How would it be possible that nature and all of the beings and the creatures that are part of nature would not have some form of wisdom?

How do you ultimately define wisdom?

That's a really big question. One of my favorite quotes is by E. O. Wilson. He said, "We are drowning in information, while starving for wisdom." Again, when we go back to that concept of what being an elder is, you have a lifetime of all these experiences, all this knowledge, all these things that you've learned. You can be perceived as a wise person, but might not be able to get to a deeper level, to be able to see your life clearer, to really get to the meat of what wisdom is. I think that's probably one of the saddest things that I've witnessed. I can go back to the story of my mom. I don't care what your station or circumstance is, we are all given certain gifts that are unique only to us. And that gift is absolutely essential to the larger web, because we're part of this interconnected web. When one person isn't able, for whatever reason, to realize how incredibly special and unique they are, to tap into their inherent wisdom, then that is a sadness for all of us.

People often think they have to change the world. But that was another interesting lesson that I learned: The world doesn't need to be changed—it's us that need to change. We are the problem. We have to start with us. We can't go out and make bigger changes in our communities if we don't get ourselves right. Understanding that truth allows us to develop wisdom, and put it into action. So it's not just sitting on a shelf, like a beautiful book. It's something that you look at every day and say, "Oh yeah, that's that experience that kicked my ass, but wow, look what I gained from that. And look how my path unfolded from there. And if I hadn't done that, then I wouldn't be doing this."

In his TV show *Cosmos*, Carl Sagan, "The cosmos is also within us; we're made of star stuff." This is something that apparently came from his predecessor at Harvard, Harlow Shapley. I loved how Sagan looked at life and at our place in the universe. He was saying that we are a way for the universe to know itself. It always stuck with me. Again it brings up the mystery of life. We are walking, breathing miracles. Putting it into a framework like that, we can see how wondrous we truly are. So that's always been a way for me, when I feel like I'm somehow less than, or not doing enough, to go, 'Wait a second, I am made of star stuff. I am this being of love and light. I am a lighthouse. I can be this joyous being if I decide to be.' I'm not saying it's easy. I'm just saying that it gives me hope and possibility for what I can do, and the legacy that I can leave behind, for the next generations.

How can each of us develop wisdom?

Be a sponge and learn everything you can, and just be open. But it's also honoring yourself and your experiences. And this is hard. I began attempting to do this a few years ago when I started to be able to understand things that 'happened' to me, or didn't, or choices that I made or didn't make. I tried to really be as unattached to the outcome as much as possible, and also not attach a negative or a positive to any experience. I use the term 'riding the roller coaster of life'. Sometimes you're going up the hill and sometimes you're coming down. Are any of those experiences good or bad in and of themselves? Of course we can say that struggle is bad and good times are great, but it's like you're giving something a charge when you attach a value to it. If you can look at all your experiences as gifts and opportunities, then I think we can get to a place where maybe wisdom isn't so far out of reach, and it becomes a part of how we meet each moment in life. We can meet it with an open heart and mind. We meet others because they're a reflection of ourselves, as opposed to creating this 'othering'. We start to see people from a place of love. And it takes a lot less energy when you can be present and grateful for whatever comes your way. I understand that there are people that for whatever reason don't have the privilege of looking at life that way. Their lives are in a different place, and their struggles are different. But that to me is a level of wisdom and understanding that makes life so much more joyful.

Is there anything else you wish to add?

I think we're doing the best we can. Human beings are inherently magnificent, and they're inherently nuts, and everything in between. And we get lost in the minutiae. Life is a ride, and it's important to be open to that ride and enjoy it. It's not about sitting back and just letting things happen, because we still have to make choices, but don't overthink things and get into 'analysis paralysis'. Just know that we are extraordinary beings. There's a gift in the experience of living, and knowing that you are a part of something greater than yourself.

Given our current state, we must have the wisdom to recognize that we cannot bring about change, on any level, by using the same tools, systems, ideas, thought processes and knowledge that got us here in the first place. We have to create, build and imagine new ways of doing things. If we can have the courage to risk going where we've not been before, we will be able to find a more beautiful, equitable, just world, for all people, everywhere.

How did it feel to discuss wisdom today?

You're getting all these different perspectives in this book, and no one's perspective is right or wrong. It's based on our own unique experiences. But I did feel a little bit like, 'God, I really don't know what I could possibly say that would add anything to the conversation.' But that's also sort of taking what I said earlier about recognizing that we have our own unique gifts and throwing it out the window, because my experiences may be something that someone else can look at and draw from. It may be meaningful to their life experience. We're all just walking each other home.

Reuben Langdon

Reuben Langdon is an international stuntman, martial artist, actor, motion capture artist, filmmaker and video game star. He has worked on many highly successful films, TV shows and video games, and has worked with some of the biggest names in film, from actors Jackie Chan and Andy Serkis, to directors James Cameron, Peter Jackson and Steven Spielberg. In the video games industry he is internationally recognized as Ken from *Street Fighter*, and Dante from the *Devil May Cry* series.

While working on James Cameron's *Avatar*, Reuben had his first UFO sighting, inspiring him to research the subject. In 2013 he co-produced the historic five-day event at the National Press Club in Washington, DC called the Citizen Hearing on Disclosure. He is now the host of the popular TV show *Interview with E.D.* on the Gaia Network. reubenlangdon.com

What comes to mind first when you think about wisdom?

When I first read the question, I was trying to go deep. Then I realized I need to just go with this and not overthink think it, because when you start going down these different rabbit holes and pathways you can get a bit lost. But when you asked me just there, and I heard it a second time, the first thing that came up is awareness. I get: wisdom equals awareness. And that has a lot of different meanings for different people. Mindfulness may be another way to put it.

Wisdom to me is an understanding of things and seeing the bigger picture. Awareness comes in many shapes and forms, and typically we think that an elderly person will have more wisdom than a younger person, but that's not necessarily true. Because many children today are born with this deeper awareness. They're not necessarily versed through experiences on the planet, and our traditional wisdom teachings and stories from the wisdom keepers, the elders. And I think the elders know this. When I talk to the elders, they recognize that these children are born into this reality with this incredible awareness. We still have to teach them how to do the normal human things, but at the same time the rest of the world is learning from them and what they naturally bring through.

We are born with intuition, but we also develop it through experiences. We are taught it through storytelling and teachings from the elders. And when I say elders, I go back to many of the indigenous cultures around the planet, because they embrace this idea of wisdom, of passing knowledge and experiences down through stories and customs. In the Western world we kind of have that, but not to the same degree.

I started with wisdom as awareness, then mindfulness, but maybe the next label we can put on it is intuition. That's a form of wisdom in my book. And the more we're following our guts, following our hearts, the more we're tapping into this sort of universal wisdom and letting it guide us through this reality. It's experiential, as the elders of the planet have gone through so much in their lifetimes. And it's also intuitive, as we're seeing now with the children coming through; they're born knowing what the right choice is. And then mindfulness: stepping back to view things from a wider perspective.

Finally I have to add integrity as being an aspect of wisdom. Because ultimately, I think that integration is a big part of what we are doing here in this Earth experience. We are in a constant state of integration, taking all the experiences, knowledge and learned teachings from our personal lives and family, culture, school or religion and integrating this into the current moment. Wisdom in a sense is integration, or at least wisdom comes from the process of integration. In the knowledge form it can be about having an understanding of different archetypes and how they interact with each other. This 'integral knowledge' can be learned from experiences or can be passed down through stories. Mostly it is a combination of both. This is why the elders in the indigenous communities, the story tellers, are also called the wisdom keepers.

Do you recall the first time you witnessed wisdom in action?

I don't know if I have a specific situation that comes to mind, but I definitely found it in readings. When I was young my interests were heavily focused on the martial arts and Asia, so I moved to Japan at the age of 19. During that time, when I was learning about Japan and Asia, Bruce Lee became a big influence in my life. I loved his movies as an action guy, but there was something about him that the other guys didn't have. I dove deep into studying him and his martial arts, and I soon came to realize that what he had, that the other folks didn't have, was a philosophy. He talked about the martial arts being not just a form of combat training, but a way of life. It's both an art form and a path. Bruce had many books and writings, and even in his movies he would incorporate a lot of these teachings, like in *Enter the Dragon*. In the opening sequence he's the master and is teaching a kid about kicking. He says, "We need emotional content, not anger. Don't think; *feel*. It is like a finger pointing away to the moon. Don't concentrate on the finger, or you will miss all that heavenly glory."

There's other guys that are just as good as martial artists, doing amazing things. Like Jackie Chan and others. But there was something different about Bruce and I wanted to really explore that. And through his teachings I was learning about Lao Tzu, about Krishnamurti. I was learning that Bruce studied a lot of these philosophies that were different to the Western approach to religion.

As a young kid, this philosophy, this way of life from the Far East, was something new and exciting. And it heavily influenced me. I moved to Japan and started learning martial arts. From then on I always had that philosophical background, and it influenced the direction of my choices in the martial arts, and my understanding of them. So it's not just a punch or a kick; there's a whole energy component, in terms of the qi, that you go deeper with. And then you learn where that comes from, the flow, and how to generate that. And the role that emotion has, in generating these movements. If you're not focused, if you're moving out of anger, or some sort of knee-jerk reaction and emotion, you can lose control. So this was all about focus and control. I learned that early on from the martial arts, and particularly from Bruce Lee, and the wisdom teachings that he held and passed on. That aspect of him really resonated with a lot of people around the world.

My first major martial art that I studied was aikido, at the Aikikai Hombu Dojo in Tokyo. There are many different branches of aikido, but this was set up by the founder of aikido, Morihei Ueshiba. So this dojo holds that lineage. Guys like Steven Seagal started out there. And as I started diving deep into that martial art, it definitely has its own philosophy. It's about redirecting the energy of the opponent, and going in circles, not taking the direct line. And then I branched off into other styles, like Wing Chun and Kali. All the martial arts have a philosophy behind them. They're all generally the same philosophy when you boil it down, but they have different ideas around movement. The hybrid style that Bruce created, Jeet Kune Do, translates as 'the way of the intercepting fist'. His idea was to read the intent of the opponent before they move, and then intercept their strike and neutralize it. Aikido was more about getting out of the way, taking the energy of the opponent and redirecting it. So you're actually waiting for them to do more. There are subtleties to all these martial arts, but they all rely on reading the other person's energy, feeling into it, using your body to redirect, move or intercept it.

As a young guy, I had gone into it just wanting to look cool and be a badass like Bruce Lee. But then the underlying philosophical aspect of martial arts really caught my attention. And that gave me the building blocks for who I am now and the direction I've gone in, in terms of my series, and connecting with the ETs and understanding those wisdom teachings. If I didn't have what I call the 'Bruce Lee basics', I would not be the person I am now at all.

In Wing Chun, I love the 'sticky hands' component. It's an amazing drill, especially blindfolded as Bruce often did it, for feeling and understanding the subtle motion of the opponent and keeping that flow with them, but then detecting when the flow is broken. It's critical for understanding the greater picture. It's like boiling it down to the micro and the macro. We can use our bodies and even take our mind completely out of it, and get into those sensations and feelings. Our body knows, and it learns quickly and adapts to these different energies and feelings, and the push-pull thing. We're teaching ourselves to automatically tap into these movements without the thinking aspect. So it becomes second nature. In fact it already is second nature, we just need to tune into it.

Who is the wisest person you know, and why?

About 10 or 15 years ago, I would've said Bruce Lee, but since walking through this doorway into the wacky world of channeling and indigenous teachings, it's changed. I've known so many wise people, and I've taken all these different teachings from many modalities, and to try to put one over another, it doesn't feel right.

You're always a teacher, you're always a student. Those rules never really change. And the more you move from student to teacher, the more student you become. You realize that the learning never stops. Recently I've become a teacher of this information in a sense. I'm interviewing these channelers, but I'm also integrating the wisdom teachings from our ET families, as well as our indigenous families. I've been doing a lot of research and spending time with indigenous cultures and wisdom keepers. And the role feels more like a sharer of this information. Through doing this work there's an integration process of the teachings, which are becoming their own entity. With Bruce Lee you can study his teachings, but some of them have become so essential in my life that they almost have a personality of their own. So instead of going to a person, I'm really going to the specific teaching, or modality. And it's interesting that no matter who I go to, whether it's Bruce Lee, Lao Tzu, Krishnamurti, Deepak Chopra, or the Pleiadians, Arcturians or Orions, they're all saying the same things. So my focus jumps past all of these labels and goes right to the teachings.

With my show I say I'm supplying the world with a buffet of channelers, so people can pick and choose. They're not all the same, and they're not all saying that exact same thing, but at the root, they are. It's like ice cream. There's all these different flavors, but it's essentially made from milk and sugar. And with my show, there's now over 50 episodes, with 28 different guests so you get 28 different flavors. And we like the taste of some more than others. Some are easier to digest than others.

So I've adopted that philosophy in doing the show. I'm always looking for the lesson in everything. This is part of the wisdom teachings from the ETs; no matter how much you may disagree or not resonate with that person or situation, it's showing up in your life for a reason. So take a look at it. Even if looking at it is just to declare that you don't resonate with it. But at least taste the food before you say it's not for me.

So with that viewpoint, you're not pushing anything away that comes into your life. You're accepting the things that show up, and giving value to it all, knowing that it may not be for you, but recognizing that somebody else out there may resonate with it. And this is where I trust the universe implicitly, the intelligent design of this amazing experience that we're having. By taking this wider view of reality, I don't get caught up in the details. It's more fun that way.

With what's happening across the world right now, it's amazing to watch it unfold, but not necessarily have the emotional charge. I'm not this guru that can just walk through life and not have any issues. We all have that. But compared to the old Reuben, that would get angry or upset about the little stuff, it's really nice to navigate the world through this lens and not get as charged as I used to. I think a big part of that is just having this understanding that these things exist. They don't have to be for me, but they're there for a reason. When you understand that, you can relax into it a little bit. You don't have to be so uptight.

Looking back on your life, what is the wisest thing you ever did?

There have been several. I've had a number of lifetimes within this one. I'd say the first one was moving to Japan as a teenager. I had this passion for the country. Even in elementary school it was there, mostly from movies about martial arts, and samurai and ninjas, in the late 80s. Young boys love that stuff because it's cool, right? So I just kept focusing on getting to Japan. In junior high school I was looking into exchange student opportunities, but my grades weren't good enough. And my family didn't have the money to send me, so how do I make this happen? A lot of people came to me and said, "You can't go. How are you going to do that? How are you going to pay for that? You don't know anybody there." So there were a lot of obstacles constantly being shown to me, but I didn't listen. I said, "I don't care. I'm going to get there." Luckily my parents weren't too against it, though they were concerned. They said, "We've been hearing this for years, but are you sure you're going to go? You still don't know anybody there, you don't have any real connections."

But sure enough, at the age of 19 I had saved up some money and was able to buy my own plane ticket and get there. So just listening to myself and following that drive, turned out to be very wise. I started my training, learned the language, and through various circumstances got into the entertainment industry and landed a job as an actor on a TV show there. It was just a roller coaster after that, and I became a stuntman, stunt coordinator, actor, motion capture artist and filmmaker. I worked on some of the biggest video game series, TV shows and movies. I worked with Steven Spielberg, James Cameron and Peter Jackson. I did the motion capture for Jake Sully in *Avatar*, which was an incredible experience. In fact I had my first UFO encounter during production. I also ran a motion capture studio in LA. And currently I have the number one show on Gaia TV, which is

Interview with E.D. All these things happened because I followed my path and I didn't listen to anybody telling me I couldn't. So I learned at an early age to listen to myself, to that drive, and to follow that wholeheartedly.

What is the hardest-won wisdom that you have?

Sometimes I didn't fully use integrity. When you act on your excitement without integrity, you can easily upset people and create extra drama for yourself. So I learned that lesson at a young age too. There were some good wisdom teachings through that entire experience. And I think because I did that at such a young age, that was my basic operating system from then until now. It has continued to serve me. And it's an example to others: follow your passion, follow your joy. It's your guiding light. You cannot go wrong as long as you do it with integrity, and no insistence on the outcome. Going back to the teachings from all the channelers, they're essentially saying the same things, just in different words.

Going to Japan and embedding these teachings, really diving deep into the martial arts, you learn that anything you do physically, it's going to go deep into the cells and you're going to learn those lessons. Whether you mentally or psychologically understand them or not, you start to live it. Anybody who's done martial arts will understand this. Even if you've only done it for a little bit, there's a way you carry yourself through the world. Once you've committed yourself to the discipline of learning specific moves and kicks and punches, tuning the body, it's a way of life. And once you learn that you can't go back. It's always with you.

But the number one lesson, that constantly shows up to kick me in the ass—and we all forget it—is about trusting yourself, trusting your gut. When you meet somebody, especially in business relationships, you get an instant gut feeling about them. But then there's all of these other circumstances around them, in terms of their connections or wealth, for example, that we get caught up in. We use that to tell our gut that it's okay, because look at all this other stuff. But if your gut tells you not to get involved, you need to trust that. And trust that you don't need to figure it out. You don't need to judge the person or figure out what this person is doing to make you trigger and feel this way. That's where we get caught up in the craziness. But over and over again, especially in Hollywood—but in the world in general—we get caught up with people because we think they may be able to help move us forward. But your gut says, 'No, go the other direction.' Sometimes it has taken years for me to finally act on that gut instinct with someone.

In the world today, where do you see wisdom, and its lack, being demonstrated?

There are so many goofy things going on in the world right now that we could say are not very wise. Yet a lot of people are tuning in, getting access to good information, or going deep within through yoga, meditation or breath work, learning from eastern traditions, or the ETs, or the indigenous teachings, or medicine plants like ayahuasca. The human collective as a whole is really tapping into these teachings, getting exposure to all of these amazing wisdom teachings from around the world. Yet at the same time, we buy in to the exact opposite, the political mumbo jumbo, the polarity game that is constantly being presented to us. Most countries have it, but some more than others. The States is probably the most extreme example right now. Yet we have all of this wisdom at our fingertips. The solutions to all the problems on the planet are right there. We don't even need to talk to the ETs anymore. When we buy into this polarization known as the political arena, we somehow drown out what we already know collectively, and make excuses for buying into this political stuff.

And these teachings are super accessible. We've got books like yours, shows like mine. You can get what you need from a video, you can get a meditation download, or some wisdom from an indigenous elder. We're flooded with this information and we all have it inside, yet we're still buying into the polarity game. And I think that with this current situation we've created for ourselves, we can finally address that issue and say: this is just not working. We know it in our hearts, but now it's time to physically implement that. We literally manifested a pandemic so we can address the problem.

How do you apply wisdom to the care of your mind, body and soul?

Care of the mind, body and soul is wisdom. They all need good nutrition. I have to remind myself of that, because it's easy for me to get caught up in the mind, trying to dissect and understand and give a language to all of this information. And for those of us who are sharing information in the way that we do, it's a mental game to try to label things, and use the right words that connect to the right emotions. As a filmmaker, I'm trying to find those images that connect to the right emotions. It's a very technical game. By getting caught up in that you forget that, 'Oh wait, I just need to go out in the woods and breathe.'

And you can be so focused on the task that you forget that the body needs food, nutrition, exercise and sleep to function properly. All aspects of the mind, body and soul trinity need their own nutrition. And you need to understand what yours needs, uniquely, as we're all different. You have to tune in.

Is wisdom a uniquely human concept?

No, wisdom is not just limited to an individual human. It's something that exists everywhere. And we can tap into that. The children that are coming through now, they carry a certain universal wisdom. They are not taught it, but are born with it. The elders, the wisdom teachers, they also tap into this universal understanding of how things are, and then bring that back through their teachings. These days we can even find some of these amazing children on the internet. Children who without being taught know how the universe works. They mimic the same teachings from some of the best channelers and indigenous elder teachings, without having learned any of it. They just know it. I think that's proof that there is a natural wisdom to everything.

We can also look at wisdom in terms of evolution: the design, the natural intelligence that we see in the animal kingdom. Their adaptation to their environment is a natural wisdom. If you want to compare evolution and wisdom, they are both about becoming more aware of and tuned into our environments.

Do you have a favorite parable or anecdote on wisdom?

One comes to my mind right away. I think even Bruce Lee wrote about this. There was a frog sitting by a river, and a scorpion comes up to it and says, "Hey, can you give me a ride across the river?" And the frog says, "No, you're a Scorpion. You're going to sting me." And the scorpion says, "No, no, I'm not going to sting you. I just need a ride across the river. Trust me." They go back and forth and finally the frog gives in and agrees. And sure enough, halfway across the river the frog feels the sting. So he's dying and they're starting to sink. And he says, "You stung me! What the hell?" And the scorpion says, "What do you expect? I'm a scorpion." And they both drown. It goes back to what I was saying about listening to your instincts!

How do you ultimately define wisdom?

After this conversation, it shifted a little bit. Now, what comes to mind is universal intelligence, which has a whole lot of definition behind it. It syncs up to awareness, to knowingness, to mindfulness and integrity. But that universal intelligence is already built into all beings, including the animal kingdom. Wisdom is maybe just another word for that.

How can each of us develop wisdom?

A lot of that came up in the conversation today. In terms of our discussion about feeding the mind, body and soul, there's wisdom in learning and tuning into how best to do that. For the mind, there are so many modalities, like martial arts, philosophy, even religion. Many religious texts are sought after and studied because of the wisdom they contain. I'm not a big fan of religion in itself, because some of it turns into dogma and then we have a lot of issues there, but I believe as a scholar, as someone who's seeking to gain wisdom, it's good to have a basic understanding of all religions and philosophical texts, from Plato to Lao Tzu, to Egyptian teachings, to indigenous South American and African teachings, and so on. And as we go deeper with all that, we begin to find the connections between them. To have engaging dialogue like this, I think helps bring this stuff to the surface, to understand and to develop a language for these teachings.

And then the soul aspect; you need to feel into the body and into your heart: What resonates with me? Does this teaching resonate or not? The more we build the other aspects of the body and the soul, the more we're able to develop discernment, in terms of which teaching is going to best serve us, and guide us to our next step.

How did it feel to discuss wisdom today?

It felt really good. It's been a great way to start the day. Because it's a reminder, especially the question about the mind, body and soul, that all of this is truly in sync and harmony. And to reflect on these moments in my life where maybe I could have implemented a little more of the wisdom teachings. But that's part of the lesson. Now I have this toolkit that I can use moving forward because I can reflect. The art of reflection is a great part of the wisdom teachings.

Whenever I ignored my intuition I got a hard lesson. It's like: 'See? You already had the answers, but you ignored them.' A big part of learning who we are is learning who we're not.

Frances Moore Lappé

Frances Moore Lappé is the author or co-author of nineteen books, including *Diet for a Small Planet*, which has sold over three million copies. Her latest work is *Daring Democracy: Igniting Power, Meaning, and Connection for the America We Want*. Co-authored with Adam Eichen, it focuses on the roots of the US democracy crisis and how Americans are creatively responding to the challenge.

Frances is co-founder of Oakland-based Food First, and the Cambridge-based Small Planet Institute, which she leads with her daughter Anna Lappé. The recipient of nineteen honorary degrees, Frances has been a visiting scholar at MIT and UC Berkeley and in 1987 she received the Right Livelihood Award, often called the Alternative Nobel Prize. smallplanet.org

What comes to mind first when you think about wisdom?

The theme song of everything I'm going to say is that wisdom suggests always thinking in, and being in, relationship. For me that means continuous awareness of all the ways in which we are connected to others' ideas, and how we affect, and are affected by, other people. It means letting go of the illusion that we are independent entities trying to figure it out. That concept of relationship was what led to my 2013 book *EcoMind*, which is a reframing of the environmental crisis. But it goes even deeper than that. The core of my ideas, starting with *Diet for a Small Planet*, is that we are fundamentally relational creatures, and that wisdom is not just a general theory about human beings, it is very personal. It's about who we humans are, and the fact that each of us is affected, moment to moment, by all with whom we interact in the natural world, and all that occurs within us.

So wisdom for me means living in that world, rather than the notion that I'm a single force in the universe and I'm going to do what I do. And we can really enjoy that way of seeing. Instead of being terrified by it, we can enjoy how much we are each the relational embodiment of all the relationships of our lives, and certainly our early lives. I'm 76, and the older I get, the more I appreciate my parents' continuing influence on me, though they've been gone a long time. They were courageous people, yet never fully appreciated for that. Their influence is no doubt a key to why I place courage high in my ranking of virtues. Without courage, it's hard to realize any other human virtue. So for me, understanding the relational nature of existence is the grounding of wisdom.

And a second realization about wisdom hit me at a young age. In my 20s, what motivated me to write *Diet for a Small Planet* was seeing that our mental frame—the core assumptions about a problem—was blinding us. And at that point it was world hunger. That frame prevented us from seeing the obvious: there was no food shortage. So over the decades I began to say, "Believing is seeing," not the other way around. Grasping the power of one's mental map is a grounding of wisdom.

Do you recall the first time you witnessed wisdom in action?

I go back to my parents and their choices. I never used the concept of wisdom to think about them, but your question really brought that up. They were seekers. They were always questioning, and this is key to everything I'm going to be saying. I was brought up in the very racist, reactionary, sexist environment of Texas in the 1950s. But every day, wisdom was embodied for me in my parents' action not to absorb that culture, nor just react to it, but to help transform it through their relationships. They co-founded a very liberal Unitarian church and chose to integrate it when the city was still segregated. That meant risk. So to me, their choices were an embodiment of wisdom; not just being reactive to one's culture, but helping to transform it through one's own actions.

Who is the wisest person you know, and why?

The book that most reoriented me was a little-known book by Erich Fromm, called *The Anatomy of Human Destructiveness*. I'd read some of his other work and was touched by it, but in the late 90s a friend recommended *Anatomy* to me. A lot of it is about the Holocaust, and what I took from it became the framing of all my work about democracy, and what you read in *Getting a Grip* and my other books. We human beings so often frame our challenge as evil people versus good people, as if these categories are either genetic or fixed in some other way. Many identify the problem in the individual, and therefore we either deem a person good or bad.

But what I got from *Anatomy* was that not just a few of us, but most of us, will behave with incredible cruelty under certain conditions. And we don't know if we'll be one of those until we're tested. And so one reason I focus so much of my work on democracy is that I never want to be tested! I can't know what kind of German I might have been during the Holocaust. No one knows, right? So, the wisdom of Fromm's book is to remind us all of that fundamental reality. And a related book that does that for me is called *Ordinary Men*, by Christopher Browning, about Reserve Police Battalion 101 in World War II. At the outset, 90% of the men resisted going into Poland and killing Jews point blank. But by the end, only 10% resisted.

These works were a huge influence on me, reinforcing my understanding of the power of the cultural norms and rules that we create to determine what aspects of human nature show up. Erich Fromm certainly gave me that insight, which has shaped my life and work over decades. But there is more to his influence in my life.

I have developed two trilogies that orient my way of seeing the world. One explores what human beings need beyond the physical.

What are our emotional and psychological needs? And from Fromm, and then my own thinking, I came to define them as three things:

1. He emphasizes our need for a sense of agency. I quote him often as describing the human "need to make a dent." We need to know that our lives accomplish something.
2. Closely tied to the first, we need a sense of meaning or purpose.
3. We need to feel connected in community.

So power, meaning and connection have become my trilogy that is the raison d'etre of democracy. Democracy is the only positive pathway that enables human beings to meet their deepest needs, both physical and emotional. Of course these needs can be met through terrorist groups as well, right? Power, meaning and connection. You can satisfy these needs negatively through a gang or through a lot of bad things. But in one way or another these needs must be met.

For me, Fromm's wisdom reminds us that we need to assume that we are vulnerable to evil, and must therefore work for the conditions that bring out the best in us. And those conditions comprise my second trilogy. They are: the dispersion of power, transparency in public affairs, and the ethic of mutual accountability. Mutual accountability means, to quote Rabbi Abraham Joshua Heschel, that "some are guilty, but all are responsible."

So, Fromm echoes Heschel, teaching me that we're all responsible for creating the conditions that bring out the best in us, and my parents demonstrated that through their courage.

Looking back on your life, what is the wisest thing you ever did?

I think it was having the insight, when I was 26, that I had to leave graduate school. I was pursuing a graduate degree in social work, having left a job in community organizing in the War on Poverty. But I was lost. Leaving school meant living in the unknown, and I cried a lot. I was scared I'd never find my path.

But my wisdom was in the realization that I had to stop before I could start. I just had to stop and face the void. Yes, it was terrifying, but as a result I ended up at the University of California, Berkeley agricultural library, trying to figure out why people were going hungry, which was a huge crisis. I discovered the wisdom of following my curiosity, which is to ask the question most pressing on you and the world, and then ask the question behind that question.

At that time, we were told that there was not enough food for humanity, and widespread famine was just around the corner. I wanted to understand whether this was true. And in so doing, I found my path. I was fortunate to be married to a very supportive person, Marc Lappé, who was completing a postdoc at UC Berkeley, and we could live on $7,000 a year. So I didn't have to work, and I could just stay in the void and follow my path. This eventually led to me publishing *Diet for a Small Planet* in 1971, which sold over three million copies. I was extremely fortunate. But first I had to have the wisdom to stop.

What is the hardest-won wisdom that you have?

There have been plenty of tough lessons. In terms of my career, my first book really blasted out and sold millions of copies. But I kept saying that hunger is not caused by scarcity of food, but by scarcity of democracy. It's been challenging to move to that underlying cause, from being associated mainly with the food movement. But I've tried, over the last few decades, to redefine democracy as more than a structure of government. Democracy, to succeed and to last, must be what I call 'living democracy'. This is a culture of engagement striving for the three conditions I spoke of earlier: the dispersion of power, transparency and mutual accountability.

At this moment we're coming up to the 50th anniversary of *Diet for a Small Planet*, so I'm deep in the food and agriculture questions that, of course, I will tie to democracy. But the hardest part is that, while food and farming can feel visceral—embodied in what we do every day—democracy can be seen as this dull duty. My struggle is to connect specific 'issue passions' that people feel strongly about, such as food, racial justice or the climate crisis, with underlying forces.

I've come to appreciate that people can engage through different doorways. A friend of mine once said, "Frankie, you can love two children at once." So, I've got to love these two dimensions of me and my life's work: the food and agriculture part, and the democracy part. The constant struggle is being true to what I believe are root causes of our needless suffering and planetary destruction, and trying to figure out how to actualize it.

In the world today, where do you see wisdom, and its lack, being demonstrated?

Being a US citizen, it's pretty easy to see a lack of wisdom in allowing our country to be governed by somebody who is mentally ill. I have compassion for people who are mentally ill, but it's shocking to me. I'm sure some of the people in the Trump administration are kind to their children and are living decent lives, and yet they are so trapped by whatever frame they're in. So clearly there is a profound lack of wisdom right now in the Washington power structure. It is beyond anything I imagined I would ever live to see.

Yet on the other side, I feel incredibly touched, almost to the point of tears, by very young people who are speaking out on deeply rooted racial injustice and the climate catastrophe facing us. The foresight, courage and inner strength they demonstrate gives me hope. They are recognizing that together we can create solutions that will also improve our lives.

In the democracy movement, I think particularly of African Americans. At the moment, I'm reading the biography of Frederick Douglass, who was a major anti-slavery activist in the 19th century. I'm so struck today that with Covid, African Americans are being particularly hit. I have a dear friend who is African American and his family is just being devastated by Covid-19. If I were a black person in America, I can't imagine how I would function as a human being, because I would be so angry, in every moment, at the injustice, both historical and present. So, I see African Americans taking leadership in a range of movements, including anti-poverty and democracy movements. It takes tremendous self-knowledge and wisdom not to give in to your rightful anger at the way you've been treated in this country. It is just horrendous. I try regularly to express how much I honor those who are suffering, yet don't just strike out with anger, and instead are working toward solutions.

How do you apply wisdom to the care of your mind, body and soul?

Not well enough! I've just been beating myself up about the fact that I've never been able to stick with a serious meditation practice, even though two of my closest friends are Buddhist teachers. One is a Lama in the Tibetan Buddhist tradition, and the other is a leader in insight meditation and relational practice. But I am not giving up. I'm still striving for a meditation practice that works for me. I try to live the core insights that I've learned from great Buddhist teachers. Of course, core insights of Buddhism are about relationality, which is the premise of my wisdom definition.

For me, one aspect of wisdom in self-care is the ongoing cultivation of deep friendship, often over many decades. I had Covid-19 for about five weeks, starting in March. When I got to the point that I could actually talk and not just lie there, I started calling people that I hadn't talked to in decades. So, it's not just about maintaining but cultivating these long-term friendships. One of the people who called me regularly to check in when I was sick is a woman I've known since I was three years old. Our parents co-founded the first Unitarian church of Fort Worth.

Being in good relation with others, and caring for my mind, body, and soul, makes me think of my two children and three grandchildren. They help sustain me. I had the great blessing of traveling the world and writing *Hope's Edge* with my daughter. And my son is a regular source of support and insight. And I also have a partner of 20 years who is wise and courageous and models selflessness. He definitely sustains me. Together we sustain ourselves physically with regular outdoor exercise and eating a plant-centered diet.

Is wisdom a uniquely human concept?

As a human being, I don't think I have any way of knowing that. I had one very close pet who died in 2017. But I certainly felt as a human being that she had great insights into me, and acted on them. And so that felt like wisdom. And she didn't take unnecessary risks. That's wisdom.

How do you ultimately define wisdom?

Wisdom means seeing all in relationship to all else—as much as is humanly possible. So, it involves complexity: the capacity to think from multiple angles, and incorporate many variables, and yet not be paralyzed by that complexity. It means being able to act, make choices, and to constantly be learning from those choices, as they draw on many variables and many experiences. Wisdom is being able to learn from those experiences—always. So, wisdom is a pathway, not a state of being.

And, for me, all that means staying in the mode of curiosity, of questioning, and never thinking, 'Oh yeah, that's it. I got it. I figured it all out.' Remember I said earlier that leaving graduate school was a 'wise' act. Now I see that decision as the moment that I began to trust and to follow my curiosity. That's when my learning began.

My path has been all about questioning and learning. More and more, the word 'curiosity' holds great power for me. And in that sense, one is never a wise person. Wisdom is continuing to ask questions. In fact, the highest compliment I was ever paid by a friend was, "Frankie, you ask the question *behind* the question." I liked that a lot! So to me the essence of wisdom is not a state of being but a pathway of following one's curiosity.

How can each of us develop wisdom?

We have to identify what are our greatest fears are, and then learn to live a life in which fear is a given but is not an obstacle. Years ago, I wrote a little book on fear with Jeffrey Perkins. We'd both had a lot of recent challenges in our lives and talked with each other a lot about fear. We share what we learned, and intended to call our book *Fear Means Go*. But the publisher said no. He said Americans are too afraid to buy a book about fear. So, the company named it *You Have the Power*. It's about seeing fear with new eyes, because you're always in new territory. Jeff and I talked about fear as pure energy. Your heart can pound when you are afraid, right? But fear can be a source of energy. It tells us we're right at our edge. And, what's new at that edge? What can you see that you couldn't see before? And I think the essence is to look beyond the horizon, not to leap over in despair or to pull back out of fear, but to see the horizon ahead of you and make choices that get you to the next ridge. Wisdom is redefining what fear can offer us when we transform it.

And I can't say that I always live up to it, certainly, but I think I've learned to appreciate that fear is not a stop sign. It's not telling you no, you're in the wrong place, wrong time, get out of there. It's just information and energy that you can use as you choose. Wangari Maathai, a winner of the Nobel Peace Prize, tells an amazing story about this. She shared it with my daughter and I when we interviewed her in Kenya for our book *Hope's Edge*. She introduced us to Reverend Timothy Njoya.

He had been threatened by the then dictator Daniel Arap Moi, who told him that if he preached anything critical of the government, he would be killed. But Rev. Njoya kept preaching. And sure enough, a group of armed men came and attacked him. As he was lying on the floor, grievously wounded, he started giving away his precious treasures to these men, including his favorite Bible and his library. I was stunned. I asked him how that was possible, given the fear he must have been experiencing. And he said, "Fear is just energy. We can do with it what we want." He rose from his chair, pretending to be a lion that sees its prey. "It doesn't just pounce," he said. "It acts with intention. It readies itself properly, harnessing and targeting its energy before leaping."

Rev. Njoya was telling us that fear can be seen a source of energy, instead of a trigger for going into self-judgment. Like, 'I must be weak because I'm afraid.' And this is where connection comes in. As I experienced recently during my bout with Covid, just talking to one another person, just connecting, can strengthen our courage and ease fear. The key is to transform our definition and experience of fear, from a stop sign to evidence that we're at a new horizon.

Is there anything else you wish to add?

All my life I've been emphasizing that we humans see the world through the story that is written by the storytellers of a culture. And these mental frames, these filters, mean that we literally cannot see what we don't expect to see. And I think that's another key. My understanding of wisdom is recognizing that our vision is very limited by inherited and culturally-formed filters. And how do we learn to recognize those filters? That seems impossible. I think putting ourselves into new situations with people, and taking risks, is a way to break through the frames that limit our vision.

Going back to our relational reality, in *EcoMind* I compare what I call 'scarcity mind' with 'eco-mind'. Scarcity mind is composed of the three Ss: Scarcity, Stasis (the idea that things are pretty static) and Separateness, the notion that we're all separate from one another. Ecomind is the three Cs: Connection, Change and thus Co-creation. We're all connected; change is the nature of life and therefore we are all co-creators.

So if it's true that we live in this connected world in continuous change and co-creation, then it's not possible to know what's possible. We can drop the whole idea of optimism or pessimism. I think wisdom is accepting this truth—that it's not possible to know what's possible—and therefore we are free to make choices for the world we want. That was a life-changing realization for me. I argue that for most humans, we don't need high probabilities of success to act. We just need to have some sense that our action can make a difference, however small. I think right now, when more is at stake than ever before, a sense of possibility is all we need to jump into action.

How did it feel to discuss wisdom today?

It felt great! When you posed the core question of wisdom, I wasn't sure what I would say. But then when I started talking, I said to myself, wait a minute, my whole life is about developing wisdom. And I can say that without claiming I'm a wise person, because I would never claim to be such. But I have discovered a pathway of curiosity to move me along.

In this life that I've chosen, I never expected to be a writer; I got a D on my first English paper at college. I never expected to be a public speaker. After my first speech, it was a big auditorium in Boston in probably '72. And I thought, 'Oh, I didn't do so bad.' I walked off the stage and a man handed me a note. It read, 'Have you ever considered speech therapy?' I smile now, thinking about both of these messages telling me: stop. But my curiosity and desire for sharing, thank goodness, have kept me pressing ahead. I find this interview empowering, as you've asked me to put it all together, and I'm surprised that it seems to cohere. So, I loved talking about wisdom today. And it is, of course, partly because I love and respect you, Miguel. Knowing that we go way back and we're still in touch confirms what I said about the importance of relationship. So, thank you, from the bottom of my heart.

Francesc Miralles

Born in Barcelona, Francesc Miralles has a degree in German philology and has worked as an editor, journalist and art therapist. Currently, he participates in conferences all over the world and writes about psychology and spirituality for different media. His books are published worldwide. His inspirational novel *Love in Small Letters* has been translated into 27 languages. Together with Héctor Kirai he has written *Ikigai: the Japanese Secret to a Long and Happy Life*, which is translated into 54 languages and has been at the top of the best-seller lists in the UK, USA, Holland and Turkey, among other countries, with almost a million copies sold.

What comes to mind first when you think about wisdom?

I relate wisdom to discovery. Many people confuse wisdom with knowledge. Knowledge is accumulation of information. But if you put a lot of things in the hard disk it doesn't mean that you understand more or better. So I think that the difference between knowledge and wisdom is that knowledge is accumulation. And maybe wisdom is the opposite: it's liberation. It's to free your mind so that you can comprehend more about the world, about yourself. So the first thing I would say, is that the keyword for me is discovery.

Wisdom comes to you in a way that the Japanese Zen Buddhists call satori, which means comprehension, or understanding. Satori is a very different approach to illumination from the Tibetan Buddhism. In Mahayana Buddhism, illumination is a moment of extreme change of perspective, and it's forever. For the Japanese, satori is an insight. It's a small illumination, a clear understanding of yourself, or another person, maybe the heart of a child. Wisdom is when the veil is removed, and you are liberated from prejudices, ideas, expectations. That wisdom is the clear vision of something that was there that you were not able to see.

Do you recall the first time you witnessed wisdom in action?

Before meeting any master, guide or guru, I remember that when I was a child, maybe in the woods or at a lonely beach or someplace in nature, I noticed that there were messages there, that moved very deep feelings in me. I remember a moment when I started traveling, going to Morocco. One day I was in a sea of dunes, that were moving and changing all the time. I was somehow aware that this was some kind of wisdom that I couldn't express with words. There was something happening inside me, but I couldn't explain it. It was moving my inner attitude. I would say that was the first time I felt that sense of wisdom in nature.

And then of course I have seen wisdom in action when some master, friend or traveler gives you a quote or idea, and maybe it causes something to click in your head. And I would say in my life there have been many fragments of books, conversations and observations that have made me look at life from another point of view.

Who is the wisest person you know, and why?

We could talk about books and about real people that I have known. Maybe the wisest person I have read is Buddha. But when I was a teenager I was reading a lot of books by Jiddu Krishnamurti. He was an Indian philosopher, not religious. And Krishnamurti had a lot of talks about any topic that you can imagine; things like truth, fear, love, silence. They made me think, even though I felt a bit frustrated because he never gave any answers. He offered many questions, but he never said, "You must live like this, or you can do it like that." Because I was very young, I thought, 'Yes, I love these questions, but what is the answer?' And then I discovered that I had to find the answer myself.

In the world of literature, I was profoundly influenced by the British novel *The Magus* by John Fowles. It's an initiatic novel that many students in university read when they are studying literature. Inside this novel, there are so many lessons from life that when I finished reading it I felt I was a totally different person.

If we talk about a real person, I have never had a master or been part of any movement or any school of thought. But I have worked for many years as a journalist and have interviewed many different people. Some people were very famous, but I would say the person that impressed me most is Boris Cyrulnik, a French neurologist. He's the father of resilience, the theory that a painful past cannot determine your future happiness. When I interviewed him I had the feeling of being in front of a very wise person. He explained resilience to me, and the history of this approach. But what was very important for me was to discover that he was an extremely humble person. At no point did he try to be above me. He was talking to me in a very natural way with a lot of respect, with a lot of heart. I had read that when he was a child he had been in a German concentration camp where he lost all his family. But he escaped. I was interested in this part of his biography and I asked him how he escaped from the concentration camp. And he said, "Francesc, if you don't mind, I would prefer not to tell you, because every time I remember this, it is so painful in my heart." and I appreciated it very much that he could explain in an emotional way, yet such a respectful way, why he didn't want to share that part of the story. This told me that he was a very human and wise person. I was impressed by that.

Looking back on your life, what is the wisest thing you ever did?

Quitting my job, when I was around 30. I had the fear that everybody has, that you must have security, you must have a job, a fixed salary, you must have money every month, you must buy a flat, and so on. I was also inside this illusion and I worked very hard to accomplish that. I love books and I wanted to be a publisher, so I did a master's in publishing industries. Then I got hired by a very important Spanish publishing house. After two or three years working there, 12 hours a day in the office, I discovered that I was extremely unhappy. I loved the work, but I didn't love being there every day, working long hours with people who were in a constant fight for power. There was a lot of stress. There was very little humanity there. In the beginning it was okay because I was learning a lot, but one day I thought, 'If I go on here, I will fall in a very deep depression.' Then I looked out of the window and thought, 'While you are here, spoiling your life, beautiful things are happening in other places of the world.' And then I imagined that in some place in India, maybe in Bengal, there was a very nice sunset, and masters to learn from, and colors to discover. And then I had the satori moment to say: let's end all this. I stood up and went to see the boss and I said, "I am going to quit my job in 15 days." That is the legal requirement in Spain. He was very surprised, but he had to agree. And 15 days later, I took a flight to India with my girlfriend. We were there two months. And then I returned to become a freelance journalist for the rest of my life.

I never missed being in an organization, because when you work for a company, you're prostituting your soul. So I prefer to be free and to depend on myself. That was the wisest thing I did in my life.

What is the hardest-won wisdom that you have?

I think that the hardest-won wisdom that I learned has to do with love. When I was a teenager, I was a very romantic person, always in love with some strong, charismatic girl in the classroom. And I imagined many things of how this person is, what would we do together. I wrote letters to these girls. I suffered a lot. I waited years for somebody and then I discovered something important. Writing novels helped me to discover the true nature of love. What I was looking for in these girls was actually something that I needed to develop in myself. There were values, powers and capacities inside me that I needed to bring out.

So I think that the hardest lessons I have understood are the ones relating to love. Because love is like a mirror, where you see everything you are lacking at the time, and you project this on the other person. And through this suffering I understood that these girls were not better or worse than me, that everyone is evolving into something else. And I stopped seeing any difference between me and the other, thinking that they have something that I don't have, or can give me the happiness that I don't have. When you break this wall and you understand that this beautiful woman or man is exactly like you and is in the same shit, then everything goes alright.

In the world today, where do you see wisdom, and its lack, being demonstrated?

This is a very interesting question because I work as a journalist for *El Pais* and for many magazines in Spain, and the question that many people want to know is: are we going to change after this pandemic or not? I have been interviewing psychologists, neurologists and other experts. And the answer is: some will change, and some will not. I think we are in a moment of history in which there will be a part of society that is going to live in a different way. Because we have discovered, while being in the lockdown, that we need much less than we thought, that we don't need to travel so much, that actually, life is more simple than we thought. And we were complicating that with imaginary needs. When you are locked down at home for two months you discover that you need very little to live, and this brings on a spiritual evolution. I think many people are going to live in a different way. Maybe they will eat more organic food. Many will become vegetarians. We will think longer before planning a trip. I was the kind of person that if I had a free weekend I took a plane to go to Oporto for a day and a half. This now seems stupid. It's not even ethical to make so much pollution for such a brief trip. So I think a part of society will change priorities. We will become more frugal, more focused on the essence of things. I don't know if it will be 50%, but part of society will go back to the old world, with less money, but they will be a bit more illuminated. And the other part, the biggest part, will have much more suffering.

I don't think we will be able to remake the old world, because that would require too many changes. But we have had three months of reflection. We now have more awareness of the value of time. Before, we didn't have time. But during lockdown we have discovered that we need time to read, time to talk to our loved ones, time for ourselves. I think we may move to another kind of capitalism, and companies will have to adapt to this new humanity, because the people who have more economic power will be the people who have changed more, because they had the opportunity to learn more about themselves and what they value.

We don't know exactly how this world will be, but I am sure that it will be different. For instance, we will start moving in closer circles. In Spain it was unthinkable to take a vacation 20 kilometers from home, where there may be local woods and beaches. A vacation meant traveling abroad. This will change. I think many of us will reconsider our relationship with the places where we live. Nobody knows what the new world will be, but it will be maybe a mixture of what we know and what we are going to create.

Wisdom is the only thing we have for sure because the economy changes and it can fall from one day to the other. Security is also not a very strong value. I think it's an Indian proverb that says: "You only have what you cannot lose in a shipwreck." The only thing you cannot lose is your wisdom, your vision, your idea of the kind of life that you want to live. And nobody can steal this from us. So I think wisdom will be very important individually and collectively.

If we look at the United States at the moment, it looks like the movie *Joker*, when you see these images in the streets: riots and chaos. It's like the image of a system, of a world, that is falling apart. And so we need, individually and collectively, the wisdom to decide what kind of world we want to create. It starts with the people in our circle, then expands. It's in our hands, because we have discovered that politicians don't have a clue about that in Britain, in Brazil, in the States, in Spain. No one is leading this process. So the people will have to do it. And I think we are going to take much more responsibility in our lives and our community.

How do you apply wisdom to the care of your mind, body and soul?

For my mind, the main thing is choosing which content I offer it. If I am all day connected to the news of what happens in the world, it's an endless stream of other people's opinions. It's noise. In the end I am intoxicated. There is a new word for this: infoxication. Intoxication through information. There is too much information, and it is of bad quality, and it's not balanced or contrasted. So I try to connect to the news maybe for a few minutes a day or not at all. When I know that something important has happened, maybe I read the newspaper for a while, but I choose what enters my mind in the same way that you choose what you want to eat. I choose what kind of content I consume because I am living with the quality and the effects of this content.

I try to read good books, have good talks with people who are positive. When choosing a movie or a TV show I avoid violence, because that is going to affect me on several levels.

For my body, the good thing about lockdown is that after 20 years I started cooking every day. I used to do it when I was a student and I liked it very much. But my lifestyle meant I was always eating out, because having lunch meant having a meeting. I would have lunch meetings with publishers, agents, journalists and so on. So I was never eating at home. And I have discovered that when I cook I feel much better, more energetic. And then when I have a takeaway, I feel worse.

And for my soul, I think of ikigai. If you feel that your life is going in the direction that you like, then your soul is at peace. Your soul is not at peace when there is no consistency between your needs, your priorities, what you want to do in life, and your actual life. My father, for instance, was a very spiritual person, but he never had the guts to live in the way he wanted because it was another time. He worked for 40 years in an office that he didn't like at all, but he thought it was his obligation, and he had to live his real life in his imagination, reading and writing and escaping sometimes. So I think the peace in my soul comes when I am consistent with what I am and what I want from life.

What is ikigai?

Ikigai is formed by two Japanese words. One is iki, which means life. And gai means something worth doing. So ikigai would mean literally: a life worth being lived. In 2015 I was with my friend Hector Garcia, who is married to an Okinawan woman. His father-in-law said that north of Okinawa there is a little village called Ogimi where they have the Guinness world record for longevity. Ogimi has the most centenarians per thousand people in the world. We were very curious to go there. So we started this field work. We interviewed all these people to discover how they live such long, happy lives. Okinawa is not only a blue zone—a place where people live very long lives—but it also has a very low rate of mental health problems.

People there are very happy, very open-minded. They live in community. We interviewed 100 people from the village and we discovered that following the ikigai, having a passion in daily life, was one of the secrets of longevity. Ogimi is a very rural place, so these people don't have the education to be artists or something like that. For them, following their ikigai was working every day in the garden. It's a passion they all share. And they visit friends every afternoon. They taught us that these two things were enough for a happy life. When they weren't working in the garden, they were practicing exercise. It gave them a sense of meaning because, in their gardens, they saw the miracles of life being represented. Being with other people, even if they are not married or they didn't have children, gives them a sense of security and belonging.

And so these two things were for them enough to have long and happy lives. Before we started the field work we read a lot of medical papers and books, because the Okinawan diet has been studied a great deal. There are a lot of specialists on that subject. We also studied the history of the island. It is in fact the poorest place in Japan. In comparison with big cities like Tokyo, Kyoto or Osaka, the Okinawa prefecture is like 50 years back, because in the Second World War they suffered more than even Hiroshima and Nagasaki. They had a very long war, the battle of Okinawa, and in the end everything was destroyed.

And these people have developed a very nice philosophy of forgiving. They have forgiven the past and they have forgiven the people who did them harm, because nowadays there are thousands of Americans who live in Okinawa. They have married Japanese people, they speak Japanese perfectly, and the Okinawans treat these Americans like brothers and sisters. So maybe one of the secrets of Okinawa is this philosophy of forgiveness.

What are the principles of ikigai?

In writing the book, we identified ten laws of ikigai.

1. Stay active, don't retire. We discovered that in Japan generally, people don't retire like we do in Europe, in the way that you stop working and you are like a plant waiting for death. When they finish official work in a bank, in a company, in a shop, they have already thought of a second life, a second occupation to stay busy. They love being busy. In Ogimi they never retire. They may do less hours, or maybe they do their work sitting down, but they are always active and it brings them a lot of energy.

2. Take it slow. As the old saying goes: walk slowly and you'll go far. And this slow way of life that we have experienced now during the lockdown, it's much better for our health, and for our life expectancy. Running from here to there, always having the adrenalin very high, is not healthy. So we can avoid many health conditions by taking it slow.

3. Don't fill your stomach more than 80%. In Japanese this is called hara hachi bu. They say if you overeat you put too much stress on your digestive system. It's like driving a car always at the maximum speed; in the end you are going to break the engine.

4. Surround yourself with good friends. There are many studies that connect loneliness, solitude, with lower life expectancy. In the cities of Spain and Britain there are so many people who are retired and they are alone at home and nobody calls and they feel abandoned. Eventually they start not taking care of themselves. They start not moving because they don't need to go anywhere. They stop using their brain cells because they don't have much social contact. They may eat bad food maybe, and maybe every day is the same and so they get old quite quickly. So, having good friends is a way to keep yourself well.

5. Get in shape for your next birthday. It relates to the Japanese obsession of having birthdays. Here in Spain, many people from 50, 60 or so, they don't tell you their age; especially women—I don't know why. But in Japan everybody's going to tell you when they are going to be 100. It's a source of pride. And, actually, what we show in Okinawa is that when all these people were 98, 99, they prepare like a sport to become 100, because when they become 100, the government gives them a certificate and they show it to the whole the village. It's like having a doctorate in life. So get in shape for your next birthday.

6. Smile. Okinawa is a part of Japan with a quite Latin style of life. People make jokes all the time, something that is unthinkable in Tokyo or other major cities. They smile and laugh a lot. They have a light view of life and problems, and this is also important for their life expectancy.

7. Reconnect with nature. There is even a Japanese expression for this: shinrin yoku. It's a new discipline. It's like 'forest bathing' in English. And there are a lot of studies that have proved that if you go each week for five hours to the wilderness, to nature, you gain many health benefits, mentally and physically. It's good for stress, your heart condition, the cells that fight against cancer, etc.

8. Give thanks. People who are always complaining, accusing, being

in a negative mindset have more stress and they have worse health conditions. So instead of complaining, give thanks for the things that you like in this life.

9. Live in the moment. That is something very typical from the Eastern cultures. Trying to know the future is impossible. Do the best with every day. That is what the Americans say: seize the moment, seize the day.

10. Follow your ikigai. It means putting your passion, what you love, at the center of your life.

Do you practice these laws?

We put these 10 laws together as a kind of summary of the whole book, and the whole investigation. We try to practice it in our everyday lives. We cannot do it all the time, but it has become our guiding philosophy.

People who read *Ikigai* are interested in self-development. They try to apply what they learn in the books, using the approach of kaizen, another Japanese word, that means doing something a little bit every day.

The word ikigai already existed, but it was not used in this way. They used it sometimes to say: I have an ikigai, a passion. But the book changed the concept, even in Japan. Now they have ikigai coaches and courses, which they didn't have before. The word now has a different meaning or importance.

There are some connections between ikigai and other philosophies. It has two clear connections. One is with the work of Shoma Morita. He was a psychologist and psychiatrist in the 1940s. He was working with motivation, with purpose therapies, but he's not very well known. The clearer connection in Europe is with the work of Viktor Frankl, the creator of logotherapy. This therapy is the search for meaning. And if we read his 1946 book *Man's Search for Meaning*, we see that his therapeutic approach puts purpose in the center. The ikigai.

At that time, after the Second World War, the patients who came to him for consultations had lived terrible dramas. Many had lost their whole family. Their lives were broken. So psychoanalysis that focused on the past was not helpful. Instead, Dr. Frankl explored the question of what his patients could do to get them through the day. And he understood that having a purpose was of primary importance. So this purpose therapy, this logotherapy, became a search for at least one thing that can be a point of motivation, a goal so that you want to live one day more. And it can be something small like playing an instrument, starting a new hobby, or something bigger, like starting a new relationship. And so logotherapy focused on finding the happiness in some little thing in your everyday life that you can do tomorrow. And there is a strong connection between ikigai and logotherapy. Because of that, we dedicated a whole chapter to the work of Frankl.

We have had a lot of feedback from readers on how this book has changed their lives. I think that this book is translated in 55 languages and last year was the number one bestseller in India in nonfiction books. So many people have written to tell us about changes that they have undertaken in their lives. Many psychologists, many teachers, many people who work with other people use this book. And, we receive a lot of mails and messages all the time. We are very happy about that.

Is wisdom a uniquely human concept?

In the way we consider wisdom, I think it's only a human concept. Of course, animals have a wisdom and have intelligence, but it's something that comes from intuition. It's something that is already built inside themselves. So it's not something that they developed. Animals learn things and adapt to their circumstances. But, they don't learn from external teachers. That is what you understand by wisdom. I would say that animals have a natural wisdom, but that increases in a very slow way through experiences, but they don't have the insights that we have, and that is what makes human beings different.

How do you ultimately define wisdom?

As we said in the beginning, I would define wisdom as the liberation of useless information. So wisdom for me would be this discovery of the essential truth that was always there, but I couldn't see it because I had too many filters in front of me.

How can each of us develop wisdom?

By letting go. We have discovered during the lockdown that we don't need so many things. We can let go of material things, people even, or obligations, or rituals that are useless. So the more you let go, the more free you are and the more clear your view becomes. So letting go would be the natural way to wisdom.

Is there anything else you wish to add?

wisdom is a permanent aspiration of human beings. If you are a full human being you will aspire to have more wisdom until the last second of your life. So wisdom is what gave us this advantage in front of the other species: we are always growing. If you look at animals, they learn a lot when they are very small and then they stop. If you live with a dog, the dog does exactly the same things every day. They stopped at some point of their development. What makes human beings different is that we never stop growing unless we decide to.

How did it feel to discuss wisdom today?

It was very interesting and I discovered things that I had not thought about before. Normally what happens when you write books, is that everyone always asks the same questions. So 99% of my interviews are about ikigai, and I am always answering the same questions. You asked new questions and it was exciting for me. It was very interesting.

Juan Pablo Orrego

Juan Pablo Orrego is a Chilean ecologist, writer, musician, educator and activist. He completed his bachelor's in Fine Arts and master's in Environmental Studies at York University, Toronto. Through his studies he began to spend time among indigenous communities in North and South America, which shaped his deep ecology outlook, and his relationship with people and planet. From 2005, he worked with a large coalition of organizations from many countries, and concentrated on the Patagonia Without Dams campaign, preventing the construction of a complex of five hydroelectric dams in two wild Patagonian rivers. He achieved similar success with dams in the Biobío River. His contributions to environmental protection in Latin America were recognized with the Goldman Award in 1997, and the Right Livelihood Award in 1998. He is President of the NGO/Corporation Ecosistemas, Councilman of Amigos de los Parques de la Patagonia, and a member of the board of International Rivers, USA.

What comes to mind first when you think about wisdom?

Knowing our place in the natural order and acting accordingly. It sounds simple, but it's not. I'm an ecologist, and it totally astounds me that we still don't understand basic biospherical principles. If we did, we would not have acted the way we have for the last few millennia, and increasingly so during the last few centuries, and particularly the last 50 years. We don't understand the biospherical reality and our place in the natural order.

You can condense these into a few fundamental facts that we need to understand, contemplate, and then comply with. Metaphorically I call them biospherical directives. For example, everything is interconnected. This is trendy now; there are mainstream documentaries where this is said repeatedly. But we're not behaving as if we understand what this means. Everything is interpenetrated. The biosphere's atoms, molecules and elements are all flowing from one place to another. From the so-called inorganic to the so-called organic, from one organism, such as a lettuce, to our bodies, and then out of them. We exist within the recursive flow of matter, energy and information of the whole biosphere. It's a space-temporal continuum. We are continually disintegrating and reintegrating thanks to the food, the air, the water, the heat, the light. We breathe air and give back a different gas with less oxygen and more CO_2. So, we are within the gaseous cycle of the atmosphere. We eat solid food and then we give back a degraded form of that matter that flows back into the environment. So, we are within the cycle of matter. We are constantly losing cells from our body. We are a process, a sphere of life; we are a dancing galaxy of molecules, and everything is moving, being metabolized. As far as I can see this is an observable scientific truth. It is also poetic and beautiful. And if you really look, it is easy to see the reality of this. Or it should be. But civilization doesn't seem to perceive it.

Another biospherical reality is that the whole biosphere is a water-based entity. So, the care of the hydrological cycles and water, and water bodies, should be a way of orienting the development of our societies. We are water-based entities. We need to really tend to water bodies, oceans, rivers, lakes, glaciers, clouds. It's incredible that we have this capacity to destabilize the biosphere, but also the choice to flow within its strictures.

Then, we should also know that the champions of the biosphere are photosynthetic organisms. They are the only pathway of solar energy into the biosphere; plants, trees, forests and marine photoplankton. I call them photoplankton rather than phytoplankton, after Lynn Margulis. She states that there are no plants living in the ocean. The plankton are microscopic photosynthetic organisms. What have we been doing for the last millennia? Cutting the forests down, soiling the oceans, diminishing the amount of photoplankton. All of them are carbon absorbers and emitters of oxygen.

These ecological facts are simple. Once somebody points them out to you, they are solid as a rock. There's no ideology here. It's so amazing that both individuals and civilization as a whole, cannot seem to grasp these simple facts and behave accordingly. I say that humanity needs to realize that nature comes first. This is historical and pragmatic, not ideological. Humanity needs to be at the service of nature. You want air, water, healthy food? You want climate regulation? You want regulation of the pH and salinity of oceans? We are nature, so caring for nature is caring for ourselves, and vice versa. We are a continuum.

I'm relaying this idea all the time: "Nature comes first!" My 22-year-old son said to me, "People will think that you care more about the birds and the trees than about people. So why don't you fix it a bit? You can say, 'Nature comes first, because we are nature.' Then you're going to be okay." So, we must get to know our place within the natural order, an order which is also cosmic: the sun is far away, 150 million kilometers from the Earth, but still totally part of life. Actually if the sun turns off, the biosphere vanishes in a nanosecond. We take too many things for granted. When do modern cultures revere the sun?

Do you recall the first time you witnessed wisdom in action?

I see wisdom often in simple acts, as there are little wisdoms in everyday life. So, when my parents and grandparents acted virtuously towards themselves, the family, us, these acts carried bits of wisdom, without doubt. There are levels of wisdom, but today I really appreciate the small wisdoms. Better for wisdom to be evenly distributed among all the people than concentrated in a few illuminati.

I worked as an agricultural laborer for three years with these underpaid agricultural workers. These guys had many wisdoms. They can build houses, grow fruits and vegetables, handle animals, they know how to move in the mountains in any weather, and then they cook and sing wonderfully. They have all these virtues but have been caught by history in a servile social position. I learned immensely from them. It was a pleasure to work hard with them. Despite my youth and good physical condition, it took me eight months to strengthen my body and mind for the jobs. Shovel, pickaxe, iron bar, hoe. That was tough.

For me, baking a fantastic bread is a sort of applied wisdom. It is a wisdom because somebody can put the flour together and the water and throw the dough into the oven and the bread won't be the same as a person who has what we call here 'el toque', the touch. That touch is wise and has to do with care—cariño. To make good bread is a kind of wisdom.

I participated for four years in a spiritual development school with Oscar Ichazo, at the Arica Institute. He just died in March 2020. He was a Bolivian master. He was living in Maui, in Hawai'i, when he passed. He was teaching us at the end of the 60s, and he already knew about the enneagram, Gurdjieff, levels of consciousness, Sufism, Qigong. He ended up teaching first here in Chile. There was a group from Esalen, Big Sur, who came to train with Oscar at the end of the 60s in Arica, in the extreme north of Chile. There are several books about him. So for a few years I was a disciple of a person who really had a lot of knowledge and wisdom. But that same person was captured by North American businessmen in New York. His method became a business for a while. He became an alcoholic. He got trapped in spiritual materialism, as Chogyam Trungpa used to say, but then he finally saved himself from that and retired to Hawai'i. So somebody can have wisdom and knowledge, but that does not mean that he is a perfect human being. I go back to a phrase that I heard from an Ecuadorian Shaman. "I'm not what I am because of what I know, but because of what I am." He was talking about the synergy, the gestalt of everything you have inside your mind and your heart and body. So, wisdom is complex.

Who is the wisest person you know, and why?

I don't think there is a wisest. Oscar without any doubt was a wise one, despite of all the contradictions. Gregory Bateson was also wise and important in the development of my thinking, though I never met him. I based my thesis to a great extent on his writings. He wrote *Steps to an Ecology of Mind*. He's a pioneer, a systemic and transdisciplinary thinker. I discovered his work by chance in a library in Toronto, Canada when looking for books related to my environmental studies. I saw the title and it attracted me. In fact, Bateson was also very influential with a famous Chilean biologist and philosopher, Humberto Maturana. Another epistemologist. Bateson wrote that humans can incorporate epistemological errors in our cultural matrix and that this is a sure way to trouble and even extinction. Errors such as the idea that we are separate from nature and superior to it, made in the image of a patriarchal god.

I have had flesh and blood teachers, people who have influenced me that I think had a lot of wisdom. And others have taught me through their books. There are several, but one that has really touched me more recently is Lynn Margulis, the microbiologist. Reading her, I feel that she gets you a little bit closer to what reality really is. She modulated the theory of evolution. She demonstrates that evolution is moved by cooperation and symbiosis. Which is the exact opposite of Neo-Darwinism. Darwin was a genius, and a heretic. He would have been burned at the stake in earlier times because he said that all species on Earth are interrelated and subject to evolution. Until the time of Darwin and Alfred Russell Wallace, people believed that God created species immutable, unchanging, and that humans sit at the apex. Darwin and Russell's insight was profoundly important, but what was done with their theories afterwards is like the difference between Jesus Christ and the Catholic Church. The distance is immense. His theory was transformed into the survival of the fittest, the pyramid of power and so on. It's totally erroneous.

My own gestalt reading Lynn was the realization that we ascend from bacteria. And in fact, now we are learning that we have 10 bacteria per cell, and we are filled with viruses. You have at least 10 viruses in your body permanently. Some people have many more. In each gram of our faeces there is around one billion virions, individual viruses. So, we are more viral and bacterial than cellular. This is science. I was reading a paper about virus dynamics in the processes of life. The author talks about how this new, more accurate vision somehow erases our concept of individuality. We are a galaxy of bacteria, viruses and cells. And all elements of this system are constantly interacting. We have bacteriophage viruses in our gut that infect and destroy pathogenic bacteria that could make you sick. So, they are our symbionts. As Alan Watts said, we are not an ego trapped in a bag of skin. We don't end here at the skin, we continue down into the microcosmos, and we extend up to the macrocosmos.

This information, if you can process it rationally, emotionally and viscerally, should change your way of behaving. We are co-operative galaxies of beings. Many things, like this Covid, can go into your galaxy. And if you are unlucky because of genetic factors, predispositions, that galaxy can be disintegrated by the virus. So, what's holding our galaxy of atoms, molecules, bacteria and viruses together is a miracle. You do what you can to help that miracle with food, water, air and sunshine. You try to eat well. But some people simply cannot. They don't have clean water and healthy food. But you try in your daily life to maintain this galaxy operating as functionally and pleasantly as possible. It's daily work, actually. You need to make decisions about what you expose yourself to, on all levels. Do you go to the forest, to the ocean far from cities and contemplate? Do you play war games on the computer? What kinds of impressions do you expose yourself to? According to Ichazo, impressions are the finest and subtler form of food: alimento. Air, water, solid food, impressions.

I'm a sort of informal teacher. I would bring kids from an urban university for hikes in the mountains here. And some kids would say, "I didn't know this existed." They had never been in nature. Some kids would bring liters of Coca Cola, and I would tell them, "I'm going to take you to a place where you can drink the purest water emerging from the ground." They would say, "No professor, I don't drink water. I only drink Coca Cola." And they would have panic attacks because they are not used to being in open nature. They lose it. They don't know how to behave. That is the level of our mental disconnection with nature. But nature is ourselves. We are nature. I ended up coining a term for this: ecopathy. In large cities we are becoming ecopaths. A sociopath is a person who, because of childhood trauma, becomes disconnected from fellow beings. I think the precondition to be a sociopath is to be an ecopath because that is the fundamental connection, with nature, the main umbilical cord. Disconnecting with nature is disconnecting with yourself. When that gets mentally severed, you can end up being anything, a sociopath or psychopath. You can never disconnect from the ecology of your environment. This is a totally mental and cultural phenomenon.

Looking back on your life, what is the wisest thing you ever did?

It would be easier to think of all the unwise things that I ever did. I don't think there is only one wisest thing. And, I'm clear that our life is steered by forces other than our will. Gurdjieff used to say that most people are asleep, don't develop their will, and die like dogs. My apologies to the dogs. He said you must awaken your potential and take control of your life with your will.

Many things that have happened to me were beyond my control. Firstly the military coup in Chile, in 1973. It destroyed our lives, socially and literally. All my family were on the political left, involved with the Allende government. My grandfather, an aristocrat, became a communist. He was married to an aristocratic lady, my grandmother from my father's side. And my grandfather became a communist because of social justice and idealism. I applaud him because he could have been a right-wing villain. But he was a sweet and generous man, the best grandfather anybody can have. And his idealism got him in serious trouble. When the military coup happened, they kicked him out of the hospital he had founded and built. He was a lung doctor. So, my grandfather was a communist, as were my uncle and my father. My mother was a socialist. I played with a famous communist Chilean musician that was tortured and murdered by the military, Víctor Jara. We arranged two of his songs, including El derecho de vivir en paz. I play the bass. It's a very famous song these days in Chile. It has become one of the anthems of the social rebellion here. Roger Waters has done an arrangement of this song recently.

I left this country in 1974, a few months after the coup. We couldn't get any work. I was totally traumatized. I saw corpses rolling down the Mapocho River in Santiago, I saw machine-gunned corpses in the streets. I didn't want to come back to Chile, ever. Not very patriotic, I know. I went to Ecuador and then ended up in Canada doing my bachelor's degree in Fine Arts. I had an uncle living in Toronto, my communist uncle, so I stayed with him at first. I finally got enrolled at York University and I did my BFA, which led me to listen to ethnic music, which led me to shamanism, and through that to master plants—hallucinogens. And all this happened because of the military coup. Life is a very interesting mixture between your little will, and the will of the environment, which sometimes pushes you to places that you never imagined you would end up in.

In between all of that, I have taken many wise and unwise decisions probably. I feel so privileged because I come from a difficult family. My mother became an alcoholic after she witnessed the murder of several friends during the coup. She was fantastic, a brave social leader, a great painter. She died of aplastic anemia in 2008. My brother, the sweetest guy, also became alcoholic. He died of cirrhosis in 2005 and was only two years older than me. And others in my family have huge issues. So, I'm a survivor. But I cannot claim that this survival has been exclusively my accomplishment. It's a strange feeling. I see my personal will within a constellation of infinite factors, variables and persons at every instant.

And then I fell in love. I had four children with my first wife. My mother said, "You will never be happy with her." I ignored her and got married. We were together 18 years. For a good while it was a fantastic relationship but then the love faded. So, was it a wise decision? We had these four beautiful kids. In many ways it was a perfect decision, even though the marriage did not last. We are still good friends.

So, for me it's difficult to answer this question. When I did my master's in Environmental Studies at York University in Toronto, that was clearly a wise decision. In many ways everything I've been doing since has to do with that experience. In between everything I was reading, all these masters like Gregory Bateson, John Livingstone, Rachel Carson, Thoreau, Theodore Roszak, James Lovelock, I went for eight months to live with the Huichol people in Mexico. I was getting a bit tired of Toronto, the city and the cement, and conceived this trip because I had read about the incredible Huichol in the literature and *National Geographic*. And my father was living in Guadalajara, relatively close to their reservation, and he had contacts. I wrote a few letters and got hired by the Mexican government to do something for these Indians up there. They said, "Be careful, buy a pistol, a rifle, high boots, and antidote for the rattlesnakes and the scorpions." Of course, we didn't do any of that.

I accompanied 50 of them on their peyote pilgrimage to Wirikuta in Real del Catorce, in the north east of Mexico. So my masters weren't only the literary ones. That was one of the most amazing experiences in my life, sharing with these rooted people. They call themselves Wirrarika. Huichol is the conventional name the foreigners gave them. And for those people, wisdom is embodied. It is in their everyday practices. They say that humans get more in trouble because of what we do not do, than because of the things we do. They are not perfect. In fact, they say that we should never aspire to perfection, that we are going to get in serious trouble if we do. They say that even divinities are not finished, complete, and they just start processes of creation. It's like the Greek perspective, that gods set things in motion, then watch amazed at the things that come out of this creation. They learn from their creations.

That shook so many of the preconceived ideas I had about civilization, wisdom, many things. The older men and women don't read and write. They don't have universities or hospitals. Now it's changing, and there are community schools. I was helping with that in fact. We often identify wisdom with universities, with churches, with cities. And these people have none of these. They live disseminated, scattered in a rough territory of mesas and deep canyons. But for me they were some of the wisest people I have met, in their behaviors, in the magical way they perceive reality. And the way they act within reality. In fact, they saved my life twice. On one occasion I got intoxicated while on a trip, and I was alone. The sun was setting, and there are rattlesnakes and deadly tiny black scorpions. And then a Huichol was coming down the trail on a horse, and I needed to go up the cliff to the mesa where we were staying. I had never seen him before. He asked where I was staying, and then jumped down from his horse, helped me to get on it and sent me back up the trail. He said he'd send somebody to get his horse later.

The experience with the Wirrarika gave me an epistemological shock, because I realized that we are trapped culturally in a very narrow corridor. In my high school education, indigenous peoples were treated like pagans, making weird ceremonies and whatever, and there was nothing we could learn from them. But when I left Chile after the coup, I passed through Ecuador to visit my mother who was exiled there. I saw the indigenous people in the streets of Quito and other places. I was totally amazed. And their music impacted me deeply. Andean music is just unbelievable. And at that point, something shifted in my brain. I was educated at the Alliance Française here in Chile for 13 years. They despised Latin America and indigenous people. This was 60 years ago, so that has changed for sure. I'm 70 now. I was born in 1949. But, in those days they really tried to put a Eurocentric paradigm in your head. They talked down about Latin American countries as underdeveloped, and claimed that Europeans had invented civilization, science, philosophy and so on. But when I went to Ecuador and I saw these people and heard their music, I realized that the reality they had shown me was not correct. And I had an epistemological rupture. When I got to Canada, I started discovering Indo America from the library of York University. I started listening intensely to what they called 'ethnic music', first of the Americas, then I jumped to India, Asia and Africa. I was taking mridangam lessons, the South Indian drum. And then I was taking African percussion.

And through ethnic music I got into shamanism and master plants, and through this into ecology. I saw that rooted peoples have a different attitude, perception and behavior regarding what we call the environment, what we call nature. It is totally different. I was really amazed by the attitudes of peoples of the Southwest of the US, the Anasazi, the Hopi, the Pueblo, Zuñi and others. Indigenous peoples became a super important reference for me. But I also learned not to idealize them. There have been indigenous peoples who have lost sight of the fundamentals, particularly the ecological directives. Look at the people of Rapa Nui, or Easter Island. They didn't see the ecological collapse coming. They cut all the trees for firewood, canoes and building, but especially to help roll down and erect the moai statues. When they lost the forests, everything else died off, and there is evidence of cannibalism at the end of that epoch. Some have used this example as a metaphor of modern humanity destroying the island of the biosphere on Earth.

I'm not idealizing Andean peoples, Quechuas, Aymaras, because there's been so much aggression and pain that have caused cultural degradation, hate and resentment, but they are one of the best examples in this world of self-sufficiency, which is a collective wisdom put in practice. In Bolivia and Peru in particular, there are some communities that live above 4,000 meters. So, we haven't been able to encroach into and degrade their world. And they have their appropriate technologies: appropriate tools, and houses with very thick walls, no windows, made of mud and stone, sticks and hard grasses, nothing from outside. And they have their llamas and alpacas, and potatoes and quinoa and so on. They can be totally self-sufficient if they need to. They can be survivors of a holocaust if it comes.

So these were important, wise decisions in my life. I did my assistantship at York in the faculty of Indigenous Studies. I've been trying to be close to rooted peoples since my epiphany in Ecuador, and have also had some heavy disappointments along the way. I call them rooted peoples, other people call them Indians, indigenous peoples or aboriginals. People who live with and off the land, in a stance of equality and even awe regarding animals and plants, and rivers and rocks, and Mother Earth. One of the ways to illustrate this wisdom is the Quechua ceremony before tilling a little piece of land for planting potatoes. They go at night to the field, the whole family, and at sunrise perform a complex ceremony involving flowers, a llama fetus, alcohol, sugar, beautiful things, and then they ask for permission before working the land. They ask for permission because they know they're going to be contributing a little bit to entropy, erosion, by that action. That attitude totally rocks me. They know about entropy and sustainability and ecosystem limits. They are culturally wise.

I went with the Huichol to Wirikuta, where the peyote is endemic and grows naturally. After five days riding on a truck, fasting, no solid food, only liquids, no washing or sleeping, in sexual abstinence, we reached Wirikuta up in Real del Catorce. When we arrived I saw the whole group of 50 pilgrims gather around a huge cactus. They acknowledged the existence of, and our relatedness with, a huge barrel cactus in the middle of nowhere, in the chaparral. All these tough guys and ladies revering a cactus after five days without food and sleep. And I've seen similar attitudes, for example, with the Hopi and the Pueblo, who plant their corn in the desert. It's a semi-arid ecosystem, to say the least. And they sing to the clouds to bring the rain. They call the rain with songs, with music, with prayer. And, of course, it doesn't work every time. Maybe after a week finally the rain comes. It's not an automatic response, but you keep doing the calling. But they are demonstrating their understanding that everything is interrelated. And they know that what we think, feel and do affects the environment, the land, the clouds, other living beings, and that what we do to the environment affects us. They've known about interconnection, interrelatedness and interpenetration for centuries. After reading all the literature about the Huichol and my eight-month stay with them, I think that they have developed a powerful collective cultural system that includes the alkaloid mescaline of the peyote, to somehow break the illusion of the social world and even of the senses. It is very Buddhist to transcend and remember things like the unity in multiplicity, and for the deconstruction of the excessively human construct that blinds us from higher earthly and cosmic realities. It seems we need to deconstruct the arrogance of anthropocentrism to remember who we really are and what is our place in the natural order.

Though not all indigenous people achieve such wisdom. For example, the Maya were incredible artists and astronomers, but they didn't see that you couldn't concentrate such amounts of people in the tropical ecosystem without it collapsing. And they ended up dying through famine and eating each other. This is an archeological truth.

It's curious that human beings of all races can have this blind spot regarding the most basic thing: ecology, the logic of home. Many of these peoples that I've been mentioning that have made that mistake were pretty amazing in many other ways.

So going to York University, and spending time with the Wirrarika seem like wise decisions in my life in hindsight, because I learned so much. But again, they were not entirely the product of my own will. You can try to steer your life through the power of your will, but I also see that I am moved by all these other currents.

What is the hardest-won wisdom that you have?

It would say it was the military coup. When it happened I was a hippie musician, training with Oscar at the Arica school. The Allende government was quite wonderful while it lasted. And then suddenly it all changed, and we experienced true evil. There's no other word for it. It was a really wisdom-inducing, life-changing event, that fell on us like lightning. And then you start questioning, asking how can something like this happen.

As an ecologist, sometimes we end up talking with people, students, about God and all of this, about wisdom. And it begs the question: why can human beings unbalance a whole biosphere? Why can we get so lost as to bring down our own world and not see it coming? Why were we made with this capacity? This is an understanding we are still working on.

Then, the lessons from the deaths of my relatives have been deep. My mother, my father, my brother, my paternal grandparents. I assisted them until the last second, down to their last breaths. I don't repent, though I don't know if it was so wise, particularly with my mother, to see her die so close. And my brother died literally with our foreheads touching. And I was telling him, "Go, go, go." And I don't know how and why I got into that position. I just acted. In fact, my first relative to die was my paternal grandmother. And even my grandfather, who was a strong man, an MD, he and the rest of my family ran from the room where she was dying. And for some reason that again I can't explain, I was the only one, with the nurse, that was there by my grandmother until the end. In those last moments she was struggling. Her breath would stop for many seconds, and I would say with relief, "Okay, she's gone." And then she would breathe again, because the body doesn't want to quit. And I was telling her to let go, that she had done everything she needed to, and done it well. She was the sweetest lady. And it was incredible, because after, when my grandfather died, the whole family was able to accompany him to the end. It seems I broke that ingrained cultural fear, and since then, the whole family has been able to accompany family members when they pass. Those death experiences are super important, deep learning experiences in my life in ways I cannot fully explain.

And I have also assisted eight deliveries. My six kids, I was there. And also with my daughter's last child. I was there throughout. That's really powerful, death and birth. The rooted peoples are always there for these processes. What is this thing of withdrawing to let only professionals handle the birth and death of your loved ones? So those have been important experiences, in terms of acquiring wisdom, in the sense of seeing how life really is. And life is tough. "It's not only roses, it's also thorns," as Gurdjieff used to say. People tend to think that we should just think positive, but life is also putrefaction and death and disease. And all the organisms are eating each other so life can continue. These are hard biological facts, and we need to confront them.

So in that sense, all those experiences are for me wisdom-inducing. But in the Buddhist sense, wisdom is wordless, like contemplating the hard and soft and beautiful facts of earthly biological, ecological realities. And if you are more in touch and seeing the ecological reality, then you should act accordingly. And for me, this means putting ourselves into the service of nature, which is ourselves.

But another reality is that if we manage to dismantle this biosphere, and humanity disappears, life is going to continue. The paleontologists say there have been at least 12 extinction-level events in the last few hundred million years. And five of those have been major. The Permian–Triassic extinction event took place 252 million years ago. It is called the Great Dying by paleontologists. According to their studies, around 96% of marine life and 70% of terrestrial vertebrate species were lost. It was also the largest mass extinction of insects that we know of. The theory is that there was an eruption of a chain of volcanoes in the north of Siberia that melted the Arctic, like what's happening now because of our hyper industrial activity. And then the dinosaurs appeared. And then an asteroid impacted planet Earth 66 million years ago and wiped them out. This allowed the flourishing of mammals, and among them humans. So even if we manage to dismantle the biosphere, this is no problem for life. Life is used to this. Bacteria, viruses and fungi are there, waiting to recreate a new biosphere. And who knows what kind of new living biospherical community would develop. Some people say we are destroying the planet. Forget it. Life will return, no matter what we do. At least while the sun is in its beneficial phase.

Biodiversity is always changing and developing. It's a process. So, we shouldn't even get so attached to the present biodiversity. The experts say that 99.9% of all species that have existed have disappeared. So maybe here you see another cornerstone of the paradigm we should have, which is humility. We are tiny specks of water with a little bit of dust. We are quite extraordinary, though, with these amazing hands and fingers, and voices, and this peculiar kind of intelligence. And also this self-destructive bent.

If you look at the kid in the city, wearing headphones, sitting on the floor of the subway, looking down, listening to heavy metal or whatever, that is the total anti-shamanic disconnection. They don't want to breathe because the air is foul. They don't want to look because everything is graffiti, and the cities, at least here, are so ugly. The shamanic quest is exactly the opposite. It is about connection, connection, connection; augmenting, strengthening interconnection. They even use master plants for this purpose. Ayahuasca is for recovering, strengthening and empowering your connection to the environment, which again is an aspect of yourself. The Amazonian peoples could not survive one morning in the jungle without that connection. Fundamental to that connection is intuition—the sixth sense. The ethnobotanists wondered how these barefoot, naked Indians invented the formula for ayahuasca. They take the crushed vine, *Banisteriopsis caapi*, which is rich in harmine and harmaline, two very complex alkaloids. Nobody knows why the plant has those alkaloids, which can play with our neurotransmitters. It's an amazing specificity. They mix this with the leaves of a bush they call 'chacruna', *Psychotria viridis*. It has high quantities of DMT, dimethyltryptamine. They mix them in a clay pot, ideally, with spring water, and then boil them over a sacred fire and create a powerful potentiated alkaloid. On top of everything, we have an enzyme in our digestive system, monoamine oxidase, that naturally destroys DMT. But ayahuasca has an inhibitor for monoamine oxidase, thus allowing the DMT to work on your nervous system. The ethnobotanists asked the Indians, "How did you come up with this formula?" And they answered, "The plants tell us." Decades ago, the ethnobotanists or anthropologists would laugh at the superstitious Indians. But what they were talking about was intuition, taken to another level. This is something we have lost and cannot comprehend. For the indigenous people it is essential. You cannot survive long in the jungle without that intuition, without those antennas, without that connection. And that poor kid in the subway with the headphones, he's lost that. And once you lose that connection mentally you are lost, like a kite cut adrift, blowing in the wind.

So much of our life is determined by our environment. We are open-ended as a species and can become different things depending on the environment we are born into. We could grow up in a country at peace or at war, with nurturing or abusive parents. So, how we end up becoming a saint or a serial killer is part of the mystery of life, and of this peculiar open-ended nature of human beings. A lion is born a lion, lives like a lion and will die like a lion. There can be a grouchier lion than another, but their nature cannot be as divergent as a human being's can be.

In the world today, where do you see wisdom, and its lack, being demonstrated?

I would go looking for wisdom in rather faraway places, in the inner frontiers of planet Earth, in the mountains, in some islands. Among people who have been less manhandled by civilization and urban life, and less poisoned, mentally and physically.

I don't think I would look for wisdom in a university. If somebody gave me a scholarship, I would go for a PhD without doubt, because I would be in charge of the subject and I would study the biosphere, its metabolism, physiology, these kinds of topics, to try to better understand the directives of the biosphere.

In seeking wisdom, we see tens of thousands of universities and libraries in the world. It seems there is an inverse proportional relationship between wisdom and academia. There are so many universities, books and PhDs, but where is the wisdom? By their fruits you shall know them. Look at the shape of the world.

I certainly would not go to any church seeking wisdom. I'm anti-Catholic, for a number of reasons. Researchers have calculated that the inquisition murdered millions of women over four centuries. Any woman that had a 'suspicious' relationship with nature could be thrown into the dungeon, tortured, raped and burned alive by men dressed in black. The church was really trying to extinguish the divine feminine, the feminine power in humanity. Women were the healers, the midwives; they knew the pharmacopeia, the medicinal plants, and they handled natality. The Church saw this as too much power in the hands of women and moved to take away their power.

Of all the spiritual traditions, I like Buddhism. I'm not a practicing Buddhist, but I do appreciate their attitude of contemplating the void, reality, without any adornments, the way things are.

Certainly, I don't respect evangelists, one of the most retrograde social forces today in the world. They put Bolsonaro in power in Brazil, and Piñera here in Chile. When those guys give the order to millions of followers to vote for a certain person, all right-wing, they all go and vote for them, without question. There is no dissent. It is an army.

For wisdom I would go to nature. I hiked nonstop for 35 years in the mountains. No competition, no sports. Hiking for contemplation, connection. For pleasure. We would hike up all these mountains around here. We even put little votive shrines on all the main surrounding peaks. We started imitating rooted people, but then it becomes your own practice, deeply felt. This is common in the Andes. The Huichol in Mexico do it too. Perhaps it is a manifestation of the collective unconscious.

I would sometimes go alone to a spring up here, and put up my little tent. I would fast for a few days, sometimes take some psilocybin mushrooms or the San Pedro cactus that we have here, rich in mescaline, like peyote. I would spend time with a fire, and pure water, clean air, watching animals, the birds, listening to the sounds at night, looking at the stars. Going into nature always helps. Fasting is a good practice. You are hungry, so your senses start to expand and sharpen.

You absorb the environment in a powerful way. Among North American Indians in the southwest, a key rite of passage is to go alone into nature for days and fast until they have their vision. Eventually they will develop a special relationship with a plant or animal and make a powerful connection. If you spend a week in the mountains there, in Chaco Canyon or Mesa Verde, you're going to see it all. You're going to see beauty, the sun and the clouds, but also death. You're going to see the fox killing its prey, the ants eating another insect. You're going to see the reality of life. By connecting like this you gain basic wisdom about life.

Is wisdom a uniquely human concept?

No, not at all. I feel that we can have consciousness, awareness, or wisdom, in your terms, because that is in the environment. We participate in the consciousness of the cosmos, of the planetary system, of the world. And in that sense, for me a tree is a sentient and wise being. Trees are pure synergy. Many other beings, animals particularly, are synergic and entropic; we create thermodynamic ripples. We burn energy into heat. Instead, trees grow, and give us albedo, regulation of the gases of the atmosphere, create soil at their feet, give niches, fruits, they give lipids, proteins, collaborate with fungi, with mycorrhiza. These beings only radiate synergy into the environment. They're photosynthetic, autotrophs. They don't generate entropy like us. On the contrary, right now humanity is an entropic agent for the biosphere.

And that's another interesting issue. The dance of synergy and entropy. Gregory Bateson talks a lot about the laws of thermodynamics, and this dance. According to the second law of thermodynamics, life should not exist. Not even Einstein's relativity has been able to debunk the first two laws of thermodynamics. They're still there, unmovable. The second law says that the whole cosmos is moving into disorganization, loss of structure. So, it's a puzzle for scientists, how life somehow goes counter to entropy. I think it's the wrong vision. Life is in between, the Shiva-Vishnu, yin-yang dance between entropy and synergy, creation and destruction. Life is dancing between these two poles, the tendency to disorganization, destruction, erosion, loss of energy, loss of structure, of sense, and on the other side, the tendency to grow, build, interact and cooperate, starting from the atomic and molecular level, that generates and miraculously sustains the biosphere.

Do you have a favorite parable or anecdote on wisdom?

I think of my father's wisdom. He would take us for a month during the summer holidays to camp in utter simplicity by a beautiful river in southern Chile. He always brought along a box full of wonderful books which he graduated in content and difficulty according to our ages. Every day he would go out at sunrise to fish for wild salmon for the most delicious meals around the fire. He would take us for whole day walks in the forests and hills, contemplating and admiring nature. This created in me an enduring love for nature.

My mother's wisdom was to live with her door always open to everybody in a risky neighborhood in downtown Santiago, and to always put the wellbeing of others before her own.

My paternal grandparents were also very wise. They were always there for us. And they generously offered the family a well-provided house by the Pacific Ocean, where we would spend, at their expense, most weekends and holidays, year after year, during my infancy and teenage years. The ocean, the ocean. We became so fond of the sea; we could as children contemplate it for hours on end. Not to speak of the storms.

For me, all that was offered to us by my family is a most valuable human wisdom put in practice, given that it offers children the chance to connect with the environment, to grow up in good mental and physical shape. Then maybe they can spread the same loving wisdom in their familiar, social and ecological environments as adults.

How do you ultimately define wisdom?

There is so much wisdom spread around in the heads and hearts of humble, anonymous people. Young people, old people, urban, indigenous. So why does the dark side have the upper hand in such a powerful way? I think again that the issue is connected to entropy. It's so much easier to corrupt, to destroy. With a chainsaw it takes you half an hour to topple a 2000-year-old Sequoia. It's much easier to fall than to rise and ascend. And I think it has to do with entropy. If you look at indigenous people, some of the wiser people that I have shared with, they're skinny people, fibrous, they eat just enough, and maybe save for the next winter. There's no capitalism. I stated metaphorically in my master's thesis that 60% of their time is dedicated to their spiritual, shamanic lives, even more than to survival. They spend a lot of time performing ceremonies and rituals in the mountains, the rivers, the lakes, the sea. It is all about keeping you on track. Because it is so easy to fall.

Their whole culture, their rites, symbols and myths, are about trying to keep you in the real reality, in the right perception, in the right behavior. And in different ways, because cultures are so different. But the aim is the same. The internal pattern is the same: correct behavior within your human community and your larger circle of life.

Since the arrival of the virus in Chile, I've been going out to sing to the rising sun every morning. I sing, "Inti, Tau, Anthu, Sol, Sun, eeeee." Inti is sun in Quechua. Tau is sun for the southwestern US indigenous people. Anthu is the Mapuche word for the sun. Sol is Latin, and then Sun, the English word. I also try to say goodbye to the sun every evening. I don't know why. But I know that a traditional Navajo, Dineh, that respects him or herself, is going to do that every single day of their life. And he or she brings some corn pollen in a pouch and throws this golden seed towards the sun in a gesture of reverence. Golden pollen of the blessed plant that feeds us. I'm not sure why I started doing this in the middle of this mounting crisis; social, sanitary, ecological, economic—everything is crumbling down here. Going out to greet the sunrise each morning feels good for our household. For logistical reasons I've been separated from my wife for seven weeks. The whole family is trying to deal with this crisis, and I'm working here and taking care of my younger son. And in this situation, I'm going out to salute the sun every day. It feels super healing for all of us, without doubt.

I've found an increasing respect for domestic duties that we have always participated in. I've been telling my students that they are the noblest activities—washing the dishes, cleaning your house, baking bread, doing the laundry. I'm believing more and more in the small acts of creating wellbeing in your close environment. More than the big acts of important people. I had a Japanese karate teacher in Toronto. He was an impressive person. And one day he asked the class, "What does it mean to be a strong person?" Everybody was saying it was kicking ass or being able to sit in the lotus position for three days, or whatever. And he said, "No. A strong person is somebody who radiates happiness and wellbeing to his or her surroundings. Somebody who helps the happiness and balance of others." On the contrary, a weak person is always seeding anger, suspicion, fear and so on. Social entropy rather than synergy.

I think wisdom is a state of being. In its widest meaning, it's a state of being, caring for your whole being. I always ask my students, opening my arms wide, what is the first ecosystem you need to care for in your life? It's your whole being. And that being encompasses your spirit, your mind, your emotions, your body and more.

How can each of us develop wisdom?

As I was saying before, that's tricky, because it depends on where and with whom you are born and raised. That's the curiosity of human beings. If you are born in a country at war, as opposed to being born in a free, peaceful country, and then if you are born to loving parents or to abusive parents, your life can turn out very differently.

And then there is always this beautiful, intimidating randomness in life. The freedom of the creativity of nature is infinite. That's why you have side by side, a stonefish and a dolphin, or a crocodile and a gazelle, the giraffe and the cheetah. The process of life is open-ended, and there is a strong ingredient of randomness. That freedom and randomness are the only way for life to be able to adapt to a constantly changing planet and cosmos. Without it, somehow creation would freeze, it would become like an automaton. It would not exist, actually.

That element of randomness is also active in our lives. I was going to study jazz bass at York University, but I was quite traumatized by the military coup. I went to the audition, but I chickened out, from nerves. The teacher didn't give me a second chance. So, I could have been a jazz bass player but because of that karmic instant, I wasn't. That little bifurcation sent me on another path. This is why I am always relativizing the human will. I feel so embedded in all these forces that are beyond our comprehension.

Look at the Covid virus. It has a magical chemical key to enter our cells. Why does that virus have that little tendril made of a special fat that can hook into a specific protein receptor of your lung cell and inject its RNA into your cell to start replicating? Why that specificity? The virus is designed to be able to enter your cell.

So, what I'm trying to say is that we live in a mystery and miracle. And sometimes we try too hard to understand, instead of simply being, and developing the skills, the wisdom, to flow within this turbulent river that is life, that you don't understand. I would say we understand 0.01% of it. Quantum physics says that we understand little of reality, referring to dark matter and dark energy. I asked a physicist, what are the hidden variables of quantum physics? He said, "Well, we don't understand 99.9% of reality at all."

Is there anything else you wish to add?

What I'm trying to do in my writings and presentations, is to say that I don't know any final truths, as you have noticed. I cannot pretend to have the recipe for anything. But I believe in compassion without doubt, and generosity, reciprocity, cooperation. And that we cannot escape the natural order. Somebody wrote that nature cannot be fooled. We need a society that is culturally imbued with the ecological directives, which are not too many, as I said. And this is not deterministic. There is an infinite freedom to act while respecting these directives, which some would call nature's laws. Gregory Bateson used to say, "Ecology needs to become a normative science." In other words, a science that indicates norms to orient the development of our societies and our own individual development. Until now, the ecology you study at a university can be reductionist, mechanistic, economistic and narrow. The contrary is transdisciplinary and holistic, and acknowledges the interconnectedness and unity of all the elements which form the biosphere. Such shallow ecology retains all the premises that got us into trouble in the first place. That's why some people talk about deep ecology, like Arne Naess, the Norwegian philosopher. And even the Pope is talking about integral ecology. He's talking about domestic, economic and social ecology. Which is quite interesting, coming from the Catholic Church. He is saying that ecology has to do with many more things than the relationships of animals and plants.

How did it feel to discuss wisdom today?

It feels like something that flows in my life, in a way. It's not uncommon at all. With my children we often talk about these kinds of issues. We get into these conversations where I say that human beings are an oddity, that it is strange that we are open-ended. And one of my sons says, "No, we are just like animals, plants and bacteria, and the rest of the living world can do all the things that we can do." And I ask him, "How come humans are the only ones that can send spaceships close to the sun, and put at risk the integrity of the present biosphere?" And since he has also read Lynn Margulis, paraphrasing her, he says that when photosynthetic bacteria started emitting oxygen they also destroyed an anaerobic living world, and that our going out to explore outer space is also the impulse of bacteria, that became us and now want to explore the planetary system. It's the bacteria within us. In my family and with some friends we talk about these kinds of issues, so to talk about wisdom with you is part of a vital continuity for me. This conversation today flows somehow within the daily intellectual life that we have in our family and work environment.

Tiffany Patterson

Professor Tiffany Patterson is Associate Professor of African American and Diaspora Studies, History, and American Studies at Vanderbilt University. Her research and teaching areas include Africans in the Atlantic World in the 19th and 20th centuries, the intersections of race, gender, sexuality and class, intellectuals and political movements in empire, history in film, novels and art, and comparative slave systems. She is currently co-editor of *Palimpsest: A Journal on Women and Gender and the Black International*. She is a regular visiting faculty member in the Decoloniality Summer School in South Africa and Spain. She is the author of *Zora Neale Hurston and a History of Southern Life*. as.vanderbilt.edu/aads

What comes to mind first when you think about wisdom?

How does one achieve wisdom? Living with the travails that life brings, and making sense of both order and disorder, creates the conditions for wisdom, in the general sense. That's why children usually are unwise. They have to live and learn from life to be wise, and even then, not everyone who gets old is necessarily wise. They still have to learn from others such as parents, teachers and elders in their community who demonstrate that wisdom. Yet more is required: an ability to reflect deeply on the conditions of humanity, to question the contradictions of life, and to have a spiritual grounding that allows one to cope with both joy and tragedy. In other words, maturity leads to wisdom. Wisdom is the ability to act and think using formal and informal knowledge and unbiased judgement. Wisdom is grounded in compassion and self-knowledge.

Who have been your wisdom teachers?

When I think about wisdom on a personal level, I instantly go to my mom, who I thought was one of the wisest women that I knew. She was always very clear in her directions and clear about the consequences of failing those directions. She was also a very spiritual woman who equipped her children with a maturity to handle disappointment and struggle without becoming cynical. She also had an ethical vision and a sense of benevolence that informed her view of the world.

I've drawn on that body of wisdom from the elders in my family, and from teachers, ministers and historical leaders that I read. So part of what shapes wisdom is the cultural location that people grow up in. When living in a society shaped by racial thinking, self-knowledge and racial wisdom is an absolute requirement for survival.

Let's take what's happening in the United States right now, with this explosion of racism and police violence and the Black Lives Matter movement, that has also made its way to Europe. The policeman who murdered George Floyd in Minnesota, as Floyd pleaded for his life, was completely unwilling to see the humanity in Floyd. What is bubbling to the surface at this moment is the degree to which we remain deeply divided along racial lines. And this division is being created by elements in our society who seek to gain power along racial lines. Those who use such tactics are very unwise, because they will lead to disorder and chaos. At the heart of wisdom is the recognition of the humanity of all people. The police officer who killed Floyd completely rejected his humanity and the humanity all black people. His actions, along with similar incidents, have jeopardized the sanctity of life. It seems to me that an acceptance of the humanity of all people is an absolute component of wisdom, for without compassion for all humanity we are left with social disorder.

This point is being made over and over again in this political climate. Recently, United States Senator Tom Cotton from Arkansas stated boldly that slavery was a necessary evil. He made this claim in response to recent discussions over slavery that have emerged within the debate over removing Confederate statues. Confronting the history of slavery and the aftermath of segregation is necessary to resolve much of the racial conflict in former slave societies. The debate over taking down Confederate statues in the US as well as removing monuments to slave traders in England, and discrimination against blacks in France, has exploded onto the global stage.

Yet, that issue is so conflict-ridden that violence has marked the debate for more than a month. In June 2020, poet Caroline Randall Williams wrote an article in the *New York Times* entitled 'You Want a Confederate Monument? My Body is a Confederate Monument.' She stated: "I have rape-colored skin. My light-brown-blackness is a living testament to the rules, the practices, the causes of the Old South. If there are those who want to remember the legacy of the Confederacy, if they want monuments, well, then, my body is a monument. My skin is a monument […] I am a black, Southern woman, and of my immediate white male ancestors, all of them were rapists. My very existence is a relic of slavery and Jim Crow."

So when Senator Cotton says that slavery was a necessary evil, he ignores the impact of slavery on the lives of real human beings and the continuing discrimination and violence that shapes the fabric of American society. Cotton's unwise and inhumane attitude toward the descendants of slaves ignores not only the horror of slavery, but also ignores the violence toward black people that is part of the daily experience of black and brown people in the US and elsewhere.

Sentiments lacking a humanity toward others cannot occupy a space that includes wisdom. We can't reason with the ones who want to keep those monuments by telling them you're paying tribute to traitors, and treason is supposed to be a bad thing. These are people who tried to destroy the United States, so why are you so attached to them? There is no wisdom that those people can draw upon to defend slavery or the monuments to treason. One of our young journalists went South to talk to people about these monuments. To those he interviewed, these traitors are heroes. And the logic of what every nation feels about anyone who would betray the principles of a nation, doesn't work. You would need a much longer time to get them to understand that. And so in what's happening in this country and around the world, there is something about how you approach the human that is also critical to wisdom. If you have a built-in upbringing that makes you hold on to the irrationality that one human being is more important than another human being, that person cannot have any wisdom around the question of the human.

I was brought up as a Christian, but I was not brought up to hate Muslims. It's not in my social DNA. As a student in graduate school I was trained by Muslim and Jewish scholars. So to me, these external categories to your humanity do not take your humanity away. If you talk about wisdom, you have to talk about cultural wisdom as well as philosophical wisdom. Because obviously a philosophical wisdom is not working with Southerners who hold onto hatred toward people of color or people who are different from them in color or religion or in any other way. They have been steeped in a belief system that they don't want to let go of, that tells them they are superior, and that black or brown people, or Muslims, are somehow automatically beneath them.

Your question fascinates me because although we live in a country with very strong right-wing Christianity, they are demonstrating that they can't treat other people according to what they say they believe, coming out of the scriptures. They don't treat people of color, or people who don't practice their religion, as human beings.

I spend a lot of time grappling with the question of humanity, that we're human beings, and every human group shares the same characteristics, even if their cultural articulations are different. I didn't grow up where my Muslim teacher grew up. He grew up in West Africa, and we used to talk a lot about what the culture offered him as a young African male, especially when he began to move around. He went to school in Paris and then he came to the United States, and so on. We talk a lot about the importance of cultural wisdom. In this country, we have to start with cultural wisdom. The great writer Toni

Morrison has a concept called 'rootedness'. She's arguing that African people who were brought into slavery brought with them their spiritual and cultural knowledge. And because of that, they had a cosmology from which they drew strength by blending "the acceptance of the supernatural and a profound rootedness in the real world." They drew wisdom from their cultural moorings. She discusses this in her 1984 essay, 'Rootedness: The Ancestor as Foundation.'

They could believe in practical things, but they also believed in spiritual things. And throughout that 400-year period of slavery, they drew on that fountain of knowledge and it was not a contradiction. We have white people in this country who berate Haitians, for example, because they practice their traditional spiritual beliefs, which come from Africa. But those same people in Brazil, for example, will go to a Candomblé ceremony at night and worship their traditional gods. And the following morning they're in the Catholic church with the priests. And it's not a contradiction. I've seen that in every country that I've been in; in Cuba, in Jamaica, in all of those places, because they are drawing on a fountain of knowledge that is part of their cultural strength.

So wisdom is not inborn. I think it's learned in the spiritual and cultural spaces, it's learned in the family structure. As I've gotten older—and I can legitimately call myself an elder now—I think about all the things now, more than ever, that I learned from my family. I have a very large extended family. I've traced my ancestors back to the 18th century. I hope I can go back further. At family gatherings, which we have every couple of years, I am astounded when I meet relatives for the first time, and after talking for a while, we're talking about the same thing, no matter the educational level, no matter the region of the country we come from. We're always finding new ones and there's two or three generations removed from me who are at the forefront. I'm always astounded by that. So I think that's why I read so much in philosophy as well as in religion, because the human species always occupied those two spaces.

Looking back on your life, what is the wisest thing you ever did?

It's interesting you should ask that question because I've been thinking about writing down my biography as part of another research project. When my parents left the South and went north, we lived in a segregated, working-class community across the street from Michael Jackson's family. Everybody in that neighborhood worked in the steel mills in Northern Indiana except for two ministers and their families. And when I moved into whiter spaces, there was information there I didn't understand. There were reactions to me as an African American. And it took a long time for me to figure out where that came from. I'm a child of the 60s, so I was well aware of the protests around race, because we lived back and forth between the South and the North. But when I experienced it on a personal level, it threw me.

I'll share a formative experience around this. I had to work my way through my degrees, so it took longer and I always had a job. And one of my jobs, when I was about 20 years old, was in the office of the Lieutenant Governor of Indiana. And I had a conversation one day with a young white girl about abortion, which was a hot issue in the United States at the time; it was before Roe v. Wade. And she was trying to convince me that abortions were a sin, and if you were a Christian you couldn't support abortion. And I kept arguing from my own experience that I did not believe that a fetus is a human being. Because the schools were segregated, my mom found the money to put us in a Catholic school. And we went on a trip to the Science Museum in Chicago. They have an exhibit with every stage of the development of a child, from fetus to full term, in formaldehyde jars. I had seen that exhibit many times. And so when I talked with her, I was being very rational. I had learned that during the first three months, the fetus could not survive outside the womb. (My views are far more complicated today than they were then). She became very angry that I did not agree with her, and she finally yelled at me, "You are a nigger anyway." Before I knew it, I had my hands around her neck. A colleague saw the altercation and calmed the situation. It blew me away. It was my first direct contact with racism at that level. I was in my third year of college, and her response simply made no sense.

I went to my office and when I got the call that the director wanted to talk to me, I went, as I was taught to never run away from a problem. But I was convinced I had lost my job. So I walked into the office. He was a Southerner from Kentucky. And he said, "What happened?" I said, "She called me a nigger, and nobody calls me that." I was shaking with anger. He said, "Okay. Calm down." And we had a conversation. And finally he said, "Take the afternoon off. Go home and relax, and come back tomorrow." And it was never spoken of again. I still remember the calmness of this white Southerner dealing with that incident in the context of a political office. He wisely understood that the young lady had been out of line. And my reaction was not a calm one, but I was 20 years old. That was the first direct confrontation I've had with that kind of racism and I've never forgotten it. It motivated me to think about how this young woman came to think that way. I was a college student and she was not, so there was a class difference between us, but her fallback position was to attack the essence of my identity and situate me beneath her.

So that has been at the heart of my teaching for all these years. And especially in teaching about subjects like race, slavery, civil rights and so on. This is a struggle of not just politics, but of the essence of humanity. But getting that across to people is very difficult. If someone believes that blacks are a separate species, then even if they see someone who is in all other respects the same as they are, they see a monster. I don't know whether or not, if you sit those people down and talk to them long enough, you can get them to see how irrational that position is, and how criminal it is, and how unwise it is.

And at the heart of becoming wise, I think, we have to unpack wisdom the same way we have to unpack racism. You cannot just tell people racism is wrong. You have to unpack it for them. You have to break it up and show them how it's rooted in power. It's rooted in fear. It is rooted in a false science that racists repeat over and over again.

Racism for example, takes our humanity away in the hands of

other people. I watched George Floyd be murdered on television. I watched that police officer keep his knee on that man's neck, even though Floyd said 34 times, "I can't breathe." One of the officers had a tape where he showed that he did try to get him to take his knee off his neck and turn him over on his back. And the officer kneeling on Floyd's neck refused.

And now that things have calmed down a bit, more information has come out. The other three officers had only been on the job for four days. And the officer with his knee on Floyd's neck was their training officer. So he had authority, and they didn't have the self-confidence or the wisdom to say, "I'll risk my job before I let you kill this man." If it had been me, just like the 14-year-old girl that filmed it, I would have said "Get off his neck!" I am sure they wish they had now. But I'm older. So one thing that is clear is that wisdom is something you have to grow into.

Watching that murder, my first response was extreme anger. And deep hurt, seeing George Floyd saying repeatedly, "I can't breathe." For eight minutes and 46 seconds, Chauvin, the police officer, kept his knee on Floyd's neck as the life slowly left his body. My concern is to understand how a person can simply watch the life drain from a man's body and continue kneeling on his neck until he is dead. This level of inhumanity is at the heart of racism in the United States.

One of the things we understand about racism is that white men feel empowered as men when they kill a black person. It's one of the peculiar pieces of American culture that Americans don't want to face. About six months ago we had a case here involving a skinny little 15-year-old kid. His mother moved out to a white neighborhood and he didn't know the area. Walking to his new school one day, he got lost. He walked up to someone's home to ask for directions. After knocking on the door, a white woman came down the steps and saw this black kid at the door. In her mind he was there to rob her, so she called her husband, who came out with a rifle. When the kid saw the rifle, he started to run. But the man opened the door and fired at the kid and tried to kill him. He missed. The wife actually tried to convince the world that he was a big black man. The kid was about five-five and skinny. He didn't weigh 120 pounds. Now in that case, fortunately, the husband was convicted of attempted murder and went to prison. Thirty years ago, he wouldn't have gone to prison. The system would have justified her fear.

If I had these people sitting in the room at my age now, who did that, I could talk to them and talk through their madness. But they're absolutely mad around race. And it's coming out, as the whole world has been seeing. Here we are in this moment where the Black Lives Matter movement has brought these issues to the surface. And as I tried to explain to my students before we had to quarantine, what they have to look at is how progress happens. We're still fighting the same old fears around race, but progress has happened. If you look at the marches for Black Lives Matter, there were almost as many non-black people out there as there were black people. Younger people, two generations removed from me, young white teenagers, young black teenagers, Latinos, Jews, Muslims, they're all engaged and see that this is an issue for this century.

Now let me circle back to the question of wisdom. No matter how angry I still become, because I've spent my life writing, reading and teaching these materials, I maintain a conversation with myself on how I treat people that I have every reason to hate. And part of how I am able to do that is to recognize that they're caught up in a system. And this is where wisdom comes in. You can't scream at every insult. You can't respond to every slight, no matter how you see it, because most of the time you need to stop and consider the other ways you can explain what happened, other than it being just about race. In other words, I don't see every slight as proof positive that the person is racist or sexist or any of that. But it took a long time for me to get to that place. To have a conversation now is much easier for me than it would have been 40 years ago.

My physical therapist is a young, white man. He and I had a long conversation recently, after we finished a therapy session on my knee. He said something, and I have learned to wisely listen to what he has to say, and not launch into a frontal attack, telling him "No, that's not right. This is the way you have to think about it." I let him talk. He kept saying, "I hope the Black Lives Matter movement doesn't get so intense that somebody who says something that's wrong is instantly jumped on." And I said, "I think you're right." But I'm old enough to allow that to happen. So when my students say things, I have the ability to process them quickly, so that my response does not overwhelm someone who is searching for answers. I take time to center the other person's humanity. I have taught long enough now to know when someone is trying to understand, even if they do not know how to frame the questions, or if they do not have all the information they need. It takes skill to hear between the lines and to understand where each individual is located in relation to racial matters. For example if they are southern, rural or wealthy, they may not have had access to racial issues on the ground, and therefore their statements or questions may seem naïve. But more often than not they are simply inexperienced or searching for answers.

I have a requirement in my classes: every person must be listened to. Because if you cut people off, you lose an opportunity to persuade. This comes with age and experience too, but I want to provide a space for my students to put their fears on the table. Or their beliefs, for that matter. If you're going to teach about race, you must have more than statistics. You have to understand that you're engaging human beings. At the heart of racial discrimination is an inability to see other people as part of the human species, with all their gifts and shortcomings. Now it took a long time for me to develop that human approach in my teaching; I am not afraid now of any question that comes at me, no matter how right or wrong the person may be. I take time to listen.

I'm impressed with the young people all over the world, actually, because they've taken it to the next step. But they will have to develop the understanding that how you navigate that complexity is vital when you're engaging people with ideas that may in fact trample on your identity or your culture. But it takes an enormous amount of wisdom to maintain that in a confrontation.

What has been the toughest lesson you have learned?

When I was young, I thought of university as a place where there was a free-flowing level of ideas, and your ideas would be respected. And that much of what I saw in the world will not operate as much in that space. I was absolutely wrong. It was a naïve assumption anyway, but it was still different for me as a young black woman. I worked very hard to write a book on Zora Neale Hurston, who was a famous writer and an incredible personality. She was an anthropologist and a literary artist, and she worked among the poorest of the poor in Florida in the 1930s. She had such respect for black culture. She collected the folklore, she studied the religion. She went to the Caribbean to study in Haiti and Jamaica, because she was convinced that there was a cultural connection between black people around the world. So when I was writing as a historian, I wasn't aware that there were such strict limits on what white historians thought was legitimate, but I did it anyway. Many traditional historians were very critical of my arguments, though not all were. For one thing, I was making arguments about what constitutes the nature of evidence.

These older, white historians thought evidence was only in institutional records, such as census data, court documents and letters. But Hurston was working among a group of people who had no education. These were turpentine workers. When slavery ended in the United States, turpentine and lumber became two of the biggest industries across the Atlantic world; not just here, but in Latin America, in Europe and so on. Woods like mahogany were used to make fine furniture that sits in Queen Elizabeth's home today. And these workers were one step removed from slavery, if that. These industries practiced debt peonage, which was illegal. They were put into these camps for petty crimes and forced to work for debts that were never paid off. The police departments would pay the fine, and then sell the fine to a company and the men were forced to work for very little money. This went on from the end of slavery in the 19th century till the mid-20th century, before World War II. And these are the people she was working with. But they were also talented artists. They laid the foundation for blues music. She found material to write novels on, from their experiences. But they're not in the institutional records, except for police records. And I knew there was more to it than that. So I drew on folklore. I drew on the cultural material that Hurston had found. How dare I suggest that these are legitimate historical documents? They said I didn't read census data, but I did. I read 30 years of census data. Some of them are in the census, some of them are not. I took the interdisciplinary approach through the literary work, the poetry, everything. I think, as you've forced me to talk about it, that by that time I had become wise enough to know that I was never going to convince them. Yet one American historian did say, "You made your point. You proved it. Don't ever forget that." And because I had that kind of support, it helped contain the anger.

I am able to have patience. I think you can't be a wise person if you don't have patience, because you fly off the handle, you'll act irrationally. And you can't be a wise parent if you slap your child every time they make the mistake. I learned that from my mother. She was very judicious. She was Southern. She was old school. Because a child has to make mistakes. A child has to learn lessons. It's only when they do things that may harm them that they learn. That learning can turn into wisdom in time.

To me, I have grown in wisdom in the midst of struggle. I don't think you can be wise if you don't have any struggle in this life. You can't learn if everything is given to you or everything comes easy. My mother used to say that and I didn't understand what she meant by it. If everything is easy for you, then you act foolish.

When the civil rights movement started, I remember hearing Dr. King say that you have to think through every decision; you have to consider the consequences. And also, if my Christian principles have any value, I have to be able to do something for somebody else. And so, wisdom is not something you're born with. It's something you learn from living.

Wisdom also doesn't come quickly. You have to make mistakes and you have to take the right lesson from those mistakes. In my early work I took a lot of criticism for stepping outside of the canon. But my sister—who is very wise—and some of my former students said, "You are where you're supposed to be."

Staying in the university was a wise thing for me because I love to teach. I like my department. We're struggling right now in the midst of the pandemic. Are we going to open on time in the fall? Most of us are going to be teaching virtually. And I hate that. I like to be a close to my students, but you do what you have to do. And that's what a wise person does.

In the world today, where do you see wisdom, and its lack, being demonstrated?

We're in the midst of the most unwise presidency that we've ever had. Donald Trump is a fool and he's dangerous. His niece Mary Trump, who holds a PhD in clinical psychology, has today published a book about how crazy he is. He has no wisdom or empathy for all the people dying from the Covid virus. He seems to think that this is a TV show. If there is an example of someone who doesn't understand wisdom at all, it is the president of the United States. It's dangerous for him to be in that position of power.

Wisdom has to be learned through experience. That's what W. E. B. Du Bois meant when he said that wisdom comes to you in old age, it doesn't come right away. And that is not to say there aren't young people who make wise decisions, but the true depth of wisdom about living has to come with experience. And not everyone has it. In this country we're struggling with people who don't believe the virus can get them. They're angry about wearing masks. They're angry about closing down businesses and suffering for a while. Personally, nobody had to tell me twice to put a mask on. Four of my relatives have had Covid-19. Now my niece has it. I don't have any children so the closest thing to me are my nieces and nephews. And so I'm calling home to Chicago every day because my niece is trying to survive Covid-19, and her daughter who's only 18 years old is terrified that she is going to lose her mom.

So when you come down to the simplest thing, people are so confused here. And part of this is about racism too. They're white. They think they can do whatever they want to do, and they'll be fine. But now we're spiking again, while Europe has got it under control, as have some other countries.

I would say Governor Cuomo in New York has acted wisely. He ignored Trump and took control of the state and did everything that the scientists said to do in terms of containing the virus. Just today the governor of California had to close down the state again, because he reopened too soon.

So I see it in the pandemic a lot, with the scientists, like Dr. Fauci, who Trump is trying to attack right now. I see it in the political arena. You don't always see it there, but there are good people coming to the forefront. I see it in the young people that they're interviewing a lot now, who are part of Black Lives Matter. The journalists, various other professions, some just college students, are beginning to grapple with, in a sense human rights, in the way that generation did in the 50s and 60s with Dr. King, Malcolm X and others.

This pandemic has brought out how many wonderful black women have grown up since the civil rights movement and are now leaders, such as the mayor of Atlanta, Keisha Lance Bottoms. She and her husband have been diagnosed with Covid-19, but she's still on television doing her job. There's Stacey Abrams, another woman from Georgia who ran for governor and lost. She's become a leader on voting rights. And she speaks with such depth of understanding.

I see it in a place I didn't expect to see it: among black athletes. They have stepped up to the plate in important ways. Michael Jordan, through his Jordan Brand company, has pledged $100 million to racial equality organizations over the next decade. They're saying, 'I'll never spend all this money, but the kids need help. Our poor people need help.' So I think a crisis brings out the best and the worst in us at the same time.

Wisdom is a philosophical concept at one level, but at another level it is about practical living. We've been talking for a long time about gun violence in this country. I am hopeful that, if we can defeat Trump, we can make progress on gun control. In February a young black man named Ahmaud Arbery was shot dead while jogging in Georgia. A month later a young black woman named Breonna Taylor was shot dead in her home in Louisville by police who entered with a no-knock warrant. So I hope we get the police under control, as well as guns.

Unlike some of the critics, I am not anti-police. I'm anti-untrained, rogue, racist police. Because they don't think before they move. And the police force does not do the testing that they need to do before they put a gun in somebody's hand.

I've seen countries other than the United States making good decisions on dealing with Covid. Some European countries have done well. And South Korea. They brought it down because they put the humanity of their population ahead of everything else.

How do you apply wisdom to the care of your mind, body and soul?

I'm doing that at the moment. I don't talk often about it, but I have four areas of compromised immunity. I am struggling with my second bout of cancer. And at my age, which often happens, I had to have an operation on my knee. So when Covid came, I self-isolated. We don't go out very much. I'm in a very small department of African American and Diaspora Studies, but we talk to each other on Zoom. We haven't risked seeing each other. We haven't risked being out very much. I have plenty to do, but I stay in this house to protect first of all my husband and I. And to make sure I don't get an asymptomatic disease that I may give to somebody else. Our church is on lockdown. And as much as it's lacking in some of the things that we like, I put up with it.

I don't expect to go anywhere at Christmas. Because if this comes back around here, I cannot afford to be around my relatives and either get the disease or carry it with me. The wise thing to do is to protect yourself and others. So in this crisis, I am seeing a great lack of wisdom, where people are so selfish. They think they don't have to wear a mask. And we've had these images of packed beaches in Florida. And now their cases are spiking. So you have to apply wisdom to how you treat other people, because I do believe it comes back on you.

I meditate. I pray. I don't proselytize, but I do believe that there is something in the world bigger than me. You can call it God, or intelligence, or whatever you want.

In spite of my health struggles, my doctor was very clear. He wants me to keep working. He said that his patients who stop working don't do as well. When you have something to do, you stay healthier. And I have managed very well. And I believe I'm blessed, because I will listen to somebody about the best way to handle any dilemma. I certainly am not the only one that has this dilemma. A couple of days ago, Kelly Preston, the wife of John Travolta, died of breast cancer. In my case I don't obsess about it. I just live with it.

How do you ultimately define wisdom?

Wisdom is taking positive life lessons, as well as negative lessons, and learning from them. I have taken the negative lessons and processed them over time. It takes time to be wise, and it takes living to be wise, and you learn almost more from your mistakes. That's a better source of wisdom. Your successes can lead you into focusing too much on how wonderful you are. But your mistakes will show you the pitfalls in life. And if you take the right lessons from your mistakes, your future endeavors are far more successful.

Finally, wisdom is also accepting the positives that your life has given you, and not wanting more than it has given you. That's a big one for me. I'm not a Pulitzer Prize-winning scholar, and it doesn't matter. I know I'm a fabulous teacher because my students keep telling me so. A number of my students have told me that I was the most important experience of their academic life. If you do your job right, you should take pride in the fact that others benefit from it. If you're obsessed with yourself, you won't make wise decisions because you'll hurt people. But if you see that the work you do, whatever it is, is benefiting other people, that's the ultimate outcome of a wisely-lived life.

How can each of us develop wisdom?

It's not wise to judge people by their worst act. You judge them by their best act. Because otherwise you cut yourself off from human resources that are valuable. No person is perfect. I certainly have made my share of mistakes. And if you're smart, you own them. You don't blame everybody else for the mistakes you make, you own it. And then you go from there. And you don't ever get everything you want, or you think you want.

How did it feel to discuss wisdom today?

What I feel now is I would like to read about wisdom. I'd like to reflect on it some more. It may sound trite, but I do believe a wisely-led life is one where you are not always at the center of every experience. And by that I mean: so many people don't care about their engagement with other people. And that's something I have learned. I'm old enough to really think about that. There are people in the university who are some of the most self-centered, egotistical people. You would not believe it, with all their education, but they are. And I never want to be like that. So I think reflection upon yourself and the world we live in is absolutely at the center of a wise person. So you've made me think about things I hadn't thought about lately.

Elisabet Sahtouris

Elisabet Sahtouris, PhD is an internationally known evolution biologist and futurist, author and worldwide speaker teaching Living Economies, current human evolution, and How to Navigate our Perfect Storm of Crises. After a post-doctoral fellowship at the American Museum of Natural History, she taught at MIT and the University of Massachusetts and contributed to the *Horizon* TV series. She is a fellow of the World Business Academy with an honorary Chair in Living Economies, and Advisor to Ethical Markets and other organizations. Dr. Sahtouris is a co-founder of the Worldwide Indigenous Science Network and has convened international symposia on Foundations of Global Sciences in Japan and Malaysia. She has appeared in many films and is currently a Professor of Business at Chaminade University in Honolulu. Her books include *EarthDance: LivingSystems in Evolution*, *A Walk Through Time: From Stardust to Us*, *Biology Revisioned* (w. Willis Harman) and *Gaia's Dance*. sahtouris.com

What comes to mind first when you think about wisdom?

What comes to my mind first is philosophy—a Greek word, philos-sophia, meaning lover of wisdom. It was the ancient Greek word for natural science, expressing the quest of science to be the search for guidance in human affairs through the study of nature, which is, of course, all there is to study. That search for wisdom by studying nature was actually my own intention in becoming a biologist.

In my work as an evolution biologist, I identified a pattern, a repeating cycle of maturation, by looking at evolution from the very first bacteria, up through the evolution of single cells and then multi-celled creatures. Reaching each new stage seemed a kind of maturation following a youthful phase, because being acquisitive and competitive was always followed by mature cooperation. New species take all the space and resources they can get, reproducing as fast as possible, duking it out with each other, until that competition gets very energy-expensive and small trial attempts at cooperation turn out to be more effective and efficient. Eventually they go into the mature cooperative phase. This cycle, from a competitive to a cooperative phase, mirrors that which we humans go through individually—a feisty adolescence followed by becoming a cooperative member of our community.

We were all so immersed in the Darwinian theory that we did not see that it only described the youthful, competitive phase; we simply did not see beyond it. Early capitalist entrepreneurs and economists promoted the Darwinian model because it suited their values, goals and methods perfectly: competition, may the best man win, play king of the hill. So we were not prepared for its eventual unsustainability. Had we studied nature more completely, as we now do, we would have gained the wisdom to see why we must transform our economy into a sustainable, cooperative one.

Our capitalist growth economy sees nature as subservient, as a collection of resources to be exploited for human ends. And so we keep turning nature into stuff for human use, whether it's the fossil fuels that run the machines or digging up the minerals to make the machines themselves, making chemicals to grow food while killing off living soils, manufacturing all of the consumer goods, up to plastics and all the rest of it.

What if, instead of making our ecological systems subservient to our economy, we invert that, fitting our economy into nature's ecology in ways that don't destroy it, and that are in harmony with it? The 'eco' in the words economy and ecology comes from the word for household in Greek, which is oikos, pronounced 'eekos'. So, seeing the economy as our collective household and fitting it into ecology as nature's household, you get what I call the ecosophy, the wise society.

So, again, if we let nature guide us, we gain wisdom ourselves.

Do you recall the first time you witnessed wisdom in action?

In retrospect, the first wisdom I experienced was during childhood. I was born in Athens, New York during The Great Depression that began in 1929 and lasted into my childhood. What I experienced was grownups all taking care of each other in my extended rural neighborhood of Hudson Valley farms in New York State. The wisdom of that community was to feed each other before going to profitable markets. Shopping was getting into my father's Model T truck on weekends and driving from farm to farm, loaded up with vegetables my mother had grown. One farm had chickens and eggs, another had one cow tagged for our family, with milk so rich that we made butter just by shaking the cream in glass jars. The next farm had fruits, an apple cider press from which we filled our glass jugs, and 'Uncle Gus' the beekeeper, who we watched harvesting our honey with bees all over him, calmed by the smoke from his pipe. As there were no farm chemicals yet, everything was organic and healthy. Every family fed all the others. That was real community—indeed a very wise society in a situation where money was short and wartime food rationing severe.

Who is the wisest person you know, and why?

I'd have to put the Dalai Lama right up there in terms of people I've met personally and interacted with. He spends hours a day watching TV news, reading newspapers and otherwise informing himself about current events, so he knows a great deal about what's going on in the world, and has the wisdom to discern what's happening without judgment. I met him because he invites groups of people, including professionals from all disciplines, for conversations that last up to a week in his home base of Dharamsala, India, or elsewhere. He turns these groups of people, experts in their fields, into ad hoc think tanks. When we were with him, he quizzed us endlessly and was a great listener as well as sharing his own wisdom. I was fortunate indeed to participate in two such groups.

Occasionally His Holiness would say something that seemed almost a definition of wisdom, such as in expressing the importance of "critical thinking, followed by action." He meant this in a context both political and spiritual. Critical thinking happens as you digest information about what's going on, distilling that and asking yourself: So what do I do about it? How do I work toward a better world? What kind of action can I take? It isn't just about sitting in your spiritual cave meditating, it's about being in the real word, thinking critically and responding with action.

He also teaches forgiveness and has forgiven his enemies. Forgiveness heals the person who forgives, since anger or hatred harms only you, not your enemy. If you harbor a real grudge against someone for something they've done to you, once you forgive them, you are liberated.

Other wise people I've known have passed on. One was Leon Shenandoah, the Haudenosaunee Tadadaho (Iroquois chief of chiefs). I also know his successor, Oren Lyons, who was, like myself, a student at Syracuse University in the early 50s. Their people founded the confederacy of Six Nations, which the French called the Iroquois Indians of the New World—new only to the Europeans, of course. I'm passionately interested in this Haudenosaunee culture. Benjamin Franklin spent a lot of time with these Native Americans, who were living under a Great Law of Peace that united six warring nations to create the only existing democratic government in the world. Unfortunately, the only thing Franklin got across to his fellow founding fathers was their separation and balance of powers, which was adopted in the US Constitution. Left out were the roles of women, children, nature and seven future generations! If a man wanted to declare war in the Haudenosaunee culture, he had to put on a skirt and carry a corn grinding bowl into the parliament, to remind the people of what war would do to the women, the children and the food supply. So they had no wars for many centuries. If the founding fathers had actually emulated this wisdom culture's law, the USA might well be thriving today, rather than becoming a failed state.

Here in Hawai'i I had the good fortune of joining the MBA program faculty at Chaminade University as a professor in residence. I work with the dean and two Native Hawai'ian elders in designing four new MBA courses, which are rooted in Native Hawai'ian values and the living economies practiced here traditionally before capitalism was brought to these islands. It was a wonderful design year, interacting with Native Hawai'ian on how to prepare business people for the world of the future; how our economics must be revised to take care of each other in ways rooted in the Hawai'ian values of caring and sharing, of Aloha. More native wisdom!

In many long meetings with indigenous people over the years, I learned much about wisdom. When you sit through the night until you reach harmony on matters—not always agreement, but harmony—you find that the meeting does not end until individuals learn to give a little, to compromise, to negotiate between individual and community interests until a workable balance emerges. Quaker meetings result in similarly harmonious wisdom.

This kind of wisdom is also evident in your body. Every cell has to negotiate with the organ it is part of, and that organ with its organ system, and that organ system with the whole body. This constant negotiation goes on 24/7 at all these holarchic (embedded) levels of the body, from microscopic to macroscopic. That concept of holarchy extends beyond the body to family, community and ecosystem, all the way up to the planet, and to the whole universe. Nature is holarchically embedded all the way. A wise Mexika Indian elder named Xelonem once told me, "Anyone who knows how to run a household knows how to run a world." This going back and forth between levels of holarchy is common to many ancient and indigenous cultures. It is reflected in the well-known perennial philosophy's "As above, so below." To me as an evolution biologist it means that the same features or principles of healthy living systems repeat at all levels.

Wisdom traditions have always been about caring and sharing within Oneness. It's coming into mainstream culture at last, and is the only thing that can save us—that old, old wisdom of balancing. Nature is profoundly conservative with things that work, and endlessly creative about changing what does not! It is an ongoing division of labor, not an adversarial choice of doing one or the other by a partisan vote every few years. Until we grok this wisdom, our democracy will not be wise and cannot even be sustainable, much less thrive.

Looking back on your life, what is the wisest thing you ever did?

The wisest thing I ever did was take a 13-year midlife retirement in Greece, though I didn't know that was what it would turn out to be. When my youngest son graduated high school, I was suffering from science being too constraining—like a suit too tight for me, or perhaps like being a caterpillar in a chrysalis, needing to break out somehow from what I had been taught in becoming a credentialed scientist. I felt crippled by the foundational beliefs and rules of science. It wasn't giving me an adequate picture of evolution or anything else in my reality. I had to break free.

I was also suffering from what I called 'thing glut.' I had raised two kids, mostly as a single mom, leaving me with a big house filled with stuff—canoe, bikes, books, tent and lots of other stuff accumulated over the years. And I wanted out of that, too. My daughter was living away from home as she completed her medical internship, and my son was graduating from high school, so I announced I was going to Greece with the intent of writing a novel to explain the human condition to myself, as science just wasn't answering my big questions about life and the universe.

I ended up staying on Greek islands for 13 years, during which my son joined me there. And I married a fisherman with only childhood schooling, yet he was uniquely wise and compassionate. In those years I wrote up a storm: three novels, a huge stack of essays on many aspects of science as I reconstructed it for myself, and my first book on evolution.

My journey back to science began while combing the woods for wild mushrooms or greens one day. A walking stick insect fell on my arm from a tree, and I burst into tears as I hadn't seen one since I was a child in the Hudson Valley forest. Suddenly I knew I still wanted to know how nature works. So I walked home and started over to tell the story of evolution from scratch, first as a story for kids, to see how the very basics could be said simply. I began to correspond with scientists around the world by post and they sent me books and articles.

The Gaia hypothesis, developed by James Lovelock and Lynn Margulis, especially intrigued me, and in the late 1980s, Teddy Goldsmith invited me to his series of Gaia conferences in Cornwall, England. Teddy became a good friend. He was both a 'wise guy' and a truly wise man. The first time I met him he was jumping up and down like a big walrus, saying with passion, "First decent thing my brother Jimmy has ever done! He crashed the Wall Street stock market!" His brother James was at that time one of the richest men in the world and lived in Paris. Teddy was born with a golden spoon in his mouth, but he was a self-taught scientist who figured out things like the fact that entropy was not running down either the universe or our planet—that entropy was balanced by centropy. Nassim Haramein later called it syntropy, the point being that the universe was not running down; that the forces of disintegration were balanced by forces of integration.

Another wise person, Eric Jantsch, had written *The Self-Organizing Universe*. It's an amazing book on how nature self organizes. From the work of Jim, Lynn and Eric, I learned a great deal, and Jim actually came to visit me in Greece, for a delicious week of deep conversations. Trained as an engineer, he had developed a cybernetic model of life and non-life interacting on the planet, which he also said was alive. I argued that our Earth must either be alive or not, that you can't have part of it being alive and part of it not being alive. Those wonderful talks made for a blessed time.

Coming back to the US in 1991, Simon & Schuster had already

published my first book, naming it *Gaia: The Human Journey from Chaos to Cosmos,* which upset me as Gaia is not a human journey. Eventually I expanded and republished it as *EarthDance: Living Systems in Evolution.* My more recent one, *Gaia's Dance*, is a shorter, more storytelling book, intended especially for young people.

In California in the late 90s, I co-authored a conversational book with Willis Harman, called *Biology Revisioned*, which asks what might result if we made consciousness primary in science, rather than a late emerging product of material evolution. That one brought my cosmology in, raising further questions about the fundamental worldview of science. Another book, *A Walk Through Time: from Stardust to Us*, is based on a walk-through exhibit by that name, created by Sid Liebes as a Hewlett-Packard staff member, and with a foreword by Brian Swimme.

The Seth books of Jane Roberts had initiated me into more consciousness-based cosmologies before my Greek sojourn, along with books by the likes of Blavatsky, Gurdjieff, Hazrat Inayat Khan, Itzhak Bentov, Alan Watts, Gregory Bateson, Marilyn Ferguson and Fritjof Capra. I count as wise people a number of other authors, especially J. Allen Boone, whom I call my guru. He was known as the Saint Francis of Hollywood, and in his first book, *Kinship with All Life*, he tells how Strongheart, the first movie star dog in Hollywood, taught him direct transmission of knowledge and information—what I came to call 'communion' rather than communication; the fundamental means by which all nature exchanges information.

I seek out people in my culture who have tapped into this ability to commune with nature, with animals and plants—people who have recognized the intelligence of and kinship with everything in the natural world. I was once in a rainforest with a beautiful long-haired Amazon Indian being naïve enough to ask, "Can you teach me to talk to the plants and animals?" And he said, "They've been in conversation as long as the forest has been here. Can you hear it? Shut up and listen." More wisdom gleaned along my path.

What is the hardest-won wisdom that you have?

Probably discernment without judgment. I'm an information hound, a cosmic snoop. I dig into everything; always wanting to know what's going on. I've looked into the cosmologies and ways of different cultures, trying to discern what's going on in our world. And when you're serious and willing to look into everything, you soon find the dark side of human culture that has not been obvious, going down some very deep rabbit holes. The internet, now the source of so much we encounter in life, is rife with dark stories. I work hard at discerning what fits with other puzzle pieces in my belief system, what rings true, dealing with the emotions of having been deceived about how things really are, and the rising need to expose these things, to get others roused by them.

So the wisdom I work at is becoming nonjudgmental—to hold information and see it with equanimity as part of a systemic pattern rather than condemning particular perpetrators. Whether the evils abroad in our world are visible or hidden or both, as in racism, it is never just about bad people or bad aliens we must take out to get rid of the problem. I remind myself over and over that we cannot fight darkness by returning hate or violence, but only by turning on the light. Wise people know better than to waste energy on judgment that leads to further violence. They find ways to speak truth to power and change behavior in peaceful ways.

In the 60s I was living in Canada where I met a Bengali political activist and poet who had escaped from India. I was outraged, in anguish and anger, over napalmed kids in the ongoing Vietnam war and, while my older brother was becoming a US Marine colonel in that war, I was leading antiwar demonstrations. As the poet and I became close, he wrote poems to me, and one of his lines has stayed with me ever since. Translated into English, it is: 'Somewhere the tears and the agony are stored into the chest of thunder.' It conveyed the transmutable energy of angry anguish. It urged me in his gentle way to transmute the energy of my outrage into positive action.

So it's not about becoming all sweetness and light. Anger can be appropriate and motivational. So can be sorrow, grief at the death of loved ones, of so many species, of tortured plants and animals in our food supply. We desperately need big changes in how we treat each other and all nature. Climate change threatens us all, as do pandemics and immune system disorders in our hi-tech world. Can we, who so want a better world, avoid dissipating our anguish in blame by letting it fuel us collectively into thunderous but peaceful action?

In the world today, where do you see wisdom, and its lack, being demonstrated?

To answer that question, I need to speak first of cosmologies and worldviews. Most humans throughout history were given their worldviews by unquestioned authorities; now it is incumbent on each of us to develop our own worldviews. In a world as large and complex as we live in today, I believe wisdom depends on a very broad and inclusive worldview, as well as the critical thinking urged by the Dalai Lama.

Imagine, for example, an inclusive worldview of the whole universe as a piano keyboard, which represents vibrations arranged from low keys representing matter, to a mid-range representing energy and the fast vibrations of the high keys as mind/spirit/consciousness. Quantum physics and Eastern cosmologies, including Vedic and Taoist, all agree that the universe is made up of vibrations. So, let us use the metaphor of an infinitely long keyboard that maps the whole range of matter, energy, mind, spirit, consciousness going from low keys to high.

Western science, which gives us the 'official' worldview of secular societies, derives its universe by seeing it from the low vibrations of matter, using material instruments, including telescopes and microscopes, to detect and measure (quantify) its reality. When electromagnetic energy could be measured, it came into western scientific reality. Einstein then showed the equivalence of matter and energy; i.e. that you can, metaphorically, transpose the music up and down that range, all of it ultimately vibrations. But western science cannot get further up the keyboard because of its dependence on material instruments which cannot measure the vast human experience of non-material vibrations as reality. Thus mind, spirit and consciousness remain mysterious to western science.

All the other sciences in the world—indigenous sciences and ancient Vedic, Taoist, Greek, Islamic—start at the high end of the keyboard with a cosmic worldview of a living consciousness or spirit, and slow down the high frequency waves to get electromagnetic energy and eventually matter. Once we see matter, energy and spirit as fundamentally the same 'stuff' at different vibrational frequencies, we see them as perceptually different ranges of the keyboard (think ice, water and steam or vapor all being H_2O at different temperatures). This simple model represented as a keyboard, gives us one universe in which science and spirit are not separated.

What you now can see is how scientific concepts of the universe depend on which end of the keyboard a particular science views it from. To wit, the West (left end when facing keyboard, just as when we face geographical maps) claims that matter gives rise to consciousness, while the East claims that consciousness gives rise to matter. Opposite statements of belief, which are worldviews, about the same universe!

My proposal is to establish a Global Consortium of Sciences that appreciate and respect each other's different perspectives on the same universe as they exert 'checks and balances' on each other. Toward that end I held international symposia on the foundations of sciences, in which I had Western, Vedic and Islamic scientists write out their fundamental assumptions and distil them into a final list of around ten most basic ones. Thus we formalized the assumptions of these three sciences. Taoist and indigenous sciences are next on this agenda.

Western quantum physicists actually became aware of being stuck trying to get up the keyboard, and turned to ancient eastern sciences for their personal worldviews and their scientific advances. That in turn gave rise to what became widely known as a new paradigm shift, slowly completing from within western science itself, toward a more unified and truly global worldview.

The keyboard model can be applied to building tolerance and effecting conflict resolution—both keys to wisdom—in many human situations and experiences. Consider for example the current Covid pandemic. Looking at it from the low end of the keyboard, we see the pandemic as chasing a newly detected (perhaps not actually new) virus. Where did it come from? How does it spread? How can it be tested for? What pharmaceuticals will cure it and what vaccines will prevent it? Vaccines, hospitals, masks, respirators, people sheltered in place, airplanes grounded, businesses locked—all material aspects of the pandemic. Emotions of fear, grief and anguish move us into the energy range.

But what if you go to the other end and ask what it might look like from a higher perspective? What if this was a soul agreement among a myriad souls seeing that we are failing to change the human world as needed in a perfect storm of extinction-threatening crises? Might our souls have searched for a more dramatic way to move humanity into averting total disaster?

Might our souls have seen that the only thing everyone would respond to quickly was an unprecedented health threat to every individual and all of us collectively—a mysterious, unstoppable disease with no cure, lurking everywhere? We've given our Earth a fever; what if we experienced that fever or the mortal threat of it ourselves? Well, we actually locked ourselves up and the global economy was shut down overnight for just such a disease. Reducing the burning of fossil fuels dramatically cleared the skies in a week, as we knew it would but failed to achieve by arguing the climate threat. Money impossible to find for a clean, green economy appeared magically for bail-outs. What shortage? Trillions of dollars appeared out of thin air. And so we saw our Earth breathing and starting a little recovery as the impossible proved doable. Did the pandemic thus contribute to humanity's wisdom from this perspective?

Something else appeared to show our lack of wisdom: that national and global health systems are largely one vastly profitable sickness system dominated by pharmaceutical companies that make us sick via their toxic agricultural chemicals and then offer medical chemicals as cures! Nothing makes this more obvious than the Monsanto/Bayer merger, which dropped the M name because it had fallen into such popular disrepute. Monsanto got its patent on Glyphosate (marketed as RoundUp) as an antibiotic. It's origins were in Agent Orange, which killed off the forests and fields of Vietnam and now kills the soil and plant life of our food-growing fields, to allow only engineered 'RoundUp-resistant' crops to survive. Factory-farmed animals are filled with other antibiotics; both plants and animals pass them on to us. Statistics show clearly that poor people die of the Covid pandemic—indeed of all pandemics—at higher rates than those better off, and poverty is associated with cheap, toxic junk food.

I've been crusading on the serious lack of wisdom in antibiotic overuse—in making genocidal war on the entire microbiome—ever since the invention of antibiotics. Antibiotics literally means anti-life agents. Only recently did we discover how much we depend on our gut bacteria for our health. They make vitamins, heal damaged gut linings, indeed run our immune systems, whose health is the best preventive there is for the Covid disease! Some 80% of the people who take in SARS-coV-2 viruses do not get the Covid-19 disease. If that virus was the sole agent causing the disease, everybody who gets the virus would get the disease, but that doesn't happen. The vast majority of people can harbor that virus safely, showing no symptoms. It seems you have to have some problem with your immune system to get the disease, and so the best way to avoid getting sick from the virus is to have a strong immune system, which means having healthy gut bacteria.

The body's balance can only be restored by healthy food, destressing, rest, exercise and time in nature. Overexposure to EMFs via our digital devices, metals in dentistry, toxics in cleaning and body products, etc. are all health hazards we should eventually gain the wisdom to ban, as is slowly coming to light.

The wisest things I am seeing in my world have to do with returning to communal caring and sharing. The UN reported years ago that the only way to feed the burgeoning population of humanity in the future would be through small farms using natural methods again. There are excellent examples in the urban Mondragon Cooperatives in Spain, the rural bootstrapping development of the Sarvodaya Movement in Sri Lanka based on the spiritual principles of inner peace and generosity, the Global Ecovillage Network GEN), and The Business Alliance for Local Living Economies (BALLE). There are thousands of other local food and appropriate lo-tech sharing cooperatives around the world which offer role models of the way to mature human society—the ecosophy modeled on nature's ways.

Restoration of ecosystems has begun with massive tree planting, but must avoid monocultures and be vastly expanded by setting aside whole ecosystems to allow their self-restoration. Ending fossil fuels through clean, green energy is essential, but so is the dramatic cutback of all unnecessary consumer society production, at least until balance is restored. Far greater caution must be used in deploying new technologies such as 5G, which ignores all the research on damage to our health from the less dangerous 3G and 4G. Profits simply cannot continue to be put ahead of people if we want to survive!

Wise societies have always been about caring and sharing in a spirit of respect and love. The Polynesian canoe Hōkūleʻa that was built here in Honolulu, sailed around the entire planet without compass or other navigational technology on its mission of teaching Mālama Honua—care for our planet and each other. Such beautiful things are happening now, getting into the news, letting the young people see that we do know what to do.

How do you apply wisdom to the care of your mind, body and soul?

Among the more usual self-care, meditation—whether seated or mindfully walking in nature—is essential. As are eating healthy food, avoiding stress, avoiding wifi all I can (my computer and phone are wired at home; all electronics shut down while I sleep).

Consciously practicing gratitude and discernment without judgment, transmuting anger into positive action, as I said earlier. Getting enough sleep is also important. At 84 I wake up a lot, so I get into my rocking chair and meditate at very peaceful mid-night hours.

Self care is important. By taking good care of yourself and staying in a positive mood or mode while doing your best work in the world, you become an attractor to others. I believe everyone can find something that makes their heart sing while contributing to making the world better for all beings. Whether you write poetry or music, or enjoy campaigning and voter registration to get better politicians into office, or grow healthy food, or teach children, or develop appropriate technology, you can contribute great value toward the world we dream of, and will find your positive spirit attracting others to work with you. Rather than telling others you've got to do this or that, try saying, I invite you to come to my party, whatever its theme. Then put on your best party.

It's easy to slide into despair at the world situation, so remember that we all play a role in creating our common reality. Everything you see around you, other than undisturbed nature, was first in somebody's mind. Everything in our human world, all our artifacts, are our ideas made manifest. Coming out of a pandemic lockdown, many people realize we don't need to rush back into shopping. The consumer society is what gave me 'thing glut'. When I got rid of everything I owned to go to Greece, I was light as a feather. It was like coming out of the chrysalis, freed from the strictures of science and the oppression of possession. That was extreme 'deglutting', but in general, sufficiency trumps glut.

I love telling young people: Look at all the things your elders are doing that you don't approve of, and simply don't copy them. You don't like their going to war with each other? Their racism is abhorrent? Don't get into wars or discrimination yourselves. If it seems to you there are better ways to solve human problems, then why waste resources and do the terrible damage of war? One generation can end warfare and racism. If you don't like people dumping toxic glyphosates on your food, turn subsidies for unhealthy agriculture into supporting healthy food. Insist on clean energy and healthy food in your generation. Stop allowing big rewards for sickness care and invest in real health care. Redesign the whole education system to make it a joy to learn lifelong. Love and care for everyone as you would like to be loved and cared for yourself. The old Golden Rule is still a really good one! Just stop copying everything you see as damaging or useless in your personal life and for all. The future is yours to copy or create as you decide.

Is wisdom a uniquely human concept?

As a concept, it is uniquely human. This concept of wisdom has been with us since ancient times as a human ideal to strive for. Our wisest role models were generally people with long life experience and broad vision, elders good at resolving conflicts and making decisions for the wellbeing of their people, and otherwise guides to better behavior.

We saw such wisdom in the ways of nature, that magnificent context in which we lived and from which we learned. Many indigenous and later urbanized cultures created deities, most often goddesses as mother figures, or balanced pairs of male and female deities to represent the ways, the discerned laws, of nature. As urbanization led to patriarchal empire building, these supra-human authorities became less nurturing and more authoritarian father gods. Nowadays, when wisdom is ascribed to male role models, it is to men who express what came to be identified as feminine values of peace, compassion and caring, so in a sense we have come full circle.

Wisdom as seen in nature is invariably about cooperation for communal wellbeing—in sustainable, thriving ecosystems where all species contribute and benefit. As I am particularly fond of trees and consider them wiser than people, I like to cite the work of Stefano Mancuso, especially his book *Brilliant Green*, which describes trees as having all of our human senses and at least a dozen more. They see, hear, touch, feel, smell, and they also sense every chemical gradient and electromagnetic fluctuation, the oxygen levels and pollution in the air and everything going on in their underground microworld. They have amazing detectors in their finest roots, intertwined with complex fungi and other soil life. Merlin Sheldrake, Rupert Sheldrake's son, describes that world beautifully in his new book on fungi, called *Entangled Life*. Trees are wise, nurture their young, develop vast cooperatives. I go to them asking how to be more like a tree.

As I unraveled the story of biological evolution myself, a repeating cycle of maturation became obvious in nature's endless progressions from youthful species competition to mature, collaborative solutions to problems faced. Cooperation is what got us humans evolved, though we still need to practice it genuinely at the global, planetary level. When our economy is harmoniously fitted into nature's ecology, we will have our ecosophy, our wise society.

The explosive development of the human brain in evolution is a novel experiment. It dramatically changed the way our minds work. In short, our brain/minds traded inner knowing (instinct) for freedom of choice. We have far more freedom of choice than other animals, having to consciously choose our habitats, our food, our mates, our governance, our associations and communications, all through emotion, discernment and reason. This freedom of choice is a huge evolutionary gift; but it comes with the huge responsibility to make our choices wisely!

Many ancient and indigenous cultures found guidance for wise decisions in nature through both inner and outer ways of knowing. To believe that physical worlds are All That Is is an illusion the Vedics called Maya. Our human brain evolved to limit our perceptions in order to function with free choice in our 3D world, as we would otherwise be overwhelmed. It is a kind of filtering device helping us focus in order to make so many choices on our own. Trees and other non-human creatures can afford to perceive more than humans, as they know what to do while we flounder in choices. You can, however, cultivate the inner knowing required for wisdom through calming techniques such as meditation and listening quietly in natural settings.

Do you have a favorite parable or anecdote on wisdom?

My favorite parable is the Cherokee story of the grandfather whose grandson is complaining that somebody did something really mean to him. The grandfather tells him a story about two wolves inside him. He says, "We all have these two wolves inside us. One of them gets really angry, and can get greedy, upset and mean. The other one is a very loving, caring, sharing kind of wolf. And one is always trying to get on top of the other one." The boy asks, "Which wolf is going to win that fight?" And the grandfather says, "Whichever one I feed."

That's a wisdom parable to me. If you feed the grief and anger, it will take you over. But the love and joy can be recognized and nurtured. I can't imagine a more beautiful planet than the one we've got. Will we let the greedy wolf in us destroy it, or nurture it by feeding the loving wolf?

How can each of us develop wisdom?

Cultivate love and care for all beings.

How do you ultimately define wisdom?

I said earlier that people we call wise generally had long life experience and broad vision, and could resolve conflicts and make decisions for the good of their people. I also referred to the Dalai Lama's "critical thinking, followed by action." That, of course, requires a spiritual context, awareness of the whole keyboard on which you play. Because you can do critical thinking about making lots of money and take action to make it, thereby feeding the greedy wolf. This is not wise. I also spoke of science in the ancient Greek, labelling of it as love(r) of wisdom. So, distilling these ideas, let me try this as a brief definition: Wisdom is the ability to interpret and apply the fruits of a pursuit of truth, love and beauty toward the wellbeing of all.

If you make your life mission such a pursuit then you must also apply what you learn—translate it into something beneficial to all beings. Wisdom is more than just knowing what to do. It requires setting good examples, and providing actual guidance.

Is there anything you would like to add?

When the Western science of secular societies became the global authority on How Things Are, inner knowing was suppressed in favor of outer knowing, of rationality. The universe was declared to be material, meaningless, purposeless, and running down in a state of entropic decay. A most depressing worldview, in which getting what you can while you can, in perpetual competition with other humans, is the only way to go. Small wonder we developed an extractive, exploitative global economy! Was it not the antithesis of wisdom to abandon the search for truth, love and beauty?

Indigenous traditions persisting against these odds still see nature—and human possibility within it—very differently, and continue to offer hope for wisdom. That Polynesian canoe, Hōkūle'a, recently circumnavigating the globe on its mission of teaching care for each other and our Earth as I said, revealed the ways of ancient wayfarers. They navigated oceans in these very small sailing canoes that were never nailed, screwed or glued together. All parts of the boat were lashed together, the whole remaining flexible on the waves so it did not break in a storm. They knew that the only way to get across huge oceans was to know nature's ways so well that they couldn't get lost. One such navigator explained to me how they studied the stars, the clouds that gather over islands, the direction of surface waves and deeper swells, the floating seaweed, the fish migration patterns, and if all these indicators failed, they stood tall in their canoes until they could see the land.

He was pointing to inner ways of knowing. Every individual

consciousness is free of physical constraints. Who hasn't played on a tropical island beach during a boring lecture? You can move your consciousness easily. Can you raise it up high enough to get a bigger picture when you seem to be at the bottom of a dark well with no way out? For me, the Big Picture is evolution biology—deep 'pastism'—and futurism; seeing all the way back through billions of years of Earth's past and then into the far future in order to see what's possible, all within a conscious loving Cosmos.

When you feel like you're at the bottom of a deep, dark well with no way out, can you rise high enough to see that well as one small hole within a greater landscape? Can you see the human drama being played out on nature's great stage? We are all co-creators in a planetary improv theater production, and each of us reading this book has a great deal of choice in our role. The future is not something that simply arrives as we sit like a waiting audience; we are all on stage making it happen! Do we have the wisdom to create a show we can all thrive in and enjoy, no matter what dramatic challenges we face?

One last thing. The inner world of nature uses communion to share feelings and information, and such communion with animals and plants is a human birthright. Communication is what we do with languages, and communion is direct transmission requiring no translation. My 'guru' J. Allen Boone, learned to commune with Strongheart the movie star dog, and reported that eventually they spent hours a day in deep philosophical conversations, not as man and dog talking to each other, but as the universe 'talking them to each other'. In other words, they established a communal field in which, as he pointed out, the communion would cease if he raised the mental bridge between them at his end with the slightest feeling of superiority of man over dog. Only as absolute equals could they be 'spoken to each other' by the universe.

Few people in our modern world have cultivated this birthright, but once you have a cosmology in which the inner and outer worlds of the full keyboard are no longer separate, life really opens up!

I urge everyone, especially young people, to find something that makes your heart sing and can help build a loving, inclusive, thriving world. Choose not to do anything you now see as destructive. Encourage all your peers to know that they are agents of change with the power of your numbers. It can all be shifted by a single generation that uses our superb communication tools as well as communion—our internet and our innernet—to reach each other and make wise collective decisions. Love each other and our Earth and get on with the play!

How did it feel to discuss wisdom today?

It was fun. I enjoyed it and I thank you for issuing the challenge, which offered me and all the others in this volume the opportunity to reflect deeply on this clearly vital matter of wisdom, which we need to guide us into the future.

Mollie Semple

Mollie Semple has a master's in psychology and psychotherapy, and worked in social work for many years becoming a Principal Service Manager. She went into psychoanalysis, during which time she trained as a group therapist, an individual therapist and finally as a family and couples therapist. She worked privately with her own consultancy, facilitated groups for a university, a mental health charity and a church organization, and she supervised people in training.

Semple was a practicing Christian until the age of 20, when she started questioning rather than accepting. She then explored other spiritual paths including Buddhism, Hinduism, Wicca and nature-based spirituality. She eventually settled on a pagan path, joining the Order of Bardes, Ovates and Druids (OBOD), where she trained as a Druid. She now facilitates a Druid Grove in Glastonbury, England. druidry.org

What comes to mind first when you think about wisdom?

I suppose it's the archetypal crone, or a wise old man, such as Merlin, Gandalf, or the Druid in his Grove. That's the archetypal image of wisdom for me.

However, the more I think about wisdom, the more complex it becomes. Are we talking about spiritual wisdom, or secular wisdom? Is it about how we live, helping people provide a better life for themselves, their wellbeing? If we think of spiritual wisdom, developed from ancient religions to the spiritual paths of today, Christianity, Buddhism, Hinduism etc. and the nature paths which I follow, they seem rather different to a secular wisdom.

For example, in this time of Covid-19, we would like our government, our scientific advisors and health advisors to be wise, to use the knowledge they undoubtably have in a way that will protect us and keep us safe. They have the knowledge, but the wisdom is in how they apply it.

It is the same in our lives; we develop knowledge through life experience, which we must draw on when making future decisions. We learn from our mistakes. If not, we repeat them. Freud called this 'repetition compulsion'.

Do you recall the first time you saw wisdom in action?

No, but does that mean I did not experience wisdom, didn't recognize it as wisdom at the time, or just don't remember?

Wisdom comes through experience. Certainly when we are young, we don't always know if something was wise until after the event. Or were we just being sensible, and using our common sense?

Who is the wisest person you know and why?

When I think of wise people, I think of people like Satish Kumar, Thich Nhat Hanh, the Dalai Lama. Spiritual people. Also, Carl Jung the great psychologist and analyst, and Philip Carr-Gomm, the chief of my Druid training order (OBOD). For me they all epitomize a person with life experience plus a deep connection to nature, filled with love and compassion. They recognize our place in the world, and the fact that we have to live and work in reverence to the whole of nature and to each other.

Looking back on your life, what is the wisest thing you ever did?

Again, I wonder if things I did were wise, or just common sense? The main thing that changed my life was a decision I made early on. I was born in a small town in North Yorkshire, on the border with

Durham, and at the age of nine I declared I wanted to live in London. As sometimes happens in small towns and villages, there's an expectation of how people will be, what they will do. That certainly was not my expectation of how my life was going to be. So as soon as I was able, I packed everything into an old Ford Consul and drove down to London to stay with a cousin until I could get my own flat.

It was my first step to being independent, and doing what I felt was right for me, how I felt I needed to be in the world, as opposed to what my parents or anybody else thought I should be. I didn't fit into their mold and I had to make my own. Although life at times was very difficult, with lots of challenges, it was the only way for me to be. I think in retrospect, I was probably very wise to do it. I was following my dream, or was I just rebelling?

What is the hardest-won wisdom that you have?

I think the hardest-won wisdom comes from traveling along life's path, the experiences along our own journey. We're always presented with challenges, difficulties, blocks in what we want to do, where we think we are heading. For me these challenges were: divorce, leaving me as a single mother with a small son; serious illness and accidents; and at times, poverty. They were all milestones, crossroads in my journey. If we try to fight these challenges, become angry, adopt the role of victim, we become stuck; nothing will change and we will never move on. In fact we stagnate. Or, we can take control of the situation and after a period of time we can begin to reflect, look inward, and ask what it means for us. Perhaps we can ask: What can I learn from this? How might I have contributed to the situation?

But we must find a way to move on. After life-changing experiences, at some point we have to start living again. I have chosen to practice this reflective attitude, and it has served me well in my journey through life. This wisdom did not come easily, but it has helped during many years of psychoanalysis.

I don't think I've met anybody who can be really wise without life experience. Wisdom comes through our own experiences, knowing our own inner world and how we behave in the world.

In the world today, where do you see wisdom, and its lack, being demonstrated?

I think a lack of wisdom is the destruction of the planet, chopping down trees, killing animals. Greed, selfishness; people using any means to get what they want. It demonstrates a total loss of any spiritual (with a small s) connection to the whole—what Druids call Nwyfre, the universal life force. Where Nwyfre has been cut and people have lost their connection to nature, tragedy follows. For example, if you chop down the Amazon rainforest it has a knock-on effect that is totally destructive to all the plants and animals that live there, and the indigenous people who live and make their living from working in the forest. Those people work to preserve it, not destroy it.

Where I see wisdom happening is from the grassroots. Governments and policymakers are beginning to take notice but it is people working on the ground who are raising their voices, taking action to make the changes, thereby bringing it to the attention of society as a whole. An example is plastic. We all know the devastation created in the world by plastic. I think sometimes people get caught up in what's called 'cognitive dissonance'. They know that plastic is damaging to the environment. They possibly sign a petition to eliminate plastic, encouraging people not to buy plastic goods. They know the damage it causes but continue, for example, buying bottles of water and throwing them away. It is so much easier to continue as normal. Governments have known of the damage caused by climate change for decades but until relatively recently have chosen to deny the problem.

We have lost our connection to the whole. Our ancestors, certainly prior to the industrial revolution, worked in partnership with nature. This disconnection from nature came about in tandem with the development of technology, and industry has contributed to the dysfunctional world we now inhabit.

However, let us not become too pessimistic, as change is happening all over the world. Certainly in the Druid world, which is a nature-based spirituality, this is happening. We work all the time to preserve nature. We do not chop down trees, rather we plant trees, because of our belief that all of us, sentient and non-sentient, are connected.

Some of us join action groups such as Extinction Rebellion. I think their aims are very good, but for me some of their methods are not always terribly helpful. By damaging property and causing major disruptions eventually it just gets people's backs up and so discredits what the people in these organizations are trying to achieve. So again, it comes back to knowledge and wisdom. They know the facts, what needs to be done, but how do they use that knowledge to make it appealing to people, to attract them to the cause and get the people on board who can make change happen?

On a personal level it comes down to practicing what we preach, being the change we want to see in the world, whether working within large groups or individually to make changes happen. It is about enacting that in our daily practice, and making sure that we aren't contributing to the problem. I have an image of what is happening as being like a tree. The roots are the ordinary people who are taking action and working to attain what they believe; the branches are the governments, the policymakers etc. who hold the power to bring about change. Gradually, it is hoped, these two will meet and form the solid trunk of a fully functioning, loving and compassionate world.

How do you apply wisdom to the care of your mind, body and soul?

I'd never really thought about what I have done for most of my adult life as wise. Certainly for my body, I've always eaten very healthily. I've been a vegetarian and later a vegan for many years. I come from quite a sporty family, so sport has been part of my life since I was very young. I currently go to the gym three times a week and do a great deal of walking. I've been doing this, knowing it was good for me and enjoying it, without consciously thinking I'm wise to do it. And whether we call it wise or not, it is certainly very sensible, knowing the damage to health caused by obesity and inactivity.

I am very aware of excessive stress and the damage that it does. There are times when all of us are under stress, but if it's prolonged it can be very damaging. It gives rise to psychological problems and damaging behavior. I have had years of psychoanalysis both individually and in groups, and trained and qualified as a therapist in both disciplines. If I feel the signs that I am becoming stressed, I take action. I step outside and walk, and just be in nature. I nurture myself by being with trees, animals, birds, or walking by the beach with the waves crashing. I'm fortunate in that I live in a converted farm cottage. I look out over fields and animals. Just looking at that, absorbing it, I begin to feel calm and relaxed.

As for my soul, I've always been fascinated with religion and different religious paths but my main path is a nature path. I mentioned above how important being in nature is for me; it feeds my soul. I listen to sacred music, meditate and aim to live in a calm and peaceful way.

Being part of a social circle that is meaningful to me is very important. I am part of a Druid Grove, and our regular meetings and ceremonies are so important in reinforcing our connection to nature, the rhythm of life, the seasons, the acceptance of death and rebirth.

In most spiritual traditions, and certainly in Druidry, we work for peace. As Druids we chant peace prayers and call for peace when we're in ceremony, and aim to live our lives in a way that promotes peace.

From the perspective of my training in the Western psychoanalytical tradition, wisdom comes with gaining an understanding of our inner world. How and why one reacts, thinks and feels in any situation. Unless we're in touch with our own feelings and know how we are in different situations, we can react, we can get angry about something that's not really important. It can be difficult to keep things in perspective. I'm not saying we never get angry—the Dalai Lama talks about getting angry—it is how one reacts to that anger, expresses it, that makes the difference. It is through this understanding that we learn to gain control over our feelings and actions, so that we can mediate how we act, and gain control over our feelings rather than our feelings controlling us.

Without an understanding of our inner world, what makes us tick—revealing and facing our shadow, as Jung expresses it—then I don't believe we can be truly wise.

Is wisdom a uniquely human concept?

No, not at all. As we connect with nature, we learn from nature. As I said earlier, our ancestors had to work with nature for everything, in terms of agriculture, animal husbandry, building materials and so on. If we leave nature alone it knows how to look after itself, and we can learn from that. We know that the trees communicate to other trees to help each other. They send out messages if there's danger around. Animals are the same. There are very few animals that kill for pleasure. Most kill only to eat. And they know how to live in communities. Look at elephant families, and the way they communicate and look after each other. Wisdom, as I see it, is found everywhere in nature. If we acknowledge that and work with nature and have reverence for it, it has much to teach us. Nature wants to work with us. It provides so much that we can't live without: the trees providing breathable air, food that we eat, herbs and flowers for healing remedies.

Nature knows what is right and what is wrong. If you try to plant plants in the wrong place, they won't grow. It's a bit like ourselves. If we're stuck in a place that is wrong for us, we're not going to grow and develop to our fullest extent. Like I was saying, if I had stayed in my original environment, I wouldn't have gone through all the developments and had all the challenges that I have. Because I moved down to London it took me on a path that led me to travel to and live in different parts of the world. I don't think I would have had that experience if I had lacked the courage to leave. I feel there is a connection between that instinctive wisdom and the instinctive wisdom in nature. Nature is a great teacher.

Do you have a favorite parable or anecdote on wisdom?

For Druids, wisdom is provided through triads and stories, myths. There is one story I recall but can't remember where I heard it and it is not particularly a Druid story.

Once upon a time, a master and a young novice were traveling through a desert to a monastery, and they had to stop for the night and make camp. The master directed the novice to tie the donkey to a shrub overnight. When they got up the next morning the donkey was gone. The master asked the novice why he did not do as he was asked. The novice replied, "Because you said God would take care of everything." The master responded, "But sometimes God needs a little help."

For me, what that is saying is that we can't expect things to be handed to us on a plate. We cannot expect anyone else to look after everything. We have to take responsibility for ourselves, and what happens in our lives. It's no good telling your doctor about your problem and then not taking the medicine given to you. We all have to put in some work.

How do you ultimately define wisdom?

It begins with an accumulation of knowledge. But not just one specific knowledge, becoming an expert in one field of science, for example. We also need knowledge gained throughout our lives. However, that is not enough. The wisdom is in how we use that knowledge, for good or evil. Like the trees in the forest, wisdom grows slowly. In the same way, we also grow and mature.

Wisdom is also about being curious, being open, wanting to learn all the time. And having humility. There's no place in wisdom for arrogance, for people who claim that they know what is right.

We've seen a lot of that recently, where people know everything about Covid-19 and what we should and should not be doing. I think a lot of that comes from fear. But yes, I think wisdom is humility, compassion, living in the whole, connecting with nature, accepting that we don't know everything, and being able to admit that.

In Druidry, wisdom is gained through our connection to nature. There is an Irish story of the magical Salmon of Knowledge, that whosoever captures and eats the salmon will become the wisest of all men. In the story, Fionn mac Cumhaill believed that before he could become the captain of the Fianna warrior band he needed to increase his knowledge, wisdom and learning. He decided to visit the old bard Finegas, who dwelt by the river Boyne, to become his disciple. Swimming in this river was the magical salmon that could be caught and eaten and be reborn. For seven years Finegas had lived by this pool in the river waiting for the salmon, but it was only after Fionn joined him that the fish was caught. Whilst the salmon was cooking, juices burnt Fionn's thumb which he instinctively put in his mouth, thereby attaining the wisdom and knowledge he was seeking, and becoming the wisest of men. Finegas acknowledged that Fionn was the intended recipient of the wisdom and gave him his blessing. So, perhaps wisdom only comes to those who are ready to receive it, who are humble and know they do not know everything.

How can each of us develop wisdom?

I think we can only develop wisdom by getting to know ourselves. To some it might mean going into some sort of therapy, for others it might mean going deeper into and following their spiritual path. We can't become wise by sitting exams and reading many books; we also need to connect with life, to know our place in relation to the whole. We must realize that no matter how wise we become, we are just a small cog in a big wheel. There have to be many of those cogs connecting together to make the wheel turn. So, we must work with others and nature and accept that no matter how clever we are we do not have the monopoly on truth.

Is there anything else you wish to add?

Is wisdom a goal to be reached or an ongoing process that continues throughout our life?

I'm interested in how wisdom and philosophy fit together. How wisdom and common sense fit together. When does common sense become wisdom? Looking at the progression of wisdom as we grow and mature. I mentioned humility which is well expressed in this quote from Shakespeare's *As You Like It*: "The fool doth think he is wise, but the wise man knows himself to be a fool."

I believe a wise person only works for good, although I know some philosophers didn't agree with that. But for me, to be wise in the sense that we've been talking, we can only work for good.

How did it feel to discuss wisdom today?

I think the exploration of wisdom is fascinating. I am grateful for being given this opportunity to think and explore more deeply the concept of wisdom. In my Druid Order, we work to develop within ourselves wisdom, creativity and love. So it fits in with the way I work. Having this interview with you has opened in me a wish to continue to explore wisdom, as it is seen in the world today—and perhaps become a little wiser in the process. Thank you.

Vandana Shiva

Vandana Shiva is an Indian scholar and environmental activist who has dedicated nearly five decades to the protection of biodiversity. Shiva did her master's in particle physics at Panjab University in Chandigarh in 1973. She received her PhD in Quantum Theory at the University of Western Ontario. In 1981, she founded the Research Foundation for Science Technology and Ecology. Since 1984 she has dedicated herself to promoting nonviolent farming based on biodiversity. In 1991 she founded Navdanya. She has authored more than 20 books. She is one of the leaders and board members of the International Forum on Globalization, and a figure in the global solidarity movement which she refers to as the Earth Democracy movement. She received the Right Livelihood Award in 1993, the Midori prize on Biodiversity, and numerous other awards for her service to planet Earth, the protection of biodiversity, and people's rights. navdanya.org

What comes to mind first when you think about wisdom?

The big picture and the long term. For me, the big picture is seeing all the relationships and the interconnectedness that you have with everything around you; your relatives, friends and colleagues, but also all our relatives that are not human. I've grown up in a culture that sees life this way. And my ecological work has taught me that all living beings are related to each other. The crazy world that has been built over the last 300 years is based on a pseudoscientific view that assumes separation is necessary for objective knowledge. And this view endures, despite that fact that a century ago we learned about non-separation through quantum theory. My PhD thesis is on nonseparability and nonlocality in quantum theory. And it became clear to me that we've known this scientifically for a hundred years, and centuries through ancient wisdoms, and yet this mislearning of separateness continues to dominate. So for me, wisdom is being able to see the whole, all the relationships, and the long term.

It's really just going through many dimensions of life. Life is the ultimate teacher of wisdom. Children aren't born wise, but grandparents by and large become wise.

Do you recall the first time you witnessed wisdom in action?

I felt an imperative that came from a sense of a bigger picture and values beyond oneself. For me, wisdom is also transcending yourself, transcending your ego, transcending what is immediately important to you. This became active in me as I witnessed the deforestation in the 70s. I then joined the Chipko movement to take action. I think at that time it was the women's wisdom that was guiding. I was basically responding with a deep sense of violation, that I don't want to see this happen, I don't want to see forests disappear.

I was at a meeting in 1987 with my friends in the 'poison cartel', a group of chemical companies. They laid out their plan for the future, including how they would own plant seeds through patenting, how they'd have to do genetic engineering in order to claim patents, and how they would create a global treaty to impose it all around the world. And I think that's when I experienced wisdom in terms of: What do we do? How do we respond to this? And that's what led me to all the work I've done since then, including the seed saving, the creation of Navdanya, working on laws that respect the integrity of life, dealing with globalization, and becoming part of the International Forum on Globalization. All of that came from that one moment.

Who is the wisest person you know, and why?

Definitely the forests. Last year I wrote an essay titled 'Everything

I Need to Know I Learned in the Forest.' I was born in the central Himalayan forest, so that was my reality. My father was a forest conservator and so trees and forests were my teachers. My home was the area where the Ganges starts from. It is also the area where later in 1973 the Chipko movement started, where women said we are going to hug the trees to prevent them being cut down. Those trees were my wisdom teachers. They taught me so much. I was doing my PhD in quantum theory, and here were these women working with all that wisdom, knowledge and experience. And I was so humbled, because we are all taught that without a degree you have no knowledge. There is this hierarchy of expertise. And I had gone through that hierarchy. Why does one do a PhD? Because you think you know more. And here are women who knew more, just by living in the forest. So that wisdom teaching made me so deeply respectful of all indigenous knowledge, and gave me a recognition of the wisdom of indigenous cultures.

And it also created in me a sense of outrage when that wisdom was trampled on as ignorance. That's why so much of my work has ended up being about knowledge, whether it's in my books, or in my having to deal with patenting issues: patenting of the name Neem, of our basmati, of our wheat, all of this. I worked with communities who had done the basic work of knowing that name Neem as a pest control agent. Or the basic work of knowing that a seed can tolerate salt and they've evolved it. So that respect for the wisdom and indigenous knowledge then allowed me to deal with the violations of these cultures and systems.

Chipko itself was a very Gandhian movement. My mother was a Gandhian. When we were little we used to spin. And there was a gem of wisdom that has never left me. Being as old as I am, we saw the arrival of the first petrochemical fiber. Before then it was all natural fibers. And of course it was fashionable, as everything fake is made to be fashionable. And this was nylon, literally glass nylon. It looked like glass. And you could not print on it. So they used to have to put paint on it. It was quite ugly when I look back, but everyone around us was wearing nylon. And when my mother asked my sister and me what we wanted as gifts for our birthday, we asked for nylon frocks. And my mother explained the consequences of choosing either nylon, or khadi. Khadi is the hand-spun, hand-woven cloth that Gandhi revived as part of our freedom struggle.

I noticed yesterday that they pulled down a slave trader's statue then threw it into Bristol harbor, as part of a Black Lives Matter protest, stemming from George Floyd's murder. In a way, for the first time in the world, it has created a movement against slavery and colonization. It's quite amazing. In Australia the Aboriginal people are now counting all the Aboriginal youths who were killed in custody.

Because we've been colonized, I know this history very well. The British Empire was an empire of cotton. That's what made them take the Africans to America to pick the cotton in the plantations. Why did they have to have so many cotton plantations? Because they wanted to destroy our textiles. We had the most sophisticated textiles. Basically it's the same as dumping food right now, with the globalization of food and agriculture. So good agriculture is destroyed. Good food is destroyed. You are going through with Brexit and the whole import of chlorinated chicken and deregulation of GMO. But at that time, it was happening with clothing and textiles. So good clothing of India was being destroyed and fossil fuels had just been found. The steam engine was now taking over. And so instead of just saying, okay, we'll make this much cloth for England, they said, no, we'll just destroy all the textiles of the world. And for doing that, we need more and more plantations. So they grabbed the land from the indigenous people. And in colonialism, 90% of the indigenous people of the Americas were exterminated. And who is going to farm all this? We'll capture the Africans. So George Floyd's story really goes back to that today. And so they captured Africans and made them work on it. And the entire exclusion, dispossession and violence that we witness today against black Americans has its roots in the violence where blacks were not treated as human beings. They were treated as property to be bought and sold. At that time, 85% of the planet was controlled by the

British. And then Gandhi realized that if we don't reclaim economic democracy we'll never have freedom, because the empire is an economic empire. Empires don't exist in the sky. They exist for resource and wealth transfer. And yet we always focus on the story that the empire builders tell us. And we ignore the reality of the theft. Because that's the smartness of colonialism: it always presents colonization as progress, a civilizing mission, the white man's burden.

So Gandhi said, if we don't make our own cloth we'll never be free. So he taught himself how to spin cloth, then taught the whole country how to spin cloth. And this hand-spun, hand-woven cloth was called khadi. So my mother used to dress us in khadi because she was a Gandhian. And so when we asked for nylon frocks, she said, "If you want it I'll get it for you. But just remember, if you wear khadi, a poor woman fed her child that night. And if you wear nylon, a rich man bought the next Mercedes. So you make your choice." And this wisdom has always stayed with me. So I was influenced by her and my father, by Gandhi, and by Chipko. And when this meeting of '87 took place, it woke me to the love of the world in freedom, and a rejection of a world of enslaving all life through patenting. In that moment Gandhi's wisdom came to me.

Looking back on your life, what is the wisest thing you ever did?

I did several things. First I made a matrix. I said, okay, in Gandhi's time it was the cotton empire. So what did Gandhi pull out? He pulled out a spinning wheel. Then came the chemical revolution, which we missed, but Rachel Carson wrote about in *Silent Spring*, and the birth of the environment movement took place at that time. But we didn't have the kind of burst of agroecology and organic farming at that time, which we should have had.

They used to call themselves the life sciences industry at that time. Now they call themselves biotechnology. As the conference was on life sciences, I asked myself, what is the spinning wheel for our times? And I thought of the seed. And then Gandhi's wisdom guided me to the next step. He had a very clear idea of self-rule. No person, no culture is free if they don't government themselves. He had written a most brilliant book in 1909 while he was still in South Africa, fighting against racism there. He had done his first non-cooperation civil disobedience in 1906, when they passed a law of discrimination against the Indians. So he had come to England. On his way back to South Africa, he wrote this book in one shot. As he wrote, when his right hand would get tired he'd write with the left, and vice versa. The book is called *Hind Swaraj*, which basically means freedom for India. The word Hind is derived from the river Sindhu. The river Indus, its name is Sindhu, but as the Arabs couldn't pronounce Sindhu, they made it Hind. And so the land beyond the Indus is Hindustan. It's not the land of the Hindus, it's the land beyond the Indus. So Hind was the way we described ourselves as a land. And swaraj is freedom, and self-rule. This book has been my wisdom bible.

The second thing relates to the spinning and weaving, which Gandhi called 'self-making', or 'swadeshi'. If you're colonized economically, you reclaim your freedom not through being a consumer in the colonizing system, but by being a maker in a system of freedom, which is self-making, self-creation.

And the final one is the most powerful, which I have used repeatedly. I said, okay, if they pass laws that make it illegal for us to have seeds, we will not obey. Satyagraha is basically creative, nonviolent, civil disobedience. Satyagraha was Gandhi's word for it. It means the fight for truth. But to know the truth in the process. This is exactly what Thoreau practiced when he said he would not pay a poll tax to support slavery. He would rather go to jail. And so I said, okay, I will work to make sure laws are passed that don't patent seed. But even if we fail, we ultimately have satyagraha. So we started seed satyagraha. Those were different days. Our parliaments and our leaders weren't the fools that are there today. They were enlightened statesman. And the speaker of our parliament joined me at the statue of Gandhi leading the salt march. And we announced what Gandhi did to salt, we are going to do with seed. The British wanted to monopolize salt and they passed a law in 1930 saying that it would be illegal for people or Indians to make salt. Even though we need salt in a tropical climate. So Gandhi walked to the beach, hundreds of miles, and thousands of people joined him. He picked up the salt from the sea and he said, "Nature gives it for free. We need it for our survival. We will continue to make salt. We will not obey your laws." And this began the salt satyagraha. And people started making salt all along the coastline. In the west, Gandhi was arrested. On the east, 45,000 people were shot dead for making salt. And I did a freedom journey a few years ago, to visit every spot where a salt satyagraha had happened, including every village where someone had been killed for making salt from the sea, and honored the descendants.

So we said we would do a seed satyagraha. We worked with parliament and we fortunately passed laws. Because I think what a satyagraha does is, it raises the consciousness. Like George Floyd, one man has been killed, but suddenly people are remembering slavery. They're remembering colonialism. A totally forgotten, submerged history. I remember 25 years ago, I was saying something and I mentioned colonialism. And they said, "Dr. Shiva, colonialism has no relevance anymore. It's over." I said, "No, it's not over. New forms of colonization are found."

So seed satyagraha became a big part of my work. And the seed saving, I called it Bija Swaraj. I said, if the spinning wheel brought us freedom from the cotton empire, then seed saving is self-rule over seed. We've now established over 150 community seed banks. The movement I created is called Navdanya, which means nine seeds, which stands for diversity. Because nine is the highest digit and it's the highest diversity. So Navdanya means nine seeds, but it also means 'the new gift'. The way it's pronounced in Hindi it sounds similar.

So I said, this is the new gift of reclaiming the commons. The seed is our commons. Life is our commons. Knowledge is our commons. And in this period of privatization of everything, I said reclaiming the commons is a very big part of freedom.

Everything I'm doing now flows from that early work. It basically gets its reenergization from that source. I have been with my team in lockdown. I'm not going out, but they are all young, so they are able to go out on their bikes and then they would see me. And we were talking about when the lockdown lifts, what is the work to be done with communities? And since many of them have been with me since the 90s, I was seeing what we started in terms of the seed, we now have to do in terms of life as a whole. We must now conserve life banks, like we created seed banks. We have to conserve places where people can live in peace with nature, where people are not unemployed. Because one of the things that this lockdown has done is escalate unemployment. The ILO has said of the 3.3 billion people who worked, 1.9 will lose their work in this lockdown period. And many will never recover because another economy is being created. We already had a billion hungry people in the world. Now we will add an extra 130 million in the next few months. That is 300,000 per day. The World Food Program says they are not hungry, but dying of starvation. So these are the figures we are talking about.

And when Covid hit, I was reading very carefully the reportage on it. I've done a piece on the blog, it's called 'Ecological Reflections on the Corona Virus.' I was trying to make sense of both the creation of the virus, as well as the response. And I've written a number of pieces since then. While thinking about the coronavirus, I was seeing a lot of writings on making decisions about who the government would spend money on. They had this even in England. There was a *New York Times* article I read while rushing back to be back home for the lockdown. It said: who will live and who will die? That is the choice. So I said, we used to have inequality, which was bad enough—the haves and the have nots. And we've been pushed through both the coronavirus and the lockdown into a situation where a very easy debate has begun: who will live and who will not live? It's couched sometimes in healthcare, but sometimes in budget decisions. And I think that any society that decides that some people are expendable is no better than Hitler's concentration camps. It is that Nazi thought of: I am superior and others are expendable. Coming back to George Floyd, the blacks are an expendable part of America. Most of the people dying in America from Covid are black. Most of the people who are dying in England are non-white people. The have and have not inequality has moved to: we decide which species will live and which will be allowed to go, which human being will live and which will be allowed to go. And you can do the 'allowed to go' in three ways. You can deprive them of food, so they will starve to death. You will deprive them of work so they can't have food, so they starve to death. The third is more complex. Much of my work in agriculture is based on understanding where the chemical comes from. The pesticides came from the concentration camps. Zyklon B is the ancestor of all pesticides. It was invented in Germany in the 1920s and is cyanide-based. These were designed to kill people, so it's not an accident that 200,000 people still die because of pesticide poisoning. They just made an excuse that they would control pests. But that was just to sell it as an agrichemical. Its purpose was based on its power to kill.

Also, 1984 was when I moved into agriculture. And again, it wasn't wisdom, I don't think. It was outrage. I said, how can so many people die in Bhopal and Punjab? That's when I started to look at chemical agriculture. And so you can create things that kill people directly. Chemicals are brilliant. And there's a lot of debate about Covid-19. There's so much writing on the fact that it comes out of the Wuhan defense lab. But they were working with the Americans. So the story of the virus is couched in so many narratives: geopolitical, medical, economic. I don't think any virus has had such honor before. I don't think any image of any other living being, or any other object has had so much screen time as the coronavirus. And all they do is change the color from pink to blue. Always very radiant colors.

And I think of the children. I asked: What happens when you're locked down? What kind of imagination do you create? So I told my colleagues we must save the seed. Now we have to create systems where people can take care of their lives. So, I've been working on local living economies for a while, but we're going to put much more energy into it, into re-imagining the economy.

What is the hardest-won wisdom that you have?

When I started to save seeds and challenge GMOs, I had to do a lot of work on the biotech industry, the poison cartel, and a lot of that work was of course in India. For example, I did the first studies on the farmer suicides because of GM cotton. And this was not acceptable in the narrative of: here are GMO seeds that are going to make farmers prosperous because they produce more. It was breaking the narrative. And the assault that came on me was incredible. I knew they were powerful companies, but I had not expected that kind of organized mafia-style attack; the levels of structures they have, the journalists they hire. My Wikipedia page changes all the time. They want the world to think I've never studied science. So they removed my physics degrees. My son got angry and he sent my degrees to Wikipedia, and they changed it within the next second. Then it was back again: she's never studied science.

Those who break that narrative can be subjected to these attacks. And this means every political scientist, every toxicologist and everyone was working on the glyphosate, GMO-linked cancer was attacked. So I think my wisdom learning then was the Buddhist training of equanimity. I have received many awards, including the Right Livelihood Award. The thing with awards is, you should never let it blow up your ego. You should accept it humbly and with gratitude and use it to serve. Which is what I've done with all of my awards. That's much easier. But when this attack is coming on your very integrity or identity, who you are, it is much harder. I live by my truth and conscience. But that Buddhism teaching of equanimity helps you to stay stable. I learned that wisdom through a decade of that attack.

In the world today, where do you see wisdom, and its lack, being demonstrated?

I see a lack of wisdom in not understanding the difference between a disease epidemic, and actions needed for that, and a new economy without people that was being institutionalized, hiding behind the virus. To hide behind the virus is sophisticated. We must understand what is unfolding and what is our right choice, and not conflate what are many different phenomena.

I wrote a book a few years ago called *Oneness vs the 1%*. And the origin of this book was basically two phenomena. One was at the Paris summit on climate in 2015. I saw Bill Gates and Mark Zuckerberg on the stage with heads of state, and they were giving the recipes of what should come out of this: geoengineering, genetic engineering and so on. And I recognized that something had shifted in power, that the billionaires tell governments what they should do. I'd been studying globalization since the late 80s, but I had not studied how the deregulation would create the tech barons. That was not my focus. I was looking at seeds, biodiversity, agriculture. I was looking at the Monsantos and the Cargills. I wasn't looking at the tech giants. When I watched these tech giants strut around on the stage it was clear that something had shifted. And if they are more powerful than governments then where is democracy? Because we elect leaders to represent us. But if those leaders are listening to instructions from money, then what's our role?

Two years later, Monsanto was bought out by Bayer. And then I started to look at the economics of this. I wanted to know how much finance each company has. And my son, who co-wrote the book with me, was very good at this kind of work. He discovered that they're all owned by the same billionaires. So the idea that they are all independent corporations is over. Ownership used to be based on many small investors. But now the big investors are the companies like BlackRock and Vanguard. And when these investors are the largest shareholders, they determine the policies. Shareholder activism takes so much energy for one person to give a one minute speech, but it doesn't change too much, especially when most of the votes are on the other side.

Since our book came out one and a half years ago, I've been

keeping track of Bill Gates. A large part of the book is about him. And I'm watching every step of the economy he and his friends are institutionalizing, hiding behind a virus. I can't understand how there isn't more outrage, because for me, like I said, wisdom is about seeing the whole, and the long term. And the long term is part of your experience that helps you grow. But the long term is also about foresight. Anticipation is a huge quality of wisdom. To be able to predict the result of present trends continuing. This inability to anticipate and prepare today, while we can do something about it, is vital. I'm doing my little things, but I'm just one, and many more will have to contribute.

We should be doing more to oppose deregulation. This is the second element of my observation of the lack of wisdom in the world today. In 'Ecological Reflections on the Corona Virus,' I wrote that the reason we have regulation is because it creates the framework for societies and economies to run. So if you have environmental regulation, certain things are wrong. If you have a convention on biodiversity, then destroying biodiversity is wrong. You have a UN framework convention on climate change. We're supposed to be able to legally bind reductions in emissions, but this was destroyed in Copenhagen. And that's why Paris was not really a treaty; it was just voluntary declarations. And I had written that we can't afford to allow deregulation in this period. And I don't know what it was that taught me that this would happen. If we look in the lockdown period, the worst permissions have been given for basically illegal activity, like Bolsonaro burning the Amazon, and in India all our primeval conservation zones have been given up for coal mines. And England deregulating on the GMO question. You look around and deregulation is very big. And we are not looking enough at this unfolding future from evidence.

I will give two simple examples. I was working on my five-decade journey with biodiversity for World Biodiversity Day. In a way it was my biodiversity memoir. It's also on the blog, titled 'My Earth Journey.' And while I was writing it, someone sent me a patent document.

Because people know I have fought many battles on illegitimate patents, of biopiracy, of stealing what doesn't belong to you. And this patent is number WO/2020/060606. The title is 'Cryptocurrency System Using Body Activity Data.' You can see on the diagram the human. This is us. These are the people who should be wise, the wisdom keepers. But in this patent, we are now mines for data. Sensors of all kinds will mine the data. That's why there's a rush to use sensors in smartwatches and other devices. They will mine the data and the user's device will process the data. This will go into their giant servers, which use algorithms to determine what we are worth. This patent has the details of what they will mine. They will mine our body activity, our blood flow, every bit of our brain activity, all the time, even when we're sleeping. This is not a gas chamber in Nazi Germany, but it is a way of working out who is fit and who is unfit. Because after all this is done, the giants will allot a cryptocurrency to us, as our value. And then they're going to govern the world according to that valuation.

For me, wisdom from human beings requires waking up to this. I would love to see a global movement on human freedom in our times. I've already helped some people write letters to the WIPO, saying this is not your domain. Defining what it means to be human is beyond your jurisdiction. There isn't enough use of existing law, such as human rights law and privacy laws.

And it's happening so quietly. I was sent this by somebody. I've written about it, but most people have been put into so much fear of the virus that they're thinking of nothing else. Because if that little thing is on your TV screen morning, noon and night on every news channel, then how will you prepare yourself in wisdom to have a future that is not just worthy of you as a sovereign free human being, but is a legacy of freedom and autonomy you will leave for your children?

Because of lockdown, obviously experiences are very limited, but I think nature's wisdom is bursting forth. The regeneration of nature has been so fast. Recently the Convention on Biological Diversity had a whole thing on World Environment Day, and I said, "With all of these international treaties, you spent 30 years doing nothing, and everything has got worse: erosion of biodiversity, increased greenhouse gases and so on. You just left it to nature because you just withdrew. But look how it bounces back." So I think that is nature's wisdom for sure.

I think the second very beautiful thing I witnessed in India is how the poor are taking care of each other, while the rich are enclosing themselves in their privileges. Half of India has been thrown out. I'm seeing that if Mr. Gates has his way, there'll be three groups of people. The first are the throwaway people who can be left to die. The second group of people will be forced into a new slavery of the old kind with no workers' rights, no protections. Even in England, when the lockdown happened, who couldn't come over? The Eastern Europeans, who used to come and work on the farms. And I remember there was this little project in which we said to the students: you can come and work on the farms and there will be a stipend. So in effect, agriculture has become based on slave labor. But if you push too many people to the edge, then the amount they are willing to allow themselves to get exploited increases. And one of the deregulations that has happened in India during lockdown—and we had amazing protests of the workers union—was that we had labor laws wiped out, to allow more exploitation. So instead of the eight-hour day, now you can have them work for 12 hours. And you don't have to give them minimum wage and you don't have to have any protection. So everything that the workers' movement had gained was undone with one little thing. But there were protests.

So we have the throwaway people. We have the slaves of the working class. And then you have the digital slaves, who won't see that every phase of the higher digitalization is a new pink slip. A new ownership paper. Just look at the last two years, how many pink slips have been given out? Because the more you write the algorithms, you write the software, the more the giants can be free of you and just have the algorithm, for but which they have to pay nothing. They always say that: we don't have to pay anything for the algorithm. We had you write your own redundancy. We don't know how long that will carry on.

All three options for me are wrong. And therefore, the wisdom I witnessed is among the poor people. They might have very little, but they'll come out to the streets and serve the people who've been displaced from the cities and are walking a thousand miles. So the wisdom of caring for each other, even in a difficult situation, has not disappeared.

How do you apply wisdom to the care of your mind, body and soul?

First, never let them split from each other. Because I don't think wisdom can exist just in the mind and just in the heart. Or just in the hands. In a way, all of this Cartesian thinking has made us think that the hands are dumb, that they have no wisdom—but they do. When we did Chipko, the wisdom was the hands of embrace. When you're bringing up a child every little expression in the eyes tells you it's the embrace that the child needs. And that's why I think part of what I call 'digital dictatorship' has used this virus to create such fear of each other. For a while it's fine to be separate, but why do you want a permanent structure of never having people meet? Why do you want a permanent structure of the six-feet distance? Good, responsible epidemic management is to know when the epidemic will grow and when it will come down. When they tell you it'll never end, something else is going on in my view.

So for me, the integrity of heart, hand and head working in unison is fundamental. When I talk about the whole, wisdom is you acting in the whole. So that's my personal care.

It's wisdom that lets you know what's good for you. Advertising makes you go for the wrong junk food. Or the throwaway clothing. But wisdom is what holds you together, and allows you to live and think your deep authenticity as a being in relationship with other beings.

Do you think wisdom is a uniquely human concept?

No. I previously mentioned that as nature has bounced back, that was my sense of wisdom. I also think back to my youth. We went to a convent school and we always had dogs. We have this lovely little Tibetan dog called Sinto. And when you put his food down, he would literally close his eyes for a few moments, and then eat. So we were in a moral science lesson and were being told that only we are made in the image of God, and only we have the capacity to pray. And my sister put up her hand and said, "No, my dog prays before he eats." And she was totally punished for that.

Because of the work I've done on seeds and biodiversity, I've done a lot of work on the soil. Both on the ecology of the soil, but also how to regenerate the soil, which is the work I do with Indian peasants. Now, so much new literature is coming out on how there is a web in the soil, and the mycorrhizal fungi understand that a tree over there didn't get enough nutrition, but there's nutrition here, so we will carry it there. Now they've done radioactive tracing systems on this. So if the life in the soil can do this, we had better let go of the idea that only humans have wisdom.

For one more dimension of wisdom, you see that a very stupid, greedy and arrogant man can grab what doesn't belong to him. It means basically the death of wisdom in that person. But anyone who wise is first asking: Who needs my care? What can I give? So it shifts from taking and grabbing, which has been the way colonialism and the economy of today has worked, including every indicator, GDP and all of that. It has been extractive. Whereas wisdom makes it very natural for you to ask: What can I do? What can I share?

Do you have a favorite parable or anecdote on wisdom?

I'm remembering my dad. Right now I'm locked down in my childhood home. At one point I wanted to leave an institution. I had done some studies on mining, and I said, "What am doing in a institution where I've spent so much time just managing to be in the institution, when a six-month study can save a valley or something else?" I realized it would be so good to be free. And my mother said, "Take the cow shed and start your institute there." So where I'm sitting now is where we used to have cows in my mother's time. This was where I grew up, as did my son. When he was young he was on the veranda, playing with the dogs and feeding them pakoras. I was making the pakoras in the kitchen and he was taking them, having a bite then sharing them with the dog. And he kept playing with them till he fell over the steps and hit his head. He was unconscious and we could not get a response. My sister is a doctor and she tried everything she could. My father was there, and his wisdom has been a very big gift, especially after my mother passed away. And in bringing up my son. And of course I was panicking. But he said, "These are the moments when we realize there are forces bigger than us."

We took this unconscious boy to find help but everything was shut, and because it was a head injury everyone was worried. There was a doctor, a friend of my dad's, who came to help. And as he entered, my son, who literally was in a coma, just sat up and talked as if nothing had happened. So the doctor said, "Where is the child who was unconscious?" And I had to say, "He's right there." That's the day my dad woke me to the wisdom of higher forces. Sometimes things are out of our control and we have to leave it to trust.

The spiritual element has been a part of my life. I was born in Dehradun, and this was the home of the best spiritual teachers when we were children. Our parents used to take us, so I sat at the feet of the best masters, such as Anandamayi Ma, Swami Shivananda, Sant Kirpal Singh. And my father gave the land to Maharishi Mahesh Yogi for his ashram, where he was visited by the Beatles. So Maharishi had come to our house to get permission. We learned so much and had very beautiful spiritual masters. So we've grown up with that. My parents were steeped in this and it's here in my ancestral home. So I've been blessed with it. I haven't had to seek it.

I'm very fortunate that I realized very early in my physics studies that a mechanistic explanation of the world wasn't satisfactory. I was studying particle physics, and even that kept pushing me to understand quantum theory more deeply, which is why I did my PhD in the foundations of quantum theory. I was going to study with David Bohm, but he didn't have a fellowship, so he guided me to his student Jeffrey Bub and I did it at the University of Western Ontario. I went to Canada to study, but what I studied was this interconnectedness.

I'm a feminist, I believe women are equal. And I used to love driving my father's car around. He had an old Fiat. While I was waiting between my MSc and my PhD I was doing sculpture, and I was going around in the car. And when I went to Canada I found that everyone wanted to escape over the weekend. And in India, holidays and weekends are when you sit together with family and stay at home. So I said, 'Why is everyone escaping?' And I took a pledge. I said these prisons of aluminum and steel are not really liberation of any kind. So for me, the automobile became the crassness, but my learning of quantum theory fitted very beautifully with my understanding of non-separation, interconnectedness, consciousness.

When I worked on agriculture, producing the green revolution critique in my book *The Violence of the Green Revolution*, then all my work on genetic reductionism and genetic determinism, I suffered brutalization from the poison cartel mafia. I would say that if I hadn't had spiritual moorings, I couldn't have dealt with it. They intended to shatter me, because they imagined that the world of money is the only thing there is. And they tried in every way. Any talk I had to give, anywhere, the president of the university would get a letter before I arrived saying I should be disinvited. And they would attach a fake CV. In some places the universities would tell me about this. Some places they just kept quiet. And it actually happened in January this year, involving Stanford. I once gave a lecture in Winnipeg, and there was a lot of security in the auditorium. I said to the president who was going to introduce me, "Are you having student trouble?" He smiled and said, "No, but the biotech people have threatened to disrupt your talk." And so we had security to ensure that this event wouldn't get disrupted.

For me, wisdom flows from a recognition that we are spiritual beings, interconnected. And all our expressions in this word are shaped by that. And if you really think all you are is a bunch of tissue, and you think you can stuff this body with anything at all, the consequence is disease. So my spiritual evolution and my scientific evolution have constantly had a symbiosis. And that's why for me, when I deal with fake food and toxic food, it's a spirituality of what food is. Which also totally gets replicated in the ecology of food. In India, we say food is the creator. Food is the currency. Food is everything.

You now know that how you grow food affects your health, because we are an ecosystem too, with a gut biome and so on. I say this to people who are pushing fake food to save the planet. Even George Monbiot is doing this. I wrote a response to this in *The Ecologist*. I said, 'George, you've forgotten that we are wild beings. We have 60 trillion microbes in our gut. We are wilderness. When we are free, and when we are spiritual, we are wilderness. It's when we are controlled that we become machines.' So for me, spirituality is really the source of all. It's the spring that gives life to everything else.

How do you ultimately define wisdom?

For me, wisdom is being anchored in your relationships, in your being, and taking the right action, having the values, but having the ability to discriminate between right action and wrong action. Between right livelihood and wrong livelihood. Because what is good and what is bad is determined by relationships and integrity. In India we call it Dharma karma, Buddhism calls it Dhamma padma. And knowing the whole over time, having that guide, you're living in your action; that to me is wisdom.

How can each of us develop wisdom?

By being more mindful, by cultivating compassion and care.

How did it feel to have this discussion about wisdom today?

I felt comfortable with it. It's good. It's not usually where conversations go. It is the deeper layer and it's good to go to deeper layers.

Sulak Sivaraksa

Ajahn Sulak Sivaraksa is co-founder of the International Network of Engaged Buddhists (INEB), and the Spirit in Education Movement (SEM). He is President of the INEB Institute of higher education, and author of more than 100 books in Thai and English on Buddhism, social justice and social critique.

He is a member of the World Future Council, and an honorary fellow at the University of Wales, Lampeter. inebinstitute.org

What comes to mind first when you think about wisdom?

In the Buddhist context, to be wise is to be humble, to be compassionate.

Do you recall the first time you witnessed wisdom in action?

Wisdom in action means that you have to be able to use skillful means, whatever you do. But it should be nonviolent. It should be with love and kindness.

As a youth I was an angry young man. And I was full of egoism, and I wanted my way. But then I learned more about the teachings of the Buddha. I learned to meditate. I learned to breathe properly. And I learned to restructure my consciousness. I changed hatred into loving kindness. I changed greed into generosity. And I tried to change delusion into wisdom. I was not always successful, but I have worked that way ever since.

I was born in Bangkok in 1933. At the time the country was called Siam. It was changed to Thailand later on. I never agreed with the name Thailand, because we have many people who are not Thai, particularly in the south of the country. More people are Muslim and Malay, and they are unhappy to be called Thai. Likewise if you call Britain 'England', the Scottish and Welsh will be angry. I feel very much that the military is running the country and they don't care about the concerns of the minority. I feel very sorry for them.

Who have been your wisdom teachers?

I was brought up in a Buddhist kingdom, and was ordained as a novice at the age of 13. I remained 18 months in the holy order. Had I stayed on I would be a senior monk by now, but luckily or otherwise I left the monkhood, and pursued my worldly education. I went to the University of Wales, Lampeter and got my degree in philosophy, literature and history, and was then called to the bar in London in 1961. So I spent a long time in the UK. I also broadcasted at the BBC, and had various experiences in the West.

When I went to Wales, my college was very much Anglican, so I was exposed to Christianity at its best. I came to admire Christianity. And later on I worked closely with Muslims. My best friend, who died recently, was a great Muslim leader: Abdurrahman Wahid. He also became president of Indonesia. The country has the largest Muslim population in the world, at over 227 million. But he said Indonesia only became Muslim in the last 500 years, and it was a Buddhist land before, a Hindu land before; so to be a good Indonesian Muslim you must acknowledge your past. So he honored Hinduism and Buddhism, and I think the best of religion should be that way.

Through my contact with Christianity and Islam, and my Buddhist background, I feel that every religion is great, if you understand the essential teaching. But you have to make a distinction between the essential teaching and what developed later on. In Buddhism I differentiate between what I call 'small b' buddhism, and 'capital B' Buddhism. 'Small b' buddhism means that you take the best of the teachings of the Buddha, which is nonviolence, loving kindness. But in some places, like Sri Lanka, many 'capital B' Buddhists killed Tamils. The same happened in Burma, and in my country. So I want to warn people: 'capital B' Buddhism sometimes becomes very dangerous when it loses its essential teaching. For me, the essential teaching of Buddhism, Christianity, Islam, is very similar: love, truth, nonviolence.

If I may say so, I am one of the founders of the International Network of Engaged Buddhists. The organization is now 35 years old. It connects Buddhists all over the world. We've tried to bring the essential teaching to the people. You don't have to be Buddhist, you can be Christian or Muslim. And the 'capital B' Buddhists, the reactionaries, we don't condemn them. We have dialogue with them, and try to make friends with them. I think that's the best way to build up friendships: we don't regard ourselves as better than them.

I have had a few mentors. His Holiness the Dalai Lama is one. Although he is regarded as the 14th reincarnation of the Dalai Lama, a highly respected Tibetan Buddhist, he calls himself a simple man. And he really is a simple man. He wants to keep the message of love. And he doesn't just talk about it, he practices it. As you know, Tibet has been occupied by the Chinese for 60 years, and the Chinese government has been very ruthless. They have destroyed temples, killed many monks, tortured many nuns, but he says we must love the Chinese. For me the future of the world depends on love, not on violence. Violence is very much practiced by many dictatorial regimes, including that of my own country.

And worse than dictatorship is consumer capitalism. People want to spend more money and buy things. It's awful the way people have been worshiping greed. So I feel one has to be aware of this, and try to change violence into nonviolence.

And worse than that is delusion. Mainstream education promotes delusion: to become more important, egoistic. The more we educate, the more we should have loving kindness. We should be more humble, and should understand that all of us are related, and not only human beings, but animals, trees, rivers—we are all related. If we had that dimension, the world would be much better.

Looking back on your life, what is the wisest thing you ever did?

Speaking selfishly, I married the right woman. My wife and I have been married for over 50 years. I have been an activist, I have been put in prison many times, and I have had to flee my country three or four times, but my wife has been with me, through thick and thin. She has looked after the family, she has looked after me. We also have a small publishing house and sometimes it has been destroyed by dictators, the books have been burned. But my wife has remained calm. She is very supportive of me. I'm now getting to be 88, and my wife is 84 this year, and she has looked after me wonderfully. She has cared for my health and wellbeing, and I am so happy to have had a successful married life.

What has been the toughest lesson you have learned?

The teaching has helped me to learn about myself. I had that violent tendency as a young man. I wanted my own way. My father was a wonderful man, but he spoiled me. I demanded so much. But I tried to learn to change. The best thing in my life was that I learned who I am. I learned to be less selfish, to not take myself so seriously, to be more humble, and to be a good friend. I am lucky to have good friends around the world. Good friends are those who tell you what you don't want to hear. And I am happy to have friends from every continent, and all the major religions. Those friends have helped me along in many ways.

In the world today, where do you see wisdom, and its lack, being demonstrated?

The world today is controlled by transnational corporations, not by the superpowers anymore. The Americans have become less and less powerful. The Chinese are competing with the Americans to be more powerful. But to me, the most powerful element in the world is transnational corporations. They control everything, even in medical science. Medical science has produced many good things, but they have so many side effects. And they depend on very few drug companies, who are very powerful.

For me, to understand the world today, we must understand structural violence, and try to change things nonviolently. I am not a Marxist, but I acknowledge the Marxist approach. They help us to understand structural violence. But they use violent means to overcome things. To hate the rich and powerful I think is wrong. Hatred doesn't help you or the other. My message is more Gandhian, more about nonviolence, loving kindness. And we must change the structural violence, not by overthrowing the top, but by making the top become closer to the bottom. That's my approach.

I studied both Western and Eastern philosophy. But it only helps intellectually. The best way is to practice. In Buddhism and Christianity, for example, the practice is marvelous. In Christianity you try to love God, and by loving God you love human beings. For me that sense of love is everywhere. In Christianity, in Islam, the message of love and truth must be put into practice, not just talked about.

How do you apply wisdom to the care of your mind, body and soul?

In the Buddhist tradition, you have to learn what is the most important element in your life. And the most important thing is breathing. In Buddhism you don't have to believe in the Buddha, but if you stop breathing, you are dead. We don't realize we breathe in a lot of anxiety, and greed. The best method is to learn to breathe properly. When you breathe calmly, you breathe in calmness. Breathe in with mindfulness, breathe out with loving kindness. It's very simple. You don't have to believe in the Buddha, or God. But if you are Catholic, for example, you can breathe in the mother of God. So the sacred, the divine, becomes part of yourself. And when we are divine, we are sacred, and all our friends are sacred. Not just humans, but the animals, the trees, the river. All this is sacred. Without seeing them as friends we can become destructive to nature, and see it as something to overcome. We are not superior to nature, we are nature, and must be friends with nature.

My method of meditation is to firstly learn to be calm. And once you are calm, you become less attached to yourself. In Buddhism it is called 'samatha'. You can then develop insight meditation, and restructure your consciousness. The ego becomes less important. Make fun of the ego. And understand that all people are equal. It is about interconnectedness, that we are all related. To follow meditation is helpful in cultivating these things.

For some people, they don't realize that their lifestyle is harmful. Particularly those of the upper and middle classes. We often exploit the lower class unknowingly. So for me, with meditation, you learn to know yourself. You must also go out to see people suffering. Even in the slums, in jail. People who have been deprived of essential living. You don't go out just to help them, you go to learn from them, to be friends with them. I think that is the way we can develop meditation properly.

In the Buddhist tradition, number one: you must learn to love yourself. Not easy. We love fame, money, security, but do we love ourself? We have to learn to care for our body properly. Not too strong or weak. And our mind should be not too smart or clever. We must learn how to use our mind properly. And at the same time, learn to share with others, not to exploit yourself or others.

And to develop wisdom, we must learn that we are not just a physical entity. We also have some mental, spiritual aspects, and in the Christian term you can even be with God. In the Buddhist term, you can come to the ultimate peace, develop selflessness, void. Which is difficult to describe. But you have to put into practice all you have learned, and develop egolessness.

I am optimistic. I feel a lot of people now are thinking out of the mainstream, even in economics. Fritz Schumacher wrote the essay 'Buddhist Economics.' His idea of economics was one without greed. In Bhutan their economy is measured in Gross National Happiness, not Gross National Product. The alternatives are now available. And if we carry this out in an authentic way, it will help each of us, and help the world to survive also.

I am approaching 88 years old, and I realize that I have not many more years to live. At the same time, I meditate every day that I will soon confront death. I now confront sickness, ill health. I welcome these as friends. And eventually, when I die, I will regard death as my friend. So I am aware that I should not be afraid of sickness, old age and death. I feel that if everything becomes our friend, then I live in happiness, and will die in happiness. And I urge my wife and children to take similar steps.

When you practice mindfulness, death is nothing great. We go to sleep. You may not wake up one morning. But then after a time you wake up in a new life. After death, before rebirth, there is the stage in between they call 'bardo'. If you are serious you can learn to develop that bardo. Then in that case, if you are reborn, and are mindful, you can be reborn better than previously. But if you have bad action, mind and speech, you may be reborn in a worse condition. It's very simple. And you don't have to believe in this. You practice it when you sleep, be mindful that you may not wake up tomorrow, and say goodbye to everyone. But when you wake up you think, 'Wonderful, I have one more day.' Life is something gainful, profitable, because I hope in the way I live that I will contribute something, not just for myself and my family, but also for all sentient beings. Hopefully when I die I could also do something better in the other world.

My contribution to the world has been very small. I am a small man. My organization is a small one. But as Schumacher says, small is beautiful. I hope my life, my organization, has contributed something beautiful. Beauty need not be painting, or sculpture. Even your writing could also be beauty. If people understand beauty, then they can understand goodness. If they understand goodness they can understand truth. For me I hope I can contribute a little bit toward beauty, goodness and truth.

Is wisdom a uniquely human concept?

If you meditate carefully, you can learn the wisdom of the animals and trees. You can even talk to the trees, the mountains and the rivers. The language they talk is not our language, but if you are serene, mindful, with humility, you can learn from the river, from the trees, from the ocean. But we don't learn from nature. This is why we have this pandemic right now. We destroy nature, we feel we can control nature. We are part of nature, and should respect every aspect of nature. And then you can hear what nature is telling you. There is tremendous wisdom that we can get from nature.

Do you have a favorite parable or anecdote on wisdom?

If you are wise, everything can become very funny. Do not take life too seriously. I know a Japanese Zen monk who was accused of seducing a parishioner, and fathering her child. It was a big scandal. And the monk laughed and said, "Is that so?" A few year later, the woman confessed that the child was fathered by someone else. And the monk laughed and said, "Is that so?" Having a laugh about everything will make your life much longer.

How do you ultimately define wisdom?

Wisdom is about learning to be humble. With humility you see things clearly. With less selfishness I think that is wisdom. It is called panja in Pali, and prajñā in Sanskrit. As you become more selfless, then wisdom transforms into compassion. Wisdom allows us to be skillful in conducting our daily lives, and with compassion, we hope that whatever we do will be helpful to other people. The Buddha is known as the one who is most wise, and most compassionate. And as a teacher he put us on the path of wisdom and compassion. With compassion, with loving kindness, that is better than the greed and delusion which is controlling the world right now.

How can each of us develop wisdom?

We must first make time to learn to breathe properly. Start with one minute, then two minutes. If you breathe properly then you slow down your life. We rush too much. When you slow down you don't want to have so many possessions. You don't want so much power, so many duties. You need time to share with yourself, and your family and friends. I think that the best thing in life is to share your life with good friends. They will tell you what you don't want to hear. We must learn to change ourselves. And we can learn to restructure our consciousness, and become a better human being.

Thich Nhat Hanh, the Vietnamese Buddhist monk, coined the term 'engaged Buddhism'. He said that we must not care only about the next world. He set up Plum Village in France, and in America, and even in my own country. Again, you don't have to be Buddhist. You go to learn how to breathe properly, to walk properly, to eat properly, to sleep properly. It's that simple. It's a wonderful approach that people are trying, all over the world.

How did it feel to discuss wisdom today?

I'm very happy that you care to talk to me, an old man. In my country people are afraid of me. They think I'm a naughty old man. Because I still care very much about social justice, and about oppressed people, and I open my mouth. A lot of people feel I'm a great danger in my old age. I hope that what I shared today, the audience will not find it a great danger, that they will find the voice of an old man who tried to be a friend to all of you. And I am very grateful to those who read this. If I said something you don't like, please forgive me; and if I said something useful to you, please take it and use it.

Wendy Stephenson

Wendy is a woman who loves deeply and is most at home in the natural world. Life has been full from the get go, with a childhood that presented twists and turns and many adventures. Growing up in the north east of England, at a time of high unemployment, Wendy had more than 30 jobs over five years before going to university to study Environmental Energy Engineering because she cared about the environment. This started her 30-year career in the field of climate change and energy policy and strategy. Wendy also served on a number of regulatory and policy committees both in the UK and Europe. For the last decade she has been developing and operating renewable energy assets in India and developing programs of eco-restoration. theconvergingworld.org

What comes to mind first when you think about wisdom?

Sages. Prophets. People that have a certain energetic. People that are not caught up in their own stuff. People that are beyond the baggage of this social construct or this paradigm. It's an expanded way of being in the world that is not attached to the social constructs that we've designed. It's a kind of universal. So I got into the idea of the people, but then that form carries a universal quality that is beyond time. And they're able to inhabit that timeless space without personalizing baggage stuff. It sounds like God, doesn't it?

I have not met any of these people, not in an absolutely fully-formed sense. I think I've got idealizations, and some of those are projected on us through certain people like the Dalai Lama, for example. I look at the framed picture on my wall of the indigenous woman. I don't know why, but she speaks to me of wisdom. It's interesting that she's older. But then children can be very wise. It's the bit in the middle that is more muddled. So have I met anyone that encompasses the full, idealized version of what wisdom looks like to me? No. I can idealize someone and only focus on the qualities within that person that might feel are wise and universal. But as you know, once you get to know them a bit better you start to see their absolutely natural, human tendencies. I wouldn't call them failings, but we all have aspects that we would prefer not to focus on. And in other people we just want the idealized version. But I think I've met people with different qualities of wisdom in different amounts, and they're different ages, and often they are children.

Do you recall the first time you witnessed wisdom in action?

For some reason I've gone back to a particular time in my childhood. So whether that is because that's when I first became aware of what wisdom might look like or not, I don't know, because maybe a child might not be able to discern wisdom. They may feel it, but can they discern it? I've gone back to a particular period, and I don't know why, but I'm seeing a tramp. I don't know what that's about. So it was a particular time when I probably saw it.
   I certainly felt it in my Nana. So she comes up a lot.

Who have been your wisdom teachers?

Definitely my sister Helen. One might dismiss her as having no wisdom, but that's what I find intriguing.
   And my niece, Natalie. She feels like she was born with a lot of wisdom. One day, when she was four years old, we were in a cafe. She had a straw in her drink and kept pulling it towards herself with her mouth. And I said, "Natalie, if you keep doing that, you might spill it." But she carried on and she did spill it. It went everywhere. And I could feel the owner of the cafe was a bit tense about this. So I said, "Okay,

let me clear this up." And Natalie who could feel my tension because of the owners. She just looked at me and said, "It's a funny old life, isn't it Auntie Wendy?"

And in that one statement, there was so much. It was like, 'Don't worry about it. I know you told me, and I've done it anyway. And you know what? Forget those people over there, because they're just tense. It's just a funny old life, isn't it?' And she was four years old. And there it was: a quality of wisdom, right in that moment. She was saying, 'Get out of your head, get out of the tension, and don't worry about it. Don't cry over spilled milk.'

That was beautiful. She has this old soul really, and she has wisdom, and it's carried on in at least one of her children, maybe two or three of them. And I think she got it from her mum. Even though she might not see that, I think she does to some extent. So those are the two people in my personal life.

For a time I was part of a religious body called the Christadelphians. A number of those people worked on themselves, albeit in a Christian religious context. Some of them might not recognize it, because they associate the concept with New Age thinking, but some of them were certainly nurturing the qualities of wisdom. They took their teaching from Proverbs and other biblical books that also promote wisdom in individuals.

So I guess I've picked up these qualities of wisdom from people that I have been in touch with. It's subliminal and it's osmotic. It gets absorbed.

I look for beauty and harmony in the world, and for me wisdom has those qualities. I really appreciate those qualities in a person, and feel very at home in that. You're very at home in the presence of wisdom. It's interesting, isn't it?

And actually I'd say that for a long time, I looked for it. I was a seeker. Not necessarily for me to learn it, because I don't know how one learns wisdom, but really because I was comforted by being in the presence of my perception of the qualities of wisdom.

For example, I think John Pontin and Dennis Burn at The

Converging World have great qualities of wisdom. Herbie Girardet is another one. Some of these are nurtured, others are innate, and some are a combination of the two. Others pick it up through osmosis, with experience. It's fascinating to think about it actually, because I know that I'm very attracted to it and sit very comfortably in it. It's almost like a feeling of 'Oh, this is nice.'

I recently read *The Book of Joy*, and it's a fabulous book. It's the Dalai Lama and Desmond Tutu in conversation. They wanted to celebrate each other's birthdays. It was the Dalai Lama's 80th. He was banned from going to Desmond Tutu's 80th because they wouldn't permit him a visa to get into South Africa. So he asked Desmond Tutu to join him in Dharamsala. A guy by the name of Douglas Abrams interviewed them, then transcribed and commented on their conversations, which took place over several days. They discuss different aspects of life and how they feel about things. Abrams would offer scientific evidence to back up some of the points being made by the two men. I know we can idealize them, but in the conversation there was some real wisdom coming through.

The laughter between them was absolutely wonderful. That was a thread throughout the book: the joy.

The Dalai Lama was asked if he felt bitterness and anger towards the Chinese. He had been exiled in 1959 after a failed uprising against the Chinese. He said, and I'm paraphrasing, "If I feel bitter or angry, then I cause pain to myself. That doesn't achieve anything. But if I turn that around and if I love the people that exiled me, that energy will go out and that will change things, eventually." There is real wisdom in that, as there is no point in carrying that bitterness and anger, because actually the only one you're harming is yourself. To turn it around and proactively learn to love is quite something. So that really stands out.

And I think about Matthew 5:43, which says, 'Bless them that curse you, do good to them that hate you, and pray for them which despitefully use you, and persecute you.' So it feels like a universal quality that is worth trying to nurture within ourselves.

And there was another one that stood out. Desmond Tutu had a difficult childhood. His father would beat him awfully. And there was a moment where he intuitively knew he had to go to him, and I think he died that night. He went through a process—as I think all of South Africa did—of learning what forgiveness really means. I think the quality here seems to be one of being open, even in the pain you might have suffered; being open to learning from and processing the pain, to find a way to forgive, to start fresh, to let go of the event or the action that caused you pain. If we're willing to work through it, we can get to a place where we can move on, so that it doesn't affect us in the same way.

Looking back on your life, what is the wisest thing you ever did?

There's one quality that I think I've been wise to try and nurture. Generally in life, if someone has wronged you, people say you should go back and confront them about it. But if it's only going to feed a drama and cause more pain, there seems little point in doing that. It's easy for us to react and hit out, but actually if you can see beyond that person's behavior, most people don't intend harm to others.

I don't feel I always need to find answers. Sometimes life is as it is, and we are better served by making our peace with the past. Sometimes we have to sit in that place of knowing, in spite of how things might appear to the rest of the world. So I think one of the wisest things I have done is to keep checking in with myself, and follow my own knowing on this.

These are not world-shattering things, but I've made huge decisions in my life. I've married, I've divorced, I haven't had children. I wouldn't venture to say that any of them were based in any wise counsel that I have. They've come out of circumstances that have been influenced by so many bits and pieces, and I did what seemed right at the time.

It's hard to say if things were wise decisions. I decided to go to university, but was that a wise choice? I don't even think that you can say whether it was a wise choice or not. Those sorts of decisions, like deciding whether or not to go to university, or buy a house, don't feel like decisions that have come out of wisdom. I think of wisdom as a bunch of qualities that might help make a decision. However it does feel like a wise decision to not put someone through hell because the world thinks it's okay to do that and that's what should be done.

What has been the toughest lesson you have learned?

I know that in the world people think you should talk about your problems, and if you don't, you're kind of zipped up and that it's going to come up sooner or later, or it'll come out in disease. I've listened to that, but ever since I was a child, I've always felt that there is also a place for private counsel. Because as soon as you let it out, you have no control. And it doesn't come out the way it's really felt. So I think there is wisdom in keeping one's own counsel sometimes. That's something I've always done.

We all have treasures in our hearts, and as soon as you reveal that, it's no longer just in your heart, it's out there. And as soon as it's out there, it changes. And not only that, but it gets blemished because people will say things about it and it becomes something else entirely, and a completely different experience through somebody else's frame. So probably one of the wisest things I have done is to keep my own counsel. And I've always regretted it when I have spoken of something, and then it's taken on a life of its own, when I felt that I should have said nothing.

Another tough lesson has been about not having the courage to follow my intuition. For example, I think that the biggest one for me, which has pain, was not having children.

I went to university, I've had a career, and I've worked hard at that career. Intuitively I knew I never wanted an office job. Somebody once read my palm and they said, "Oh, I can see a desk." I laughed and said, "You must be joking. That's not me. I'll never been in an office job." And I've spent the last two decades at a desk. Intuitively I knew that it was never me, but I didn't have the courage to ignore the external pressure of having a career and just step out and do what it was that I wanted to do. By preference I would have done something much more creative, much more in nature, probably dragging a kid or two around quite freely. And outside of this awful stricture.

I did renewable energy engineering at university because I thought, 'Well, that's okay, because I'll be in the field.' And that's never happened. So I've been kind of stuck in that cycle really. Why did I go to university? That all goes into self-worth, doesn't it? You're in this society that judges, values and validates you based on your status, so that's probably what prompted me to go. That's been the hardest lesson because it's dominated my life in a way that hasn't necessarily been as healthy as it could have been. I did not follow my intuition, to be wild and free and follow my deep passions. And it doesn't model well for the next generation either.

I did a lot of mountaineering for a time, and that was a great teacher. We were climbing Chimborazo in Ecuador, which has a 6,263-meter peak. It's the highest mountain in the world as measured from the center of the Earth. This has an impact on the atmosphere and gravity and other things. It can affect your altitude sickness, in different ways.

We ate masses of food to fuel up at about six, then set the alarm for 11 o'clock at night. You feel awful, and don't really sleep because you've got a headache, like the worst hangover in the world. You want to get to the peak by sunrise because you want to get down in good time, and because as the sun rises it starts to melt the snow and there's more avalanche risk. So you have to climb during the night. You put your stuff on and set off. So you've got ice axes, crampons, ropes, rucksack etc. The air is so thin that just bending down and tying your shoelaces has you out of breath.

When you're climbing a mountain, you cannot think about the top of the mountain, because if you do you will never get there. The pressure of getting to the peak, the pressure of that journey and what you have to go through for the next six or seven hours to get there, will be emotionally overwhelming. You won't be able to do it. So the only thing you can focus on is your next step. You've got your heavy rucksack with your ropes, food and emergency kit. You're on a rope that keeps getting pulled back and forth, so you're having to balance your body, all your muscles, and you've got hardly any oxygen and it's pitch black. The only light comes from your head torch, and you don't want to use too much torch light so you've got it quite low, but you need to be able to look where you're treading. So every step is incredibly hard work and every breath is deep and quick because you're constantly panting for oxygen. And that's what you do for six or seven hours of the climb to the peak. That's all you do. You just focus on the next step, getting breath, and the next step and getting breath, for six or more hours. And that's the only focus, not the peak. And you do the same with climbing. If you're climbing on a cliff face, you literally can't think about anything else. And if you're like me and you're actually frightened of heights and you put yourself in that position—which isn't very wise—then you're terrified. And you can feel your breath pushing your body away from the cliff. So everything is focused on the next move and nothing else matters.

To actually reach the peak, it's a suppressed elation. When we were climbing Cotopaxi there was a ladder pitch, which was one of those wire ladders. It was so steep that they'd put this in. But it was one of those loose ones. Now, can you imagine, with a rucksack, ice axe and crampons, and you're on this very narrow thing that's swaying. You're trying to climb up, and you're at about 6,000 meters above sea level. Where you get the strength from in your arms I have no idea. I don't know how we did it. But just before the ladder pitch, we got to this little outcrop and the sun was just starting to come up. So we decided to stop and fuel up before attempting the ladder pitch. You try not to stop on a mountain where you've got a lot of ice and snow because there's a lot of danger. We were sitting there, and although I don't really like chocolate, on mountain days I could easily eat a Mars bar or a Snickers. So I was just piling it in. And I said, "I'm just going to close my eyes." I'm a great cat napper. My friends have got photographs of me asleep on mountainsides. No kidding. If I need to sleep, I need to sleep. So I closed my eyes for two minutes while they were getting ready. Then Graham said, "Come on Wend, it's time to go." And I came around and I was saying, "Where's Rosie?" I saw a black Labrador and a red ball. Rosie was a friend of ours that we'd climbed with in Scotland and other places. I was so oxygen-deprived that I was hallucinating. And now I had to climb this ladder pitch. And of course, when you're oxygen deprived, you don't make intelligent decisions. And this is why it's really risky.

But we got to the top and it was amazing. We stood at 6,000 meters above sea level. The world looks a different shape, like you see in fisheye lens cameras. And we're on the edge of this volcano looking down into it. You could smell the sulfur because the volcano is active. And I say it was suppressed elation because you know you've got to get down safely, and that's when a lot of accidents happen. So you can't fully enjoy the moment. It's only usually over the next few days, that you have this slow release of, "Wow, that was fabulous wasn't it?" And it stays with you forever. I walked past big, strong men that looked fitter and younger than I did. And they were just in tears because they couldn't go any further. And maybe they didn't make it because they always had the summit in their sights. It's not the summit you have to have in your sights. You have to enjoy and focus on the journey.

In the world today, where do you see wisdom, and its lack, being demonstrated?

There is a definite lack of wisdom in governance structures, whether it's in corporations or political institutions. If you look at governance structures around the world, I'm afraid the very structures that should be nurturing wisdom are sadly lacking it. And often individuals look to the authorities for wise leadership. George Orwell identified this. He did loads of different things, and worked in many roles. He wanted to experience these varied aspects of life. It helps you to understand people. And at one point he was working as a hops picker. They got paid a pittance. So he asked why they didn't do something about it. He suggested they form a collective to fight for better pay. And the other pickers said, "No. They wouldn't like it." And he said to them, "Who are they?" And none of them could answer. This attitude is especially prevalent among the working class. Whether it's epigenetic or whatever, there's been that dominant class. I know that the classes are muddling a bit, but nevertheless it always feels that there is a dominant class, or a domineering element to the system that then disempowers everyone else. Whether people don't feel empowered to be able to nurture their own wise counsel or not, I'm not sure. Whether the education system disempowers us from nurturing our intuition and our own innate wisdom or not, I'm not sure. But there is something systemic that is having that effect. So what happens is a lot of people look to them—whoever they are—in the governance structures for wisdom, and they don't get it.

And that has a massive impact on the planet. It also has a massive impact on individuals because they're modeling a way of being, and everyone feels unsure of their own knowledge and power. So they allow other people to create the models that they follow. You see this with reality TV shows. They're awful because they're modeling a way of being which has got nothing to do with self-growth and nurturing wisdom in this world. It's lacking in individuals because it's lacking in the system that we've constructed. It's systemically lacking in education. And then that goes into everything else.

It's wonderful when you see wisdom in a family structure. It's rare, but you do see it.

How do you apply wisdom to the care of your mind, body and soul?

Not very well. To apply wisdom, one first has to nurture it. If I'm to take a proactive step in applying wisdom, it would be when I set aside time for self-care. And just that action is the application of wisdom. Because without setting time aside to nurture all those things, none of it happens. And that can mean all sorts of things. So that can manifest in listening to podcasts by people who may have what I would perceive to be the qualities of wisdom. Or it might be in sitting in nature.

I have a lot on, and I can sit in Zoom calls for 12 or 13 hours almost nonstop some days, and that is not very wise. And I don't like using the word 'wise' for those kinds of decisions. It doesn't feel quite the right application of the quality.

And I'm also trying to renovate this house. It was a beautiful day and it was dusty inside because I'm taking off this old lime plaster. I tend to just keep going with whatever I'm doing, but it was beautiful outside so I thought I'd have a cup of tea. Often I will only stop when I actually feel hungry. I don't have a routine so I can go hours without eating and then suddenly wonder why my energy has dipped. And then I realize, 'Oh. I haven't eaten since yesterday.' So I'm not naturally tuned into self-care in that way. So it will hit me and then I'll need to do something about that. And in stopping for that cup of tea I did something I rarely do, which is to let myself enjoy the moment.

So applying wisdom in the care of my mind, body and spirit is about constantly coming back to remind myself to enjoy the process, the journey. Which comes back to the story about the mountain. Because I haven't always enjoyed the process. I haven't always enjoyed my work. I've sat in front of a computer and don't want to, so then why live life like that? Somehow you have to find a way of enjoying it. Either that or change it.

Is wisdom a uniquely human concept?

Aren't all such concepts uniquely human? There are all kinds of other beings in the world, like trees and animals. But they don't have all that stuff going on that we do. They kind of have a flow. Some of it may seem cruel, but we've overlaid that with our sensitivity. It's like: lion kills gazelle, giraffe fights giraffe, and that might not feel good to us.

Is wisdom a single quality, or is wisdom a collection of qualities that help us navigate the world, given our sensitivity, whereas other beings on the planet do not need to? I guess it depends on how you define wisdom. With other beings, do they need those qualities of wisdom to help them navigate this world in their form? One will never know because I can't get inside the mind of a tree or the beingness of a tree. I can only see it from this relational point of view and I can think universally about it, and try and imagine seeing that from the beingness of a tree or the form of a flower. I can't say with any confidence that I can. But from this relational place, I can say that it feels to me that wisdom is a collection of qualities that helps us elevate beyond our 'stuff', towards a more universal beingness.

Do you have a favorite parable or anecdote on wisdom?

I can't remember where it comes from, but I think it's Japanese. There is an old man and a young man. And the young man is attacking the old man, swinging at him. The old man is wise enough to know that he can't fight the young man in the same way. So instead, every time the young man hits out, the old man steps back, until eventually the young man is too tired to fight anymore. Then you meet each other at the same place and that will open up the possibility of finding a way through. So that's one which I think is quite beautiful.

The other one comes from vipassana. The story goes that there's a general in charge of an army. They're standing at the head of the river by the top of a waterfall. And he tells his men that the only way down is via the waterfall. The first soldier jumps in, goes over the waterfall and drowns. So the general sends another man down, with the same result. Yet he keeps sending the men, and they keep drowning. And then an old peasant comes along. He dives in and goes down the waterfall, then gets out of the river completely unharmed. So the general calls across to him and he asks him how he did that, when all his young, fit soldiers are dying. And the man says, "Stop resisting the water, flow with it. And it will bring you up further down the river."

And that's the same in any tide or current. So the more we resist and the more we fight, the less likely we are to survive. We'll use up a lot of energy and we're likely to drown in that resistance and in that fight.

How do you ultimately define wisdom?

This discussion has actually helped me to define it. I think it's a collection of qualities, that can be innate, nurtured, and grown out of experience. If we apply them they can help us navigate life.

How can each of us develop wisdom?

I think we have to empower people to believe that it's up to us, to every individual, to every family structure. Don't look to 'them' for wisdom. Not even the Dalai Lama, or Desmond Tutu or the Pope or whoever your guru is. Yes, be inspired by them, let them feed you, but you have to believe that you can develop and nurture wisdom. There is an innate wisdom somewhere in every single one of us, but we've lost touch with it. For whatever reason. We've been told we're not wise. And actually, if we sit still and learn to listen, we will hear it.

Is there anything else you wish to add?

There's great wisdom in less is more. There's great wisdom in sometimes just sitting in the discomfort, just sitting and waiting and not rushing to make a decision. We're all brought up to believe that we have to be doing something and we have to be making decisions. But often just sitting and allowing things to unfold is the wiser choice. And it can take courage. In the doing nothing, either the answer will emerge, or the issue or problem will dissolve. We don't always have to be the proactive activist, making something happen. In fact, the very opposite may be true, as we've seen with the pandemic. Sometimes if we just get out of the way of ourselves, just sit, be still, do nothing, many problems will just dissolve.

How did it feel to discuss wisdom today?

Amazing. I've always felt comfortable when I'm in the presence of what I might perceive as a quality of wisdom. Or in the presence of someone that I think displays certain characteristics or qualities that I might interpret as wisdom. It gives me a sense of relief, of comfort. It's almost like we're going back to some knowing that is deep within all of us. And so actually exploring this feels like it's taking us into a deep knowing that is just ages old. And it feels like home. It feels like it's the place where we should all retrench to, or journey towards. So I've really enjoyed discussing it and exploring it. It's been soul food. Or like a soul shower. It feels primal, like going back to something ages deep.

Julie Taylor

Julie Taylor, M.Ed., is an American School Counselor Association's School Counselor of the Year Finalist and Ohio School Counselor of the Year. She is committed to supporting the academic success, social/emotional development and college and career readiness of all students, and she is passionate about the role of school counselors in their work as advocates and agents of change. Julie regularly presents at state and national school counseling conferences, trains educators in interpersonal and institutional best practices for supporting grieving students, and helped write the Ohio Department of Education's school counselor standards.

Julie embraces a vegetarian lifestyle, is a certified fitness instructor and enjoys gardening, reading, kayaking and singing in her church choir. She adores her nieces Kate and Claire and her rescue pug, Penelope. In the evenings, she can often be found walking, enjoying a girls' night with friends or relaxing on the patio with her husband.

What comes to mind first when you think about wisdom?

As I was creating a mind map about wisdom, the first words that came to mind were: knowledge, insight and awareness. I also think of the desire to continue learning, growing, changing and evolving, and using what you have learned for good. If your knowledge may be helpful, wisdom is offering to share it with others. It's striving to make the world a little bit better, and always acting from a place of benevolence, compassion and kindness.

Wisdom is found in listening. Really taking time to listen.

It is also the ability to detach yourself. At times, I believe you have to step back, because only then are you able to see the bigger picture, to gain perspective. If I become too involved or attached in my work, I try to recognize it before the job overwhelms me. I think that's wisdom: recognizing when you're not in a good spot, when you need to slow down or take a break, or when you need to ask for help. Wisdom can be reconsidering what you are about to say, or sometimes to simply stop talking. Rarely have I regretted keeping my mouth shut, especially in those moments of frustration, stress or anger.

A wise person can laugh at themselves and realize, 'Jeez, I really screwed that up. I'll try really hard not to do that again.'

Seeking to understand yourself is critical, because once you truly assess yourself, and understand yourself, then that's where you can begin to change yourself. You have to know your flaws, your faults and your weaknesses. You have to be self-aware. And then you have to desire to make improvements.

Wisdom is attempting to understand others, because it's not all about you. Others have so much to contribute, and to give and to share. I have learned so much from my friends. They've enriched my life enormously, and I am different because of them. I don't think you can be wise without developing real relationships. Relationships with all kinds of people. I have my friends who love to garden, friends who love to read, friends who love to exercise, friends who love to sing. Friends broaden your being and make you a more well-rounded, whole person.

Wisdom is being slow to react, and slow to anger. It's having patience and perseverance. There is also wisdom in questioning everything you think you know, and in using discernment.

Do you recall the first time you witnessed wisdom in action?

I didn't realize it at the time, but my parents are very wise. They both grew up with challenges in their lives, but they reflected on their childhoods, and they consciously chose to create a different life for my brother and I. They decided what they valued, and then they prioritized it, taught it, modeled it and encouraged it. They taught me about unconditional love and about kindness, generosity and compassion. They taught me about being responsible and respectful and about the importance of having integrity and a strong work ethic.

Everything my parents did was done with my best interests at heart. Even their gifts were thoughtful and wise. When I got my first home, my dad bought me this very girlish toolbox—light blue (my favorite color) and frosted white. When I unwrapped it, my brother said to our dad, "I can't believe you carried that out of the store." But in it was my dad's wish for me to always have what I need. To be independent and self-reliant. But also to ask for help if I need it. Even though my dad is not here anymore, I will always have this gift.

My mom has given me so many thoughtful gifts over the years. From every trip we took or activity we tried, she almost always brought back a small trinket for us by which to remember the adventure. She also took tons of photos, which beautifully document our family's time together. And years ago, my mom gave me a little stone inscribed with the words, "Happy Birthday." When she gave it to me, she said, "When I'm not here to wish you a happy birthday, always know that I am with you."

On the noticeboard behind me you can see it says: 'Thankful for the little things.' I think a truly wise person is appreciative of and grateful for what they have. Wisdom is not forgetting your past, but also appreciating the here and now, because when you're thankful, I think it creates that sense of peace. I'm so thankful for my parents and the life they offered me. I'm thankful for their wisdom.

Who is the wisest person you know, and why?

I've learned so much from so many, but I think the person who stands out most is a professor I had in graduate school, Dr. Susan Norris Huss. She had been a school counselor for years and was close to retirement. But instead of finishing her career and enjoying retirement, she went back to school and earned her doctorate because, she told her students, she wanted to share and impart the wisdom she had learned. She was still writing, lecturing and consulting near the end of her life. Dr. Huss was incredibly knowledgeable, and I learned so much from her, not only about the profession but about qualities like unconditional positive regard. She was authentic, genuine and nonjudgmental. Her words, thoughts, actions and beliefs were all in harmony. She was real, and she listened to you, and she made you feel real, and nothing you could say or do would change the relationship.

Dr. Huss was an amazing person, and her influence is reflected in my practice. She's in the back of my mind always; to do what is ethical, to question, to consult, to listen, to validate, to advocate and to be there for others. I try to be like her. I tend to be emotional, but she was calm even in the midst of a storm. So I try to grasp that essence sometimes, and use it to ground myself, to make good decisions and to do what's best for the students I serve.

I keep a journal of quotes from wise people who inspire me and help me reflect. When I feel lost or realize I'm not being the best version of myself, I go back and read their words. I think wise people aren't always inventing new things. They reflect on what others know and that have stood the test of time. I love little inspirational magnets and plaques. I think to be the person you want to be or to change thoughts or behaviors, you have to have visual reminders. I keep a little plaque on my kitchen counter that reads, 'Life is a balance of holding on and letting go.' There is a magnet on my refrigerator that simply states, 'Dwell in possibility.' And I have a small sign at home and a larger one in my office at work that reads, 'Go into the world and do well, but most importantly go into the world and do good.' It reminds me about being successful professionally, but also being a good human. And that's the message I try to share with our students every day as well.

I think photos, like words, can also help one become more wise. There is a photo I love of one of my nieces. She's quite young in the photo, and is looking out over a forested valley in Colorado. It reminds me to never lose my sense of awe, wonder and gratitude. So when I see this, I think, 'Stop and breathe, and reflect on the beauty that is around you.'

Looking back on your life, what is the wisest thing you ever did?

Changing careers was a wise decision. My first career was teaching music. During my four years of undergraduate work and three years of teaching elementary music, I was miserable. I was in a horrible place in many ways, and I felt trapped. And one day I just decided: I can't live like this. So I quit my job, with no job to go to. I relocated to a larger city and, after a few months, got a job with a large non-profit. And I took time to figure out what I wanted to do, because what I was doing wasn't working. I allowed myself to stop to reflect.

And that's when I decided to go back to grad school. School counseling was a thought that had always been in the back of my mind, and I had even written about it in my journals as I was trying to decide on a vocation. Looking back, I think we have some innate insight in us that we need to tune into and follow sometimes. We have to be true to ourselves, and that goes back to the importance of self-awareness.

And it turns out, my current career choice has been a wonderful one because it provides me with so many opportunities to be different versions of myself. I help kids and families. I create classroom lessons integrating art, music, drama and children's literature. I run a service learning group in which students get to experience the feeling of doing good for others. And I recently became a certified kids' yoga instructor, and received a grant to purchase yoga mats, so we can now offer yoga classes for students in the fall.

But I think the thing I love most about my career is that I get to touch the future. I have the opportunity to provide mentoring and modeling, to be an advocate and agent of change, and to make the world a better place. I also have the chance to laugh with students every day, to feel appreciated by so many, and to get tons of hugs.

Wisdom

What is the hardest-won wisdom that you have?

I think my hardest-won wisdom is that my happiness is a choice. I am the only one who can make me happy. In my 20s and 30s I kept thinking I had to find a relationship to be happy. I wasn't enjoying the moment because I was so concerned about the future. I now know that if I want to be happy, I can decide to be happy; think happy thoughts, surround myself with positive people. I have to let go of hurts, disappointments and heartaches. You can let those things swallow you up. But why do that, when you have a choice? You can choose to celebrate what you have and be thankful.

I have learned a lot from our students. I've learned about choosing happiness by watching and interacting with them. I read somewhere that kids laugh an average of 400 times a day, whereas adults laugh an average of 17 times a day. So I'm very lucky to be at a job where I am surrounded by laughter. I love the lightheartedness that kids can bring to any situation. I also love their authenticity. I don't hide my feelings well. I'm very raw and honest, and a lot of people might not appreciate those qualities. I'm so glad that I can be myself at work because students allow me to be myself. They don't judge me. They show me how to be real. They express themselves. They tell you how it is.

Some of our students go through incredibly difficult situations. They can be amazingly resilient. No matter what is happening in their lives, they can come to school and still learn and laugh and play. However, other students struggle terribly with the challenges in their lives. There have been cases where children have lost their parents at a very young age from cancer, drug overdoses or suicide, for example, and I have helped them navigate some of the associated challenges. To be there for students through their sadness, fear, anxiety and anger can be demanding and stressful, and the challenge is compounded by the reality that I'm very sensitive and empathetic. So I have had to develop a way of self-preservation to continue doing the work. The knowledge that I am doing the best I can to support students' academic, social/emotional and career development is an important awareness to have.

I also remind myself that I'm giving our students a wonderful gift: someone who listens with an open heart and mind. As a school counselor, my role is to listen, to validate, and to give students a voice. I take what they give me, and I reach out to their families, teachers, classmates and others to help make their worlds a little bit better.

The job is stressful, and it can be very disheartening at times, so I have a whole other life outside my career. I've developed hobbies and interests that bring me joy, so I can lose myself in them and not think about work so much. You have to find things that bring you joy. When I'm gardening, for instance, I find so much peace. It's repetitive, it's physical labor. It's being outdoors. It's connecting with the earth. It's growth, in itself. Gardening, being outdoors and being active grounds you. It's just good for your soul. And I think for me in my profession, having the winter and summer breaks is really important. To step back from situations, to find time for other passions, and to keep your career from becoming your identity, those breaks are needed. I don't know if I could do my job if it was a 12-month-a-year career. It genuinely helps to have time with family and friends and see functional, engaged, happy humans. It helps me step back and regain perspective. It reminds me that this is a goal for all of us to work towards, and that it is possible to get to a better place, even for kids and families who are struggling. I'm constantly sharing with students the hopeful message that things may not be good now, but they will get better. And the idea that you can be happy even in the midst of struggle. That reminds me of another quote I love and share quite often: 'Life isn't about waiting for the storm to pass; it's about learning to dance in the rain.'

In the world today, where do you see wisdom, and its lack, being demonstrated?

When I think about wisdom being demonstrated, I recognize that my answer is determined by my definition of wisdom. In other words, I know my view on it is skewed. From my worldview, I see wisdom in the movement of people going back to simpler things, like gardening, cooking meals at home, getting together with neighbors and volunteering. Yoga and other mindfulness practices are becoming more commonplace because I think people are realizing they need to slow down in order to be physically, emotionally and mentally healthy.

I have been a vegetarian since my early teens, and I'm so happy more people are exploring plant-based diets, eating organic foods, supporting sustainable agriculture practices, buying locally, and joining food co-ops. I see wisdom in people choosing eco-friendly practices like carpooling, recycling, re-purposing and simply bringing their own shopping bags. I'm also glad there is more awareness and conversation about mental health, and that there are more resources available than ever before. I think as a society we are becoming more wise by realizing the importance of keeping not only our bodies but our minds healthy.

In terms of what I perceive as a lack of wisdom in the world, I think first of the destruction of our planet—our soil, air and water—and the inhumane treatment of people and animals. I think of consumerism and the buying and discarding of so much, and the prolific use of plastics, pesticides and so many other chemicals. I don't understand corporate greed, the insistence of putting money above all else.

I also see a complete disregard of wisdom when a society believes it is acceptable to lash out in anger, to say whatever you want whenever you want, to enact vengeance and to intentionally hurt others. It's the ugliness of humanity that I see, and the media bias toward covering negative stories, and only intensifying the ugliness.

And then there is our addiction to technology. I think we are using technology to an extreme, from gaming to social media. It's affecting our minds and bodies. It's not healthy. It would not surprise me if some kids are on their devices up to eight hours a day. It seems like parents are also spending extensive periods of time on technology. I believe the latest research has found that adults spend over three hours a day on their phones. In my work, students frequently tell me that dad or mom's boyfriend is gaming and not helping with anything, or that mom is often on her phone using social media. Families are becoming disengaged, and I believe technology is one of the factors contributing to this problem. It doesn't seem, from my limited perspective, that relationship-building opportunities like family meals, activities and discussions are happening in many of our families.

Fortunately, some of our students are wise enough even at a young age to know that they don't like what they are seeing. One little girl recently told me that her dad is always gaming and doesn't play with her or her sister. She feels he barely talks to them, and that makes her feel like he doesn't care about them. So at the age of eight, she knows that she doesn't want to be like that. So she chooses to play with her sister and her stuffed animals, and she dances and makes up songs and creates art. She has chosen a different path.

I address technology and so many other topics with students and families, and I try to do so in an appropriate and ethical way because it's not my job to impose my values. It's always necessary to step back in that way, especially about topics that I feel strongly about. Students typically initiate conversations with me, because they seek me out as their school counselor. They tell me they're unhappy or worried about something, or that there's a problem. Quite often, the topic they start with is only the surface concern, but the more I listen, the deeper we get. I think this is because so few people actually listen. They are so busy with work or new relationships or their own needs. So when students and I make the time to talk, we often get to the root of the concern, the underlying problem. And then that's when I talk to families.

In this conversation, I keep referring to families, but I would be remiss if I didn't mention that students and I also frequently talk and collaborate with teachers, administrators and support staff regarding the students' school-related concerns such as academics, peer relationships and other topics.

In my role, I help children and families communicate. In my conversations with families, I share general concerns and offer suggestions. I give kids a voice, but do so with sensitivity because if parents are offended it only makes the situation worse. For example, instead of saying that dad is always gaming, I'll point out that his daughter really misses spending time with him. Instead of focusing on the negative, or blaming or judging, it's about sharing with dad that his daughter wants to have that time with him. She would really love to play a board game with dad or have a daddy-daughter day. I have come to believe that sometimes the most effective practice in working with families is to find some small thing to change that addresses the bigger problem. When the family sees the good that one little change creates, and how much their child appreciates it, the family starts to evolve or change based on that positive feedback. When the dad sees how much his daughter enjoyed the time with him or realizes how good it felt to spend time with her, maybe he will want to spend less time gaming and more time parenting.

I'll also share with families some parenting strategies and techniques that research has shown to be effective. I don't want to come across as preachy or an expert, so I'll simply pass along information or ideas from others. Instead of saying, "You really need to talk with your child because she says you never talk to her," I might say sometime like, "Most kids want to spend time with their parents. If you can, try to take a few minutes to chat with her about her day. Have a conversation while you are driving to soccer practice or while eating ice cream together. Or check in with her at bedtime. These are best practices; these are just good things to do."

When talking with families, I also explain that the information I'm sharing is from their child's perspective. I make sure to clarify this fact. I also recognize and acknowledge that parents may see things very differently. It's so important not to make parents feel attacked or insecure, but to instead focus on developing relationships with them and creating a healthy outcome for everyone. Both parents and kids have psychological and emotional needs that need to be met, and that is what I constantly try to accomplish.

But I was not good at it in the beginning. It was ugly. I was making people mad and sometimes damaging relationships between parents and kids and me. I wanted so badly to stick up for children and relentlessly advocate for them that I missed the importance of building relationships. I didn't get it. I didn't have the experience. I was not wise. I'm much better at it now, but it took time. I've had six interns so far in my career, and this is something that I've seen in most, if not all of them. They are where I was at the beginning. So I try to pass along what I've learned. I'm sure it can be frustrating when I simply ask them to sit and listen. They may want to talk in meetings, and add their input. They may want to engage with families and staff, and share their knowledge, thoughts and observations. But instead I first try to teach them to be quiet and observe, so they can be better than I was early on at helping kids and families.

In my practice, I always check with kids before I talk with their parents. We go over what they are happy for me to share, and they get a sense of the process and the approach. I want our students to feel comfortable with what I am going to share, and be reassured that I will do so in a way that leads to a positive outcome. I encourage kids to talk with their parents too, after I have called the families. But at other times, I've learned, it works best when the parent, student and I all talk together. It often depends on the comfort level of the student. Throughout all these conversations, I work hard to use respectful, kind, caring dialogue. I work hard to listen, acknowledge, validate and empathize. A few staff members have commented that I communicate well with parents, and teachers often invite me to potentially challenging parent meetings because they know that I have some skills that might help. I think teachers have learned from me—as I have learned from them—and I hope my approach has helped our school build stronger relationships with families.

How do you apply wisdom to the care of your mind, body and soul?

In terms of my mind, I always try to be inquisitive and curious, to keep learning and growing. To have a variety of interests, to read, to turn off technology. I think decluttering and organizing are important because a chaotic environment creates more chaos in your mind. So fill your home with things that bring you joy. Colors. Textures. Images. Whatever makes your home environment a place that is good for you.

For my body, I exercise every day, whether it's walks, yoga or group fitness. I often engage in physical labor too, out in the garden, the yard or in a home project. Getting enough sleep is really important. Eating whole foods, not processed junk. And sometimes taking care of your body means showing restraint, like not drinking the whole bottle of wine.

For my soul, I try to be aware of when I need to be silent, and realize when I'm lost. It's especially then that I try to take care of my soul. I get outside and take a walk. I call my mom. I pet my dog. I sit on the patio and watch a sunset. I enjoy a glass of wine. I know when I need to spend time with my friends, to set up a time together like a girls' night. Relationships, friendships, family are important for your soul. I sing. I enjoy the arts. I try to recognize moments of beauty. And I always maintain a sense of gratitude.

I grew up in the Methodist faith, and I continue to attend church, sing in the choir and pray. When I sing hymns and sacred music, it reminds me of bigger things, of my God and my beliefs. Singing is a spiritual thing for me.

Is wisdom a uniquely human concept?

I struggled with this question. Probably the general consensus is that wisdom is some kind of cognitive, emotional, higher-level thinking or development, but do animals destroy the place they live? Do they murder and steal and lie? I have a rescue pug named Penelope. She is silly and sweet and lovable. She love walks, naps and treats. Every morning she wakes up happy. Sometimes I think she is wise. When she's tired she sleeps, when she's hungry, she eats. She holds no grudges. She does harm to no one. She's protective, yet gentle. I have a picture of her I love. You can see her at the window, just basking in the sun. Simply pausing to enjoy the moment. Is that not being wise?

Do you have a favorite parable or anecdote on wisdom?

Life is about balance. This is basically what I think of when I think of wisdom. It's holding on to knowledge and experiences and all the good in your life, and letting go of misconceptions, anger, resentment and all the things that take away your joy. So to me, realizing what is good and choosing to focus on it—this embodies wisdom.

I found a quote that says, 'Wisdom begins in wonder.' And one definition of wisdom I read says that 'wisdom is speaking and acting with knowledge while doubting what one knows.'

But in this moment, I'm drawn to a passage that has always been meaningful to me. It reminds me of what to hold on to, now and always. I've always loved Psalm 23:

The Lord is my shepherd; I shall not want.
He maketh me to lie down in green pastures: he leadeth me beside the still waters.
He restoreth my soul: he leadeth me in the paths of righteousness for his name's sake.
Yea, though I walk through the valley of the shadow of death, I will fear no evil: for thou art with me; thy rod and thy staff comfort me.
Thou preparest a table before me in the presence of mine enemies: thou anoint my head with oil; my cup runneth over.
Surely goodness and mercy shall follow me all the days of my life: and I will dwell in the house of the Lord for ever.

'Green pastures' makes me think God wants me to be calm, to feel the sun on my face, to embrace nature. 'Quiet waters' means to quiet my mind and my soul. 'He restoreth me' speaks of regaining strength from him or others, or finding another source that revitalizes you. He is with me and with all of us. We're not alone. We have each other. It's a gift to humanity that we can rely on each other and support each other. 'And goodness and mercy shall follow me.' So I think it's doing good and trying to surround yourself with good. And in the end, there will be good.

I see God in a sunrise or sunset, or in a flower or a cloud. Maybe I'm crazy, but when I feel a breeze and close my eyes, it's like he's reminding me to let go of whatever is weighing on my heart. I think God is all around us. I see signs all the time that make me feel like he is reaching out to us and reassuring us. I might be wrong, but I don't care. I am such an imperfect human, but at least I recognize it. There is good in me, but there's lots of room for improvement.

How do you ultimately define wisdom?

This one I lost sleep over. Here we go. I may tweak it like 10 seconds after I say it: Wisdom is the act of deliberately expanding and embracing knowledge and experience, reflecting and questioning your beliefs and perspectives, and applying knowledge and insights to make life better. All the while learning from mistakes, being open to growth and change, and remaining grounded in benevolence, compassion and kindness.

How can each of us develop wisdom?

Be open to new experiences, ideas and people. I think every new experience offers an opportunity to learn. And we can expand our worldview and knowledge by taking classes, joining groups, meeting new people, having conversations, listening and asking questions. Read. Watch documentaries. Be inquisitive. And I think breaking routines too; having novelty in your life is important.

Learn from experiences—both yours and those of others. Reflect on them and remember your reflections, so you can apply them. Reflect on your mistakes and your choices, analyze them, and grow from them. Test your thoughts, challenge yourself to look at things from different perspectives, and ask yourself how you would handle things differently the next time. I think keeping a journal and reading quotes of wise people helps develop wisdom, too.

Develop self-awareness. Notice when you're surprised or confused, or you're wrong or remorseful, and then use those moments to change. Self-reflect. Honestly recognize yourself. You have to know yourself and accept and acknowledge who you are, so you can become the person you want to be. Examine your internal dialogue, your automatic thoughts and reactions. And your prejudices, beliefs and assumptions. You have to recognize them to be able to challenge them and change them.

Pay attention and be present. Listen, observe, slow down, be silent, breathe, be still. Recognize that you are not your thoughts, and try to detach yourself from your thoughts. Drag yourself outside your own head. Watch yourself from a place outside yourself. Instead of focusing on being productive, find a space in your life where you can simply be.

Realize what is of true value to you in your life. Find your meaning and your purpose. Follow your passions. Never lose your sense of appreciation, gratitude and wonder.

Is there anything you'd like to add?

There are a few words that stuck with me throughout the discussion that I want to mention. I think someone who is wise has humility, courage, gentleness and patience. There is wisdom in being tolerant of uncertainty, in authenticity, and in laughter.

There are also a few thoughts, or I guess you could say bits of wisdom, that I have gleaned along the way and wanted to share because they resonate within me. These are thoughts that I always try to hold on to. The first is this: before you say something that might cause damage or hurt, ask yourself if what you have to say is worth the relationship. The second: give positive feedback, and give it often. It takes five positive interactions or comments, according to research, to counteract the effects of one negative interaction or remark, so foster healthy relationships through words of affirmation and appreciation. And the third is something I heard years ago in a suicide prevention training: challenge yourself to change up the maxim, 'If you don't have something nice to say, don't say anything', to: 'If you don't have something nice to say, find something nice to say.' It's a powerful shift in thinking, and it could make a tremendous impact in someone's life. You may never know when someone is struggling, and your words could make all the difference.

How did it feel to discuss wisdom today?

I'm exhausted! But I do want to mention this t-shirt I wore today because it's kind of my abridged version of wisdom: 'Be nice. Drink wine. Pet dogs.' This sums it all up. Be nice in what you do and say, enjoy the moments and the blessings in your life, and follow your passions.

Mike Wallis

Michael Wallis was born in 1949 in London to Hilda and Danny, blessed loving parents, in a working-class community in South Acton, West London. His first job was working as a solicitor's clerk in Central London in the late 1960s. He moved on to be a computer operator for a large bank, and during that time he took a trip down to the Greek island of Paros, where he found himself beguiled by the alternative lifestyle. Staying too long past his vacation period, he was sacked, and took this as a sign to go hitchhiking through Western Europe. He returned to England with a resolve to experience as much of life as possible, leading him to a wide range of people, places and work.

Wallis studied Amenity Horticulture at Sparsholt College, and Facilitating Music Workshops at Goldsmiths, University of London. He took courses in many other things, including Performance Guitar and Clowning.

What comes to mind first when you think about wisdom?

Wisdom helps us survive. It is knowledge learned, developed from an inherent instinct. It's a progression of common sense.

Do you recall the first time you witnessed wisdom in action?

When I was young I met a vagabond guy. He showed me the meaning of contentment, being satisfied with choice. And having an open mind towards opportunity. He lived in a state of benevolence, kindness and tolerance of ourselves and others. He was like an open book in a way. I always remember that he had robust health. I asked my mum about him, and she said he just travels around, and that's all he does. So that's the first time I witnessed wisdom, because he'd made his choice and he was content with it.

Who is the wisest person you know, and why?

There have been people I've known that have utilized wisdom in respect of action or non-action. They either do something about something, or they don't, according to the circumstances, and their consideration of the consequences. In some cases it's best to leave things alone, and they've realized that, which is a wise decision. Or they've done something about it, based on a principle of it being a problem that requires solving. But if they can't do anything about it, they accept that, and don't worry about it. So those who have taught me that have been the wisest people that I've come across. A number of my friends have got that attitude. Virtually all the people I know have taught me that in different ways.

The Dalai Lama is one of the wisest people whose books I've read. They resonate with me and my understanding of a wise way to live, which is based on harmony, love and kindness. They are the three main aspects of having a life that is enduring in happiness. It avoids having unease or misgivings, because there's an answer to everything in just being kind and understanding. It takes a rational approach to life, rather than being forceful with it.

Looking back on your life, what is the wisest thing you ever did?

The wisest thing I did was to choose to commit to learning the skill of being kind and gracious in the application of loving kindness. I was quite an aggressive person before that, quite forceful and intolerant. I didn't give much consideration to other people's thoughts or feelings. It wasn't until I started meeting people that had that attitude of loving kindness that I realized the value of it. They seemed to be content with their lives, and I thought that perhaps that's what I have to do to enjoy my life. I knew I had to take action, but it took me a long time to do that, because I was so embittered and angry in myself. But I realized I had to turn my life around, and I resolved to seek a means of doing that.

I started by simply being more open and observant of other people, and seeing how they dealt with their lives. Especially those who were in a situation with a lot of unhappiness. They dealt with it by adopting an attitude which wasn't one of conflict, but was about being able to adapt, to adjust to their circumstances without being aggressive. And they were quite tolerant of other people. They had a loving attitude. My aim was to find out how they maintained that. This became a quest for me. My mum and dad, and my aunts and uncles had that attitude to life, as did various other people that I started becoming aware of around me, including our neighbors. I started to develop a very open mind. I became more observant, and absorbed how other people were.

I had quite a lot of teachers after that because as my life progressed from there, when I was about 21, I started traveling and met a lot of people along the way. I took the Magic Bus from England, and it went through Belgium, Germany and down through Yugoslavia and into Greece. I stayed in Greece for a while and that's where things really opened up. I met some amazing people and learned a lot from them. I enjoyed it so much that I went back again, this time hitchhiking all the way down. I went on another trip to Munich in Germany, as I'd met a girl from there. I met some other women from Malmö in Sweden, and ended up there too. I traveled around a lot of Britain after that. On another trip I went to North Africa, into the Atlas Mountains to find the source of hashish. I also spent time in Spain, Portugal and Italy.

I found a lot of inspiration in the British hippie culture in the 70s and 80s. Living in Bristol I knew people who had connections to the hippie communities in mid-Wales. The intimate lifestyle of the place was special. People lived by the seasons and close to the earth. It gave me a broader attitude to other people's ideas, and their respect for nature. But I also realized that within that earthy existence, there was also a harder side, where it came up against convention, and rules and regulations.

What most stayed with me was the lesson of learning to live as a community. This meant adapting to the needs of a group, which involved respecting individuality and difference. We learned to avoid creating resentments. Everyone needs to feel satisfied and contented with each other, and negotiate differences. If we base our relationships on mutual respect we create community rather than destroy it. Smoking dope helped. It was a mellowing influence. It helped me to let go of preconceived ideas and narrow-minded opinions about things. It became useful in developing a greater ability to adapt and survive. Before that period I was in constant conflict with life.

In traveling I met people in poverty, and people in affluence. All of them had to learn to live with it in a healthy way. And I found that a lot of people are very kind. I also found myself in threatening situations and had to learn how to adapt and to survive those.

I realized there was a common thread involved, where people were able to live and let live—that was the way they survived. They were not closed people, they were open to learning and understanding. That's how I grasped the meaning of wisdom. Because they were gradually developing an understanding of how other people were and how we have to adjust and adapt, and learn to live with other people. Instead of having a single-minded attitude, they were open to other people's ideas and attitudes. It's learning to be more flexible. In hindsight I realized that that was the mistake I was making in my life previously. I was too rigid, and unaware of alternatives. I was like an ice cube before, but when you allow yourself to thaw, you lose that rigid definition, and join the waters of humanity.

There were quite a few moments where I realized that someone was a teacher without them being aware of it. It was just their way of dealing with situations or people that were difficult. They were very considered in their actions and reactions. It was an accumulation of knowledge that I gained from being with other people. It was a number of people over the course of fifty years or more that have taught me that. It could be a single moment, or it could last as long as I knew that person.

I realized that a lot of my anger and intolerance and frustration was being eroded, melting away in the light of being kind and loving towards other people. I gradually became more empowered, because before that I didn't really know how to deal with situations. But through encountering with and through other people I saw they had the attitude to be flexible and adapt to situations. There were ways of being that were more rational, and based on wisdom. It made me realize that wisdom is a tool. I learned how and when to use it by observing other people that had that wisdom. Approaching things with positivity rather than negativity seemed to be the best way to solve problems. Not to make trouble out of trouble. Learning to make allowances was something I didn't realize I could do before. I had a simple-minded attitude that I was always in the right, rather than looking at it from another point of view. Having an attitude of loving kindness toward other people helped me see that they were in a situation that needed resolving. Changing my perspective, and seeing their way of looking at it, and negotiating, wasn't something I knew I could do before. And that was a big blessing to me.

What is the hardest-won wisdom that you have?

I think it was when I had a problem with making decisions. I learned that a decision was something I had to be confident with, and I had to learn to make mistakes. If I hadn't made the right decision, I had to recognize that I made the choice, based on what I knew. And it was learning to be honest and trusting in that respect. Which was quite difficult to do. Up until then I didn't really have much trust in life. I'd been trying to get somewhere that I wasn't clear about in myself.

I had the realization that honesty and trust are aspects which I needed to adopt to give me clarity and purpose in my life. I wasn't really sure up until then that you could be honest, and trust in a decision based in honesty. I was always being devious and mistrusting, and trying to force things; trying to prove that I was making the right decision, by making it work the way I wanted it to. And then I would become frustrated, angry and resentful. I had a very negative response when things didn't work out; and invariably they didn't, because that failure was based on me being inflexible and closed-minded. So, meeting all the people that I did made me realize that I had to let go of my old attitude, and remodel myself on principles of being kind and loving, which was difficult because I felt I was being vulnerable. So that was quite a hard-won bit of wisdom that I opened myself to. It was difficult for me to do that because I'd become quite a hardened character. And that left me unhappy, because I wasn't being loving, and I wasn't letting love in. So the hardest thing was letting go of myself and embracing a new self, which was based on being honest and trusting.

In the world today, where do you see wisdom, and its lack, being demonstrated?

The lack of wisdom is apparent in a lot of the consequences in the world, including the present situation with the virus. Wisdom is ignored. The lessons learned in the past are disregarded in place of ignorant actions. Wisdom isn't given its true value. People cause more harm than good by sticking to a belief that their way is correct, without giving due consideration to lessons we've already learned in the past.

Wisdom, as always, is being given a back seat. Ignorant action seems to be given more importance than wisdom. I think wisdom is something which is really important before a decision is made. It seems to be an ongoing situation where that's ignored and overlooked. I accept that not every situation has been faced before, but we need to give consideration to potential consequences. And then it's a case of learning from that and gathering more wisdom from both mistakes and successes.

The world is a living organism and needs to be treated as such and given the consideration it deserves. At least as much as we give ourselves.

When we look at technology, it can be used in a positive way for the development and wellbeing of humanity, and the health of the planet and all its living creatures. Seeing the astronauts going up to the ISS this week, it struck me that that is an example of accumulated knowledge being applied to an enterprise that hopefully will be of use to the wider world. It represents our human curiosity about our nature and existence. And it represents the culmination of human technological progress thus far. It also speaks to millennia of problem-solving, which seems to be part of human nature.

There seems to be an element of fate and destiny, that we are destined to follow this path. But we can apply wisdom to that, and give due consideration to the potential problems involved in a course of action. We can adjust and adapt as we go, and use the experience to inform future decisions and processes.

How do you apply wisdom to the care of your mind, body and soul?

I use mantras to clear my mind and give me some sort of clarity. This helps me overcome obstacles. It's really to clear any negativity. I say, "Rest, relax and release, I am at peace. I heal myself with love."

Or I might say, "Is this thought causing me unease, fear and frustration?"

I normally use these if there is a disquiet in my mind. They help bring clarity and a sense of serenity or equanimity.

I also use Autogenic Training. It uses visualizations and repetitions to reduce stress in the mind and body. Using this process, and those mantras, settles my mind, which helps to settle any discomfort in my body.

With my soul, I pursue a continuity of positivity in my attitude. I will adjust and adapt things as I go along. I look to see if things are truly beneficial to myself and others. I will ask if things are constructive. Do they feel good? Are they nurturing my soul?

It is important to appreciate the benefits of the continuity of a positive attitude. A lot of that comes from being trusting and honest. What I think, feel and say is based on the idea of being honest, open and true. I do my best to maintain that attitude in order to feel good about what I'm doing and how I am relating to other people.

I've practiced Tai Chi for more than 40 years. It's like a panacea. It creates openings in my body and mind. There are blockages that occur, that have been unresolved and unnoticed. And that is something which is based on a principle of Tai Chi being a balancing process. You have light and dark, heavy and light. It's based on the principle of yin and yang. If you have too much of one thing then sometimes you have to develop the other part. If I'm too negative I have to develop the positive side of how I'm behaving. If anger is too strong I have to look at that imbalance, and work towards equanimity. Tai Chi is aiming to create equanimity without using unnecessary force. It's about using the right amount of force, if force is necessary. And recognizing that too much force is as bad as not enough, to be able to resolve a situation or a problem. Or using an attitude where force isn't used, but the mind is used; being able to communicate, understand, be aware of the different aspects of the situation. It may be a bodily thing, like not drinking enough water, or eating enough food, or getting enough rest or exercise. Tai Chi really heightens any lack, or imbalance.

Where there is harmony in my mind and body it reflects in the way I am, how my soul is. If my soul is in a harmonious balance, then my mind and body are equally responsive to that, and there is a sense of wellbeing which permeates me holistically. Tai Chi enhances and illuminates that feeling.

The only problem with it is that Tai Chi needs to be done on a regular basis, but in a restrained way. Because it can be as damaging as it can be beneficial. So it's learning to be able to recognize that. It's a matter of respecting the healing method. It can be destructive and harmful. The only way to become aware of it is to listen to what other people experience around that. And being able to apply it to my self, my condition and my attitude. I can see where I need to adjust and adapt in my way of being. And I may need to ask for help with it, from someone who has developed experience with it.

So Tai Chi is like a way of life. It's conducive to health on all levels, if practiced properly. It's like a medicine. It can help in situations where an attitude has to be adopted of rebalancing. It can be applied not just to a physical situation, but also to a mental environment. It's an enhancing appreciation of what is out of balance. It's a tangible feeling. It's like you're developing a new sense, or enhancing an inherent sensitivity.

Is wisdom a uniquely human concept?

It's apparent in all living things. You can see it animals and creatures that live by their wits, which is partly what wisdom is. It's common sense, and having awareness, with the intention of survival. A situation has been created and they will adapt and adjust to be able to solve that situation. Their accumulated wisdom is put into practice in order for them to survive. So it's not just a human concept. The word 'concept' is a human word, but it can be applied in a practical way to all living beings. We just call it a concept but it's not really a concept. Wisdom is apparent in everything.

Do you have a favorite parable or anecdote on wisdom?

It may be wise to be foolish, or foolish to be wise, but to know when to be either or neither, is wisdom. It's being able to be adaptable. A lot of people don't like a wiseguy, a Mr. Knowitall. Some people will regard that with contempt. So sometimes it's better to be a bit foolish so people feel more at ease, so they don't feel threatened. But sometimes being foolish could be damaging. So it's learning when to be one or the other. Or not be either, not try and show one is more apparent than the other. Truth and knowledge makes a wise fool, in a way. In olden times we had court jesters, or fools. And they were often consulted by the king or whoever was in power, because they were given respect which was due to them, without them clamoring for it. A wise person gets respect, and has self-respect.

The court jester was given assent to make fun of the ruler, or their policies. The fool represents us, generally speaking. We can lay foolishness at the door of the fool, knowing they will appreciate it for what it is. The fool epitomizes how foolish we can all be, and appear. But in court it was embodied in one person, and he was given that title, rather than the king being called a fool. The fool becomes the king so it can be turned around. So the wise man becomes the fool, and the fool becomes the wise man. I think that's how the fool developed, into clowns and things like that. So foolishness isn't necessarily a demeaning thing, it can be used as an indication or example of how vulnerable we are as humans to life in general. Being foolish is part of that. As is learning to accept it, which is what a fool does. A fool makes use of the foibles of being human and exemplifies it in his or her attitude. They show us this side of ourselves in a safe, non-confrontational way. We recognize it when it is presented to us by someone who has been given the permission to do so.

I learned a lot of this in doing clowning workshops. It's an alternative way of looking at mishaps and mistakes. There is both a funny side and a learning opportunity. We can learn to acknowledge and appreciate these things. As long as it's not too serious, rather than get upset and angry, we can add it to our appreciation of the silly situations which occur. And we can acknowledge that there are things beyond our control. A lot of clowning is based on things happening outside of its control. Or the clown utilizes those mishaps and we laugh at that. But if it happens in our own lives we take umbrage at it, because we think we've got everything under control and this reminds us that that was a delusion. Mishaps can happen anytime, anywhere, to anyone. We see these things happen to other people and think they can't happen to us, but they can and will. We have to be able to laugh when they arise.

If we're in a reasonable state of mind we can deal with mishaps. If we start wandering outside a healthy state of mind, we find that the effect of something going wrong is more detrimental to us. And it can be more detrimental to us mentally, emotionally and physically. But if it is physically detrimental we need to understand that it just occurred. It may not have been a lack of attention, it could be anything. A clown often manufactures a situation to be in control of a mishap, but another mishap could occur through the control over the first mishap. It could have a rebounding effect. That's how a lot of problems occur: they snowball. And often the more there are, the funnier it becomes, until it reaches a point where it becomes overwhelming. We can only tolerate so much. One thing is enough for most people, and the more things go wrong for us, the more fragile we become. But we can accept that these things often have a life to them that is beyond our control. Or we become fraught with it, and become fearful and anxious. And then you're learning about the cause of anxiety, which is fear. The distress that is caused is a product of that anxiety. So being able to acknowledge that things happen outside of our control is important. And avoid getting fearful of it. Just accept it. Or acknowledge it as part of the way life can turn.

How do you ultimately define wisdom?

I define wisdom as a tool. Its use is a method of constructive consequence in decision-making. It offers guidance appropriate to survival. If there is a situation which I need to respond to in a constructive way, then I have to be able to use wisdom for that.

How can each of us develop wisdom?

We have to be careful with it, and give it its due respect. It is a valuable tool. We have to develop a degree of patience and goodwill with it. Rather than use it in a hateful, destructive, resentful way—

which can cause other people misfortune and suffering—we have to be able to use it with an open mind and a kind heart. So we've got to be able to listen and learn. A wise person will seek advice.

Wisdom opens the heart as well as the mind. You become a more whole person. Part of the universe. You could call it God. It becomes a spiritual thing. It becomes a tangible thing. People pick up on it. Like the Dalai Lama. You've just got to look at his picture and you realize that that person is venerable. And he emanates a feeling of goodwill and good intention toward the world. I know he can be angry. He said that anger is something we have to deal with in life as it's part of human nature. That's being wise. Rather than being afraid of being angry, you've got to be able to recognize it for what it is and where it's coming from.

Is there anything else you wish to add?

Wisdom restrains the rash mind, and is a cornerstone of character building. With the mortar of sound reasoning, we may withstand fear, frustration and unease in moments of doubt. So it's pretty solid. Wisdom has a harmonizing, balancing aspect to it which needs to be developed and shared, where appropriate. It leads to a better person and a better world. Where it's ignored and everyone is single-mindedly focusing on developing their own material wealth, the wellbeing of our whole being is ignored, in place of one thing being attained. We can lose sight of ourselves as karmic beings.

Fate and destiny can play an interesting role, and offer us choices. When I was living in Bristol in the 70s, I got a letter inviting me to contact a firm of solicitors about an inheritance. It was a fork in the road. I could either go down a road in which I might become quite wealthy, or I could continue to live the quite simple, ascetic life I had chosen at that point. That path had brought many people into my life that had taught me important things. We were all on this journey together, like pilgrims on the path of wisdom. We had chosen to give up material things and pursue a spiritual way of life. So I decided to rip up the letter in favor of continuing to follow the path I was on. It was more valuable to me as a being than money.

Those forks in the road are generally quite rare. And we can either take the risk or not. But we have to make the decision, either way. That's where being honest, open and true is important. It's exciting in a way. But sometimes wisdom steps in and urges us to make a logical decision. I suppose it's fulfilling its function by saying: 'If you decide to do that, you have to be prepared to forgo other things.' Sometimes the risk is not worth taking. Wisdom is important in helping us consider our decisions carefully.

How did it feel to discuss wisdom today?

It's very enlightening. It's something that I've been aware of all my life, but I often ignore it, to my peril. It can be something which I'm quicker to give than to receive. Or I don't practice what I preach.

Talking about it has focused my awareness of what wisdom means to me and how I utilize it. I need to give it more respect. I'm more a spontaneous, compulsive type of person, and I often make rash choices. And this creates consequences that I feel resentful towards. And then, eventually, I recognize that I made that decision rashly or without due respect to the voice of wisdom. For example, I recently offered to put someone up that I didn't know, a guy that had just come out of prison. It was a hasty decision, but I based it on kindness, being compassionate towards that person. He was a relative of a friend. So I made that offer without considering the consequences to myself. The voice of wanting to prove to myself that I am a good person drowns out the voice of reason and wisdom. It's not developed strongly enough, or I suppress it by being too strong-minded. I can be too ambitious, in saying it will work out fine. But it won't. So talking about wisdom gives it more focus for me. It has reminded me that I see it as a tool, so I have to learn to use it more often. Take time over something, when it needs to be given the space for wisdom to assess both sides of the situation. Open up all different aspects of the situation to be considered, rather than just go ahead single-mindedly.

Just going through the questions, it's taken me a number of days to become clear in my mind as to how I see them. So it's made the subject of wisdom more tangible to me. And it has reminded me that I've got to let wisdom develop in its own way. I'm still learning, going through things. I have to remain open to developing wisdom, and getting better at using that tool. It's been good to have the opportunity to relate to it with you. So thank you.

Conclusion

As a seven-year-old boy listening to the story of Solomon, I was immediately struck by the central value of wisdom in managing human affairs. Throughout this project, however, there has been an evolution in my sense of what wisdom is. It is more than good decision-making. Wisdom is a spirit, a way of being. It is open and fluid, relational and respectful, insightful and discerning, humble and kind, loving and compassionate. All of the components of good decision-making can be derived from these deeper elements.

To make a good decision we must: consider the big picture and the long term; recognize who the decision will affect, and in what ways; take the time we need—within the time we have; and base it on the best information and counsel we have available.

Understanding the full context of our decision is highly complex, as it includes geographic, cultural, political, economic, mental, emotional, physical and spiritual factors. And no doubt others. Our choices will all be made within a number of dynamic, multidimensional, interweaving contexts.

The final determinant is often the most challenging: courage. Courage is found when facing that which we fear, so it is personal to each of us. Some decisions we make out of necessity, or a lack of other options. But the big ones often require a leap of faith, a willingness to let go of one thing in order to grasp something else. Many of the contributors in this book have talked about major decisions which changed their lives, and by extension, those of others. Following their passion took them to better, and often more important and influential places. Many millions of people have benefited from their courage and passion.

A major aspect of courage is about facing ourselves. Developing self-knowledge, with humility and loving kindness, may be the greatest challenge of all. The ego is a fragile yet wild thing, to be tamed with patience and compassion. There is a sweet spot between feeling good enough, and feeling superior. The willingness to commit to this work, without judgment, is pure wisdom.

Beyond the human discussions, we dove deep into the wisdom inherent in the natural world, from Gaia, the living planet, down through the world's ecosystems to a Pug named Penelope, and a little Tibetan dog named Sinto. Nature, in its wisdom, takes care of others, through reciprocity and balance. The idea that wisdom is central to survival is reinforced by the stories of indigenous people ritualizing their practices of harmony with, and respect for, their environment.

All of which begs the question: is wisdom a core feature of reality? Is it just our word for something more fundamental? If all of nature is seen as a single, self-interacting, conscious entity, then wisdom is, on one level, a survival trait. Each element of the self ensures its own heath through its contribution to that of the others. This is reflected in the mind, body and soul relationships within each of us. As above, so below.

This raises another key philosophical question: can one be both evil and wise? Not according to this study. One could make decisions that will give you a good quality of life, as say, a hitman, but this lacks some central tenets of wisdom. Wisdom here is seen as something bound up in benevolence, reciprocity, compassion and humility. Hence, the sociopath is smart and manipulative, but not wise.

But it would be fascinating to bring together champions of the prevailing order, and ask them the same questions. How would a hedge fund manager respond? Or a central bank governor? Or a right-wing politician? For that matter, how would a mafia don answer them? Or a human trafficker? Would this discussion, especially if conducted off the record, take them to a place beyond greed and selfishness? Would they tune into the wavelength that those in this book do? Do they retain a dormant facility for universal love and compassion?

Some say that this experience is all a spiritual process, and that the polarity and conflict in our world is simply a game we all play, by agreement, just as two boxers agree to collaborate in a fight. The purpose is shared enlightenment, as we grow through the experience of conflict. Frankly, that makes more sense to me than the alternative, which is that humans are, by some quirk of design, destined to wipe out ourselves, and much of life on Earth, through materialism and all that stems from it. One could argue that if wisdom were the prevailing ethic of the time, we would not have organizations called Extinction Rebellion and Black Lives Matter. Wisdom, conceived of as something ultimately benevolent and loving, could not give rise to the need to rebel against the extinction of life on Earth, or point out that different should not mean unequal. A wise society would be founded upon sustainability, equality and, ultimately, love.

The converging crises of our age, around environment, health, economy and equality, are mostly of our own making. We are not in this state because we're not smart, but because we're not wise. And we're not wise because our hearts and minds are not open. Closed hearts and minds are both cause and effect of the prevailing system. How we turn this around is the subject of many other books, but recognizing that we are responsible for both the problem and the solution is surely the first step. This goes hand-in-hand with getting ourselves out of fear, anger, blame and division. And it is essential to acknowledge that alternative economic and social models are possible. Developing one which is actually sustainable, not just a little more so, is the only option. And we have to reform the process by which we make decisions. We can only make progress if we prevent sociopaths from gaining positions of authority, and eliminate corruption at all levels. There are many experts in all of these fields, who have ready-to-go solutions for fixing these systemic issues. This book features a number of them.

If we choose a safe, just and sustainable system, facilitated by wise policymakers, with constant feedback from the people, then we have a chance. Climate change is now a fact of our existence, and the old system cannot survive it anyway. The alternative to making good choices quickly will be a kind of *Mad Max* feudalism—endless resource wars on a steadily shrinking, heating, drying landmass.

The best tools we have are the natural adaptability and resourcefulness of humans, but in the name of all that is sacred, let us be guided by wisdom in applying them. Wisdom is the only route to designing and delivering an equitable replacement for the present extinction-level materialism that defines our age. Equanimity and acceptance are useful on a personal basis, but if we collectively choose to go along with the people encouraging us to destroy anything and everything in the name of enriching them further, then we will all fail together.

In our own lives, wisdom is a kind of Swiss Army knife—it always has some beneficial application. Spending the craziest year in living memory researching wisdom is probably the best choice I could have made. It has had many unexpected benefits. These discussions have inspired me to spend my weekends in beautiful places, especially woodlands. It has been magical. My first professional training was in forestry, and my love for our tree friends remains undimmed. I'm not sure I have any poetic or psychological insight into why trees mean so much to me, but the beauty is that it does not matter—you love what you love. And when people apply themselves to what they love, they can produce great artistic, scientific, philosophical or spiritual contributions. Or simply enjoy themselves.

I have seen life more through the lens of wisdom, particularly storytelling in music, film and television, and in relationships and conversations.

Music seems to express the essence and application of wisdom. The human spirit enjoys harmony and resolution, repetition and variation. Music works for us because it reflects our need for both rules and an element of chaos. No matter how much we enjoy the conflict and dynamism in music, we want it to resolve, to close the harmonic loop. Nature is just this way. Most of life prefers structure, routine, predictability, within a dynamic environment. And wisdom echoes this. The journey to wisdom, to that moment of resolution, is often chaotic, sometimes painful, sometimes ecstatic. So nature, music and wisdom reflect the dynamics and processes of one another. There is an almost mystical beauty in that.

In films and TV shows I have become more sensitized to the wisdom, or lack of it, demonstrated in the words and deeds of the characters. Story is our way to discuss human strengths, weaknesses and relationships, to evaluate morality, to explore the quest for purpose and the need for expression. The characters have their own values and motivations which send them into conflict or alignment with one another. Over the course of the protagonist's arc we see them grow in wisdom through adversity, reflecting the hero's journey that we all take in life. We tell no end of stories, on the screen, the page, in the theater, in video games, because we are all trying to work out life's challenges and mysteries.

Despite all our human complexity, we are bound by the physical realities of this construct. If we set aside complex metaphysical and technological theories concerning the nature of reality, and see ourselves as nature, within nature, then the cultivation and application of wisdom is an indispensable requirement of our existence. It is the passenger, the vehicle, the route and the journey. It is concrete and pragmatic, as much as it is abstract and enigmatic. It is at times near and full, and at other times, far and empty. It speaks so loud we shake, and it dissolves into whisper. It is more than a tool, it is a state of being.

Our existence is such an incredibly complex proposition that reflection through art, spiritual practice and conversation with trusted allies will always be vital. As long as we proceed with an open heart and mind, wisdom—both inside and outside—awaits. Simply put: wisdom seems to be the answer to life. The two are intimately bound up. Life breeds wisdom; wisdom breeds life.

Love is so closely intertwined with these things that wisdom and love are virtually interchangeable for me. It seems that wisdom is at least as heart-based as it is head-based.

Perhaps the most meaningful thing to come out of this project personally, is that I have become more able to see the wisdom in my father. We went through the extremes of a difficult father-son relationship through my childhood. And that sticks. We feel justified in our highly-inflected view of their words and deeds. Yet now I have found myself listening to him deeply, without judgment. There is, in my life, no greater test of the development of my own wisdom, than the ability and willingness to witness that of my father. If you, the reader, gain any such progress in your life, then this book will have done its job.

Printed in Poland
by Amazon Fulfillment
Poland Sp. z o.o., Wrocław